Words & Ideas

Words & Ideas

William J. Dominik
EDITOR

Bolchazy-Carducci Publishers, Inc.
Mundelein, Illinois USA

Editor: Laurie Haight Keenan

Contributing Editors: Georgia Irby-Massie, M. Scott VanHorn

Cover & Page Design: Cameron Marshall

Typesetting & Production: Adam Phillip Velez

Cover Illustration: A young Pompeian woman in a meditative pose, holding a *stilus* in her right hand and *tabellae* in her left; from a Pompeian fresco in the Museo Archeologico Nazionale, Naples.

Words & Ideas

Bolchazy-Carducci Publishers, Inc.
1570 Baskin Road
Mundelein, Illinois 60060
www.bolchazy.com

Printed in the United States of America
2012
by United Graphics

ISBN 978-0-86516-485-7

Library of Congress Cataloging-in-Publication Data

Words & Ideas / edited by William J. Dominik.
    p. cm.
Includes bibliographical references.
  ISBN 0-86516-485-1 (pbk.)
  1. Language and languages--etymology. 2. English language--Etymology. 3. Civilization, Classical.
I. Title: Words and Ideas. II. Dominik, William J.
  P321 .W67 2002
  422--dc21

                        2002074479

CONTENTS

ILLUSTRATIONS xiv

"WORD FOR WORD" STRIPS xv

PREFACE AND A NOTE TO THE 2012 REPRINT xvii

GENERAL ACKNOWLEDGMENTS xix

ILLUSTRATION ACKNOWLEDGMENTS xx

A NOTE TO THE TEACHER xxi

INTRODUCTION xxiii

CHAPTER 1
WORD-BUILDING BASICS 1
(W. J. Dominik, J. L. Hilton, and A. P. Bevis)
   How Words are Formed and Used 1
      Word Building in English 1
      Influence of Greek and Latin upon English 1
      Terminology of Word Building 5
      Structure of Words 6
      Coining New Words 7
      The Latinate Register of English 8
   Changes in Words Across Languages 8
      Changes in Meaning of Greek and Latin Words in English 8
      Changes in Spelling of Greek and Latin Words in English 10
      Changes in the Forms of Words 11
         Nouns, Pronouns, and Adjectives 11
         Verbs 12
      Greek and Latin Plural Forms in English 13
         Greek 13
         Latin 14
   Bibliography and Further Reading 15
   Web Sites: Names and URLs 16
   Exercises 17

CHAPTER 2
WORD-BUILDING TOOLS: GREEK COMPONENTS 19
(W. J. Dominik, J. L. Hilton, and A. P. Bevis)
   The Greek Alphabet 19
   Greek Bases 19
      Nouns 19

Combining Forms 19
Adjectives 21
Adverbs 25
Verbs. 25
Greek Prefixes 29
Greek Suffixes 33
Noun-forming Suffixes 34
General Function 34
Abstract Function 34
Agent Function 35
Adjective-forming Suffixes. 36
Verb-forming Suffix 36
Bibliography and Further Reading. 36
Web Sites: Names and URLs 37
Exercises 37

CHAPTER 3
WORD-BUILDING TOOLS: LATIN COMPONENTS .45
(W. J. Dominik, J. L. Hilton, and A. P. Bevis)
The Latin Alphabet 45
Latin Bases 45
Nouns 45
Verbs. 47
Latin Prefixes 49
Latin Suffixes 55
Noun-forming Suffixes 55
General Function 55
Abstract Function 56
Agent Function 58
Locative Function 59
Diminutive Function 59
Adjective-forming Suffixes. 60
Verb-forming Suffixes. 63
Latin Expressions. 63
Abbreviations 63
Phrases 64
Quotations. 65
Bibliography and Further Reading. 65
Web Sites: Names and URLs 66
Exercises 66

CHAPTER 4
MYTHOLOGY. 75
(ed. W. J. Dominik)
What Is Mythology? 75
Beginnings 75

The Creation of the World 75
Generations of the Gods 75
    Word Study 76
Gods and Goddesses. 77
    Word Study . . . . `.79
The Underworld 82
    Word Study 82
    Divine Punishments. 83
        Sisyphus 83
        Tantalus 83
        Persephone and Demeter. 84
Heroes. 85
    Heracles. 85
        The Twelve Labors of Heracles 85
            Word Study 88
    Theseus. 88
        Word Study 89
The Trojan War. 90
    Word Study 90
    Greek Heroes of the War 91
        Word Study 91
    Trojan Heroes of the War. 92
        Word Study 92
The Wanderings of Odysseus 93
    Word Study 95
Oedipus and His Family 95
    Oedipus. 95
    Eteocles and Polynices 98
    Antigone and Ismene 98
Bibliography and Further Reading. 99
Web Sites: Names and URLs 99
Exercises 101

CHAPTER 5
MEDICINE 105
(W. J. Dominik)
Greek Medicine. 105
    Beginnings. 105
    Hippocrates and Rational Medicine. 105
        Word Study 107
    Medical Treatment. 107
        Drugs 107
        Surgery 107
            Word Study 108
    The Theory of Humors 108
    Medical Ethics and Etiquette 109

Word Study 111
Anatomy and Physiology 111
    Word Study 111
Gynecology 111
    Word Study 112
Roman Medicine 112
Beginnings 112
    Word Study 113
The Training of Doctors 113
Doctors 114
    Independent and Public Doctors 114
    Galen 114
    Female Doctors 115
    Military Doctors 116
Surgery 116
    Medical and Surgical Instruments 116
        Word Study 117
Gynecology 118
Soranus and Gynecology 118
    Childbirth 119
    Contraception 120
    Abortion 120
    Exposure 120
        Word Study 121
    Hysteria 121
        Word Study 122
Ophthalmology 122
    Word Study 122
Medical Treatments 123
    Folk Treatments 123
    Divine Healing 124
Preventive Medicine 125
Medical Humor 125
Medical Terminology 127
Importance of Medical Terminology 128
Role of Greek and Latin 128
Concision and Simplicity of Medical Terms 128
Precision and Extension of Medical Terms 128
Formation of Medical Terms 129
Key Words Derived from Greek 129
Suffixes and Combining Forms 129
Bases 132
Key Words Derived from Latin 138
Bibliography and Further Reading 140
Web Sites: Names and URLs 140
Exercises 141

CHAPTER 6
POLITICS AND LAW 145
(*J. L. Hilton and S. M. Masters*)
    The Greek Polis 145
    Latin Words for "City" 147
        Word Study 148
    Monarchy and Related Forms 148
    Democracy 149
        Word Study 151
    The Roman Republic 151
        Magistracies 152
        The Roman Class Structure 153
        The Roman Senate 154
        The Roman Assemblies 154
    The Roman Empire 154
        Word Study 155
    Roman Law 156
        The Influence of Roman Law upon American Law 157
        The Influence of Roman Law upon South African Law 158
            Roman Maxims and Legal Principles 158
            Roman Legal Concepts 158
            Roman Institutions 159
            Roman Actions 159
    Latin Derivatives in Legal Vocabulary 159
        Public Law (Criminal) 160
        Private Law (Persons) 161
        Property and Wills 161
        Commercial Law (Contracts) 162
        Other Legal Words 162
    Latin Legal Phrases 163
    Bibliography and Further Reading 164
    Web Sites: Names and URLs 164
    Exercises 165

CHAPTER 7
COMMERCE AND ECONOMICS 169
(*J. L. Hilton*)
    Ancient Economic Theories 169
        Greek Theories 169
        Roman Theory 171
            Word Study 171
    Agriculture in the Ancient World 172
        Greek Agriculture 172
        Roman Agriculture 172
            The Grain Supply 173
            Food Welfare 173

Financial Systems. 174
    Greek Money and Coinage. 174
    Greek Finance. 175
    Roman Money. 175
    The Roman Treasury and the Imperial Fisc 176
        Word Study 177
Roman Business 177
    Company Organization. 177
    Public Contracts 178
    Clubs 178
Greek Trade and Transport 179
    Athenian Sea Power 179
    Greek Trade 179
Roman Trade and Transport. 180
    Trade 180
    Road Transport. 180
    Sea Transport 180
        Word Study 182
The Role of Slavery in the Greek and Roman Economies 183
        Word Study 184
The Role of Technology in the Greek and Roman Economies 185
        Word Study 186
Bibliography and Further Reading. 186
Web Sites: Names and URLs 187
Exercises 187

CHAPTER 8
PHILOSOPHY AND PSYCHOLOGY. 191
(A. Gosling and W. J. Dominik)
    Inquiry 191
        Word Study 191
    Logos. 192
        Word Study 192
    Knowledge 192
        Word Study 192
    Greek Philosophy. 194
        Aspects of Greek Philosophy 194
            Word Study 194
        The Pre-Socratic Philosophers 195
            The Ionian Philosophers 195
                Thales. 196
                Anaximander 196
                Anaximenes 196
                Heracleitus. 196
            The Pythagoreans 196
                Pythagoras. 196

The Monists 197
 Parmenides 197
The Pluralists (Fifth Century BCE) 197
 Empedocles 197
 Anaxagoras 197
The Atomists 197
 Democritus 197
  Word Study 198
Socrates 198
The Sophists 200
Plato 200
 Plato's Forms 202
  Word Study 203
Aristotle 203
 For Consideration 203
The Epicureans 204
The Stoics 204
The Cynics 204
 Word Study 205
Aretē 205
 Word Study 206
Psychē 206
 For Consideration 206
Homer and the Early Greeks on *Psychē* 206
 For Consideration 207
Plato on *Psychē* 208
Aristotle on *Psychē* 210
Psyche in Mythology 211
 Word Study 211
Myths 212
 Oedipus 212
 Electra 212
 Narcissus 213
  Word Study 213
Freudian Psychology 213
 Word Study 214
Bibliography and Further Reading 219
Web Sites: Names and URLs 220
Exercises 221

CHAPTER 9
HISTORY 227
(*A. Gosling and W. J. Dominik*)
 What is History? 227
  For Consideration 227
  Word Study 227

Methodology and Tools of History. 229
     For Consideration 229
     Word Study 230
Recording Time. 231
     For Consideration 231
     Word Study 232
Greek and Roman Historians 233
     Approach and Methodology. 233
          Word Study 234
     The Major Historians 234
          Herodotus 234
          Thucydides 235
          Xenophon 235
          Polybius. 236
          Flavius Josephus 236
          Caesar. 237
          Sallust. 237
          Livy 237
          Tacitus 238
Source Passages. 238
     For Consideration 238
     Herodotus, *Histories* preface 1.5.3 239
     Thucydides, *The Peloponnesian War* 1.21–22 239
     Polybius, *Histories* 3.31.2–4, 7–8, 11–13 240
     Livy, *From the Foundation of the City* preface 6–7, 9–10 241
     Tacitus, *Annals* 1.1 241
     The Story of Coriolanus and Veturia
          (Livy, *From the Foundation of the City* 2.40.1–11). 242
     For Consideration 244
Key Words for History. 244
Bibliography and Further Reading. 246
Web Sites: Names and URLs 246
Exercises 247

APPENDIX 1
GREEK AND LATIN ALPHABETS. 251
(W. J. Dominik, J. L. Hilton, and A. P. Bevis)
     Diphthongs. 252

APPENDIX 2
WRITING OF GREEK WORDS IN ENGLISH. 253
(W. J. Dominik, J. L. Hilton, and A. P. Bevis)
     Rough and Smooth Breathings 254

APPENDIX 3
NUMBERS AND COLORS 255
(W. J. Dominik, J. L. Hilton, and A. P. Bevis)
    Greek Numbers 255
    Latin Numbers 256
    Greek Colors. 256

ABOUT THE CONTRIBUTORS 257

INDEX OF NAMES AND CULTURAL TOPICS 258

INDEX OF WORD-BUILDING TOPICS 264
    Greek 264
    Latin 264
    Other 265

INDEX OF ENGLISH WORDS AND PHRASES 266

ILLUSTRATIONS

This list gives the page numbers of the drawings and photographs contained in this book.

Athena with spear, helmet, and aegis. 81
Heracles and the Nemean lion. 85
Odysseus and the Sirens. 94
Oedipus and the Sphinx. 97
Marble statue of Aesculapius (Greek Asklepios) 105
Hipppocrates 106
Some clients wait to see the doctor while he treats another patient. 110
A midwife performing a delivery 115
A doctor examining a patient's eye; mourners paying their respects 122
Divine healing under the auspices of Asklepios, god of medicine. 124
The Acropolis of Athens as it is today 145
Map of the Mediterranean area ruled by Rome in the first century BCE 155
An early Greek lever press 172
Grain or ore mill 173
Roman surveying instrument (*groma*) 173
Drachma from Cyrene (north Africa) showing the head of Zeus
    Ammon (obverse) and a silphium plant (reverse) 174
Tetradrachm showing Cleopatra VII of Egypt (obverse) and
    Antony (reverse). 176
A drawing based on a mosaic showing a Roman cargo ship with a
    freight of amphorae 180
A Roman catapault (*ballista*) 185
Steam turbine of Heron of Alexandria. 185
A manual force-pump 189
Socrates 198
Plato 200
Plato's Academy. 201
Aristotle. 203
Psyche and Eros pulling a chariot containing Aphrodite and Hermes. 211
A water clock (*klepsydra*) 231
Herodotus and Thucydides 234
Polybius. 236
The triumphal celebration following the fall of Jerusalem described
    by Josephus 236
Julius Caesar. 237

"WORD FOR WORD" STRIPS

Chapter 1 ("Word Building Basics"): dish (p. 2), inch (p. 10), melodrama (p. 6), quintessence (p. 7), radiotelegraphy (p. 8), temple (p. 3), utopia (p. 4).

Chapter 2 ("Word Building Tools: Greek Components"): anosmia (p. 30), apathy (p. 27), athlete (p. 35), ecstatic (p. 31), panorama (p. 27), parallel (p. 33), rheumatism (p. 28), tropics (p. 29).

Chapter 3 ("Word Building Tools: Latin Components"): apprehended (p. 49), aquarium (p. 45), arbor (p. 61), library (p. 59), missile (p. 48), nonplussed (p. 52), preposterous (p. 53), scruples (p. 60), suspect (p. 54).

Chapter 4 ("Mythology"): Jupiter (p. 80), mercury (p. 81), stentorian (p. 91), Jovial (p. 77).

Chapter 5 ("Medicine"): bacteria (p. 117), doctor (p. 117), intoxicate (p. 138), pharmacy (p. 108), quinsy (p. 130).

Chapter 6 ("Politics and Law"): ostracize (p. 150), tribe (p. 147).

Chapter 7 ("Commerce and Economics"): engine (p. 186), fiscal (p. 177), nauseated (p. 182), soldier (p. 176).

Chapter 8 ("Philosophy and Psychology"): academy (p. 200), ailurophile (p. 217), apologize (p. 192), atom (p. 198), idea (p. 195), idiots (p. 219), science (p. 193), triskaidekophobia (p. 216).

Chapter 9 ("History"): chronic (p. 232), story/history (p. 228).

Appendix 3 ("Numbers and Colors"): octopus/octobrach (p. 255).

PREFACE

Words and Ideas is designed to broaden both the vocabulary and cultural literacy of students. It discusses key words derived from the Latin and Greek languages that are used in a number of modern academic disciplines and in the process of tracing their origins introduces students to a wide variety of topics in classical antiquity. Most general and bioscientific word building textbooks are based mainly on the etymologies of English words. *Words and Ideas* is different because it not only serves the practical end of vocabulary building but also discusses the ideas behind these words. In addition, *Words and Ideas* introduces students to key words and phrases in a range of academic disciplines instead of focusing mainly on either general vocabulary or bioscientific terminology.

Words and Ideas does not just cover word building based on Greek and Latin but attempts to introduce students to the ancient civilizations that gave rise to these languages; furthermore, it seeks to explain how these ancient languages and cultures have heavily influenced modern English and modern culture in different parts of the world. Students who are embarking upon the study of Classics, Classical Civilization, Latin and Greek naturally will find this textbook of particular relevance, but students of the Humanities and Sciences in fields such as English, Linguistics, History, Politics, Social Studies, Philosophy, Psychology, Law (and Pre-Law), Economics, Business, Commerce, Medicine (and Pre-Medicine), and Nursing will find much in this book that is relevant and helpful.

A NOTE TO THE 2012 REPRINT

 ach chapter in this reformatted reprint contains an updated "Bibliography and Further Reading" and an updated "Web Sites: Names and URLs."

W. J. DOMINIK
Dunedin, New Zealand
June 2012

GENERAL ACKNOWLEDGMENTS

Special thanks are due to my colleagues at the University of Natal, Durban, especially John Hilton, who has contributed to five chapters and three appendices in *Words and Ideas* and provided critical advice regarding its final shape; Aileen Bevis, who has collaborated in the writing of three chapters and three appendices; Anne Gosling, who has co-authored two chapters; and Samantha Masters, who has contributed to one of the chapters. Without their support this book would not have been possible. Although the contributions of my colleagues have been edited liberally in order to ensure general consistency in content and format and uniformity in style, I trust that I have not taken too many liberties in editing material that has already proven to be successful with students.

Thanks are due to a number of other people who have assisted in the production of *Words and Ideas* in various ways: Elizabeth Minchin, who read an earlier draft and suggested a number of improvements and corrections; Laurie Haight Keenan, Editor for Bolchazy-Carducci, and the anonymous referee for Bolchazy-Carducci, who made many helpful suggestions regarding the content of the original submission; Justine Wolfenden, who helped to arrange the material into chapters in the initial stages of editing; Joy McGill, who typed the first draft of Chapters 1–3; Tamaryn Pieterse, who drew the illustrations in Chapter 4; Ann Delany, who helped to edit Chapter 5 and added relevant material; Anne Briggs, who assisted in the editing of Chapter 5 and translated the source passages; Jessie Maritz, who supplied the photographs of the coins from the Courtauld Collection, Harare that appear in Chapter 7; Terrence Lockyer, who translated most of the source passages in Chapters 8 and 9; Susan Haskins and Wendy du Plooy, who helped to compile the indices; and Olivia Banks, who completed the indices and checked the final proofs. Thanks are also due to the several tutors and many hundreds of university students at the University of Natal, Durban who have read and engaged with earlier versions of the material in these chapters over the years. Their responses to the material have helped to shape this textbook.

I wish also to express my appreciation to Bolchazy-Carducci, especially Laurie Haight Keenan for guiding me through the submission, contract, editing, and production stages; Cameron Marshall, Charlene Hernandez, and Adam Velez for their technical assistance and design support during the preparation of the final manuscript for publication; and Ladislaus Bolchazy, who has done so much for Classics over the years by publishing pedagogical and other texts that help to bring life to the discipline in the university and secondary classrooms.

I wish to thank Anglo American, South Africa for funding a curriculum development grant that contributed to the publication of *Words and Ideas*. Clare Hall, Cambridge awarded me a Visiting Research Fellowship during 2000–2001, which enabled me to complete the final editing of this textbook while engaged in various research projects at the College. I wish to express my appreciation not only to the University of Natal for granting me a period of leave to work on these projects at Clare Hall, Cambridge but also to the University of Otago for its financial assistance in completing the final editing of this textbook.

W. J. DOMINIK
Dunedin, New Zealand
August 2002

ILLUSTRATION ACKNOWLEDGMENTS

The editor and publisher wish to thank Michael Atchison Enterprises for generously supplying and granting permission to publish the "WORD FOR WORD" strips that appear in this book. The strip appears daily in newspapers in the USA (syndicated by Associated Press), Australia, United Kingdom, South Africa, Papua New Guinea, and Japan.

The editor and publisher would like also to thank the following for supplying photographs that appear on the cover and in Chapters 5–9:

The British Museum, London: statue of Socrates, p. 198; coin of Julius Caesar, p. 237.

Courtauld Collection, Harare: drachma from Cyrene showing the head of Zeus Ammon and a silphium plant, p. 174; tetradrachm showing Cleopatra VII of Egypt and Antony, p. 177.

Deutsches Archäologisches Institut, Athens: votive relief of Asklepios attended by Hygieia, p. 125.

Deutsches Archäologisches Institut, Rome: bust of Hippocrates, p. 106.

Fratelli Alinari S.p.A., Florence: statue of Aesculapius, p. 105; tombstone of an oculist, p. 123.

Fototeca Unione, Rome: relief of an obstetrician, p. 115.

Giraudon, Paris: mosaic showing a detail from "Plato's Academy," p. 201; relief of Aphrodite and Hermes on a chariot pulled by Eros and Psyche, p. 211.

Kunsthistorisches Museum, Vienna: bust of Aristotle, p. 203.

Museo Archeologico Nazionale, Naples: woman holding a stylus and writing tablets, cover.

TimePix, New York: bust of Plato, p. 200; water clock, p. 231; bust of Herodotus and Thycydides, p. 234; relief with figure of Polybius, p. 236; relief from Arch of Titus showing triumphal procession after the fall of Jerusalem, p. 236.

Acknowledgements are also due to Tamaryn Pieterse, who drew the illustrations in Chapter 4; William Dominik, who produced the vase images in Chapter 5, and John Hilton, who created the illustrations in Chapters 6 and 7.

A NOTE TO THE TEACHER

Words and Ideas is designed for a course of between twelve and fifteen weeks. Its flexible format means that it can be utilized in a few different ways for the benefit of students. The word building chapters—Chapters 1 ("Word Building Basics"), 2 ("Word Building Tools: Greek Components"), and 3 ("Word Building Tools: Latin Components")—can be taught as separate chapters on their own or its sections can be discussed concurrently with the other chapters on the various disciplines. A recommended teaching method is to work gradually through the word building chapters in the process of discussing the other chapters. In this way the vocabulary technique, discipline-specific vocabulary, and cultural understanding of students are broadened at the same time. On the other hand, it may be felt that students should acquire some basic knowledge of word building before proceeding to the more specialized vocabulary and cultural topics contained in the subsequent chapters. Some teachers may prefer to emphasize the word-building sections throughout this textbook, while others, especially those involved in the teaching of history and civilization, may prefer to give greater attention to the cultural topics.

The chapters on the various disciplines may be discussed in any order, although Chapter 5 ("Medicine") in particular contains a long section on medical terminology that complements the content and objectives of the word building chapters. Chapter 5 therefore may be introduced usefully during the early or middle stages of discussing these word building chapters or perhaps shortly after their completion. There is some repetition of material between and within some of the chapters, often from a different perspective, for example, in Chapters 1–3 and 5. This is intentional on the part of the editor and is designed not only to illustrate the working relationship between the component parts of words but also to provide reinforcement of important words and concepts. An effort has been made to simplify the word building terminology and approach throughout this book and to avoid making overly technical explanations and definitions, especially in Chapters 1–3. This applies especially to the discussion of suffixes, whose grammatical functions are emphasized rather than their possible meanings.

Although the material in the chapters has been liberally edited in order to ensure a reasonable degree of consistency in style and format, it will be noted that the approaches vary in each of the chapters according to the interests and methodologies of the authors. It is hoped that these varied approaches will help to maintain the interest of the students in the topics and words discussed in each of the chapters. The "Word for Word" strips that have been included throughout this textbook are also intended to stimulate the interest of students in word origins by providing, clarifying, or emphasizing information about particular words in an interesting way.

A bibliography and suggestions for further reading appear at the end of each chapter; for second and subsequent editions of cited books I have attempted to provide the most recent places and dates of publication. Further bibliography may be found by consulting the most recent books listed, most of which contain extensive bibliographies of previous publications. The lists contain mainly publications in English; articles from journals have been excluded because of the limitation of space. In addition to the bibliography, a selection of relevant web sites accessible at the time of publication and containing the names of the web sites and their URLs (Uniform Resource Locators) appears at the end of each chapter. Some of the listed web sites contain additional information about the topics discussed in the chapters and in a few cases some helpful exercises. In addition, searching the internet using the titles of the web sites and the titles of the chapters and sections in this book should lead the reader to other relevant sites, including those that have appeared since the publication of this textbook.

The different types of questions and exercises in the body of Chapters 4–9 and at the end of Chapters 1–9 are designed to give varied practice with the words and ideas discussed in the various sections. Most of the answers to the questions and exercises in each chapter are contained in the body of the chapter; where this is not directly the case, the answer usually can be deduced from the information given in the relevant chapter or can be found in an English dictionary that provides etymologies. For these reasons it was felt that it was not necessary or desirable from a pedagogical viewpoint to provide answer keys at the end of this book or in a separate publication. The questions at the end of each chapter generally provide practice with many of the topics and words discussed; however, teachers can use these as models to write their own questions for purposes of additional practice and assessment.

Students should be encouraged generally to use an English dictionary since there is not the space in this textbook to discuss all the words that are given as examples; furthermore, students are invited in the word study sections and exercises to refer to an English dictionary when there they may feel a need to do so. When students consult an English dictionary, it is important that they use a dictionary that gives the etymologies and meanings of all Greek and Latin words from which the English words are derived. For students using American English *Merriam-Webster's Collegiate Dictionary* is recommended; it is available not only in a printed version but also can be located on-line at http://www.m-w.com. For students using English of one of the Commonwealth countries, an edition of *The Concise Oxford Dictionary of Current English* is recommended.

It should not be necessary for students to consult Greek or Latin dictionaries to complete any of the exercises in this textbook since all the information required is usually provided within its pages. The meanings of some Greek and Latin words, however, are not provided when they do not differ significantly from the modern English meanings.

As discussed in Chapter 1 ("Word Building Basics"), there is sometimes a variation in the spelling of certain Greek words that have entered the English language. Where a Greek name is well known in a Latinate spelling, that spelling is generally used in this textbook. In Chapter 4 ("Mythology"), for example, the Latinate spelling *Uranus* is used instead of the Greek spelling *Ouranos* because the Latinized name of the planet is well known, whereas the Greek spelling *Kronos* is used rather than the Latinate *Cronus* because *Kronos* as a figure or name is generally not well known today. Some ordinary Greek words, however, may appear both in their Greek (e.g., *kosmos*) and English spelling forms (e.g., *cosmos*).

For the sake of uniformity American spelling and punctuation have been used throughout this book. All English words are spelled in the modern American way and alternative spellings generally are not indicated. Since the spelling of many English words is different in Commonwealth countries from the United States, teachers in these countries may instruct their students to use the spelling system standard in their own countries.

INTRODUCTION

"By words the mind is excited and the spirit elated."

(Aristophanes)

"Words are the daughters of heaven and things are the sons of heaven."

(Samuel Johnson)

"Words are the most powerful drug of mankind."

(Rudyard Kipling)

Words and Ideas focuses on modern English words, their ancient bases, and the ancient concepts that lie underneath these words that aid in the understanding of their meanings. On a general level this book aims to help extend students' general vocabulary and knowledge, to arouse the curiosity of students about the relationship between words and concepts in different cultures, and to demonstrate the degree of continuity and interrelatedness of these cultures. On a more specific level it aims to train students in the analysis of polysyllabic words by focusing on important words and concepts that are used regularly in academic work, to acquaint them with the origin and history of some of the fundamental ideas of the ancient world and of the twenty-first century in certain key areas, and to develop in students a basic understanding of the ancient Greek and Roman worlds. The key words and phrases discussed in this book usually appear in bold print to stress their importance. Exercises are provided in each chapter for written work or discussion in class.

Chapters 1 ("Word Building Basics"), 2 ("Word Building Tools: Greek Components"), and 3 ("Word Building Tools: Latin Components") provide a foundation and framework for the subsequent chapters of the book. One of the purposes of these chapters is to provide a general background to the system and rules of word building. They discuss such topics as language families; major stages in the development of English vocabulary; the Greek and Roman alphabets; writing Greek words in the Roman alphabet; the parts of speech; the structure of English words; and common prefixes, bases, suffixes, and combining forms.

Chapters 1–3 also serve as a practical introduction to the mechanics of word building. They aim to help students develop the ability to analyze unfamiliar words in terms of their derivational components and to assist in the acquisition of standard word building and vocabulary skills. Since the words discussed in this and subsequent chapters have been brought into English according to a system, an understanding of this system makes it possible to learn and understand the meanings and usages of these often complex words. Once students acquire a systematic approach to analyzing the form and meaning of these words, they begin to enlarge their vocabulary and give it etymological precision. Although Chapters 1–3 will be the chapters that most students read first, the word building material in them can be studied in conjunction with the other chapters.

Chapters 1–3 also examine the influence of Latin and ancient Greek upon the modern English language and explain how a knowledge of this influence can aid in the understanding of English. These languages are not spoken by anyone any more. Ancient Greek was the language spoken in the Greek world some two and a half thousand years ago, while Latin was the language of the Romans before and after the beginning of the common era. For many centuries thereafter, however, Greek and Latin were the internationally spoken languages of learning, so it is not surprising that modern English, like some other modern languages, contains a large number of words that are derived from Greek and Latin terms and concepts.

This lexical influence is extensive and pervasive. About sixty per cent of words in common use in English are derived from Latin and about ten per cent originate from ancient Greek. Some English words are derived from both Greek and Latin, while the origin of other words can be found in just one of these languages. **Africa,** for instance, is the ancient Latin name for a small part of the modern continent surrounding the ancient city of Carthage, while **govern** can be traced back to Latin and Greek words that originally meant "to steer a ship."

The rest of this book examines selected groups of words and concepts that have their origin in the ancient Greek and Roman worlds. Each of Chapters 4–9 is devoted to words in one or two set categories. Some of the fundamental ideas of the modern world are examined in the fields of Mythology, Medicine, Commerce and Economics, Politics and Law, Philosophy and Psychology, and History. The classical foundations of these disciplines generally are explored first by identifying the ancient word bases that form the basis of discipline-specific discourses. These word bases then are usually examined by placing the ancient concepts they signify into their original contexts so that students gain access to the connotative fields of meaning that are still attached to the modern terms. Through this process of examination an understanding of many important and relevant aspects of the ancient Greek and Latin words is acquired, thereby providing a base for students who wish to proceed to a more intensive study of the Greek and Roman languages and worlds.

Chapters 4–9 discuss words and phrases that express ideas of fundamental importance in academic English. These chapters focus on the social, historical and political origins of these words and phrases and contextualize them in ancient Greek and Roman society. This emphasis upon contextualization is critical, since it is often through comparison with their own culture that classical antiquity becomes meaningful to students.

In Chapter 4 ("Mythology"), for instance, the discussion of the origin, meaning and history of the Greek bases in **mythology, cosmogony,** and related words encourages students to consider the connotative and denotative signification of common English derivatives from the gods' names; furthermore, the relating of some of the myths from which common words and phrases in everyday English are derived, such as **Achilles' heel, Odysseus, Tantalus, Atlas,** and the **labors of Heracles,** invite students to reflect upon what these words mean and how they have come to acquire their meanings.

Many of the words and phrases discussed and contextualized in this book have specialized meanings in a particular field, whereas others arise in more than one context, which provides an opportunity for reinforcement. The phrase **Oedipus complex,** for instance, which comes from the legend of Oedipus, one of the most interesting of the Greek mythical heroes, naturally is discussed in the chapter on Mythology, but it is treated again in a different context in the chapter on Philosophy and Psychology.

Chapters 4–9 focus on key words and phrases that not only express important ideas in academic English but also have a general utility in everyday life. They may be words and phrases whose meanings are assumed to be understood but are sometimes misused. One of the words examined in Chapter 6 ("Politics and Law"), for instance, is **democracy,** which is derived from the Greek *demos* ("people") and *kratos* ("power") and therefore means literally "power of the people." The brief analysis and discussion of **democracy** leads naturally to the different applications and interpretations of the word in ancient and modern contexts. Knowing the meanings of *demos* and *kratos*, students are then equipped to begin identifying and analyzing other words containing this base and combining form, respectively, and to consider the contexts in which they are used. Combined with their expanding knowledge of other bases, suffixes, and combining forms discussed in similar terms, the students gradually gain access to a much greater active vocabulary, which enhances their reading comprehension and improves the quality of their written and spoken English.

Words and Ideas will be of interest to all students who have a particular interest in words, wish to improve their language ability, and are interested in the origin of ideas.

CHAPTER 1

WORD BUILDING BASICS

W. J. Dominik, J. L. Hilton, and A. P. Bevis

HOW WORDS ARE FORMED AND USED

Word Building in English

English is the language with the richest and most diverse vocabulary on earth. Although it has hundreds of thousands of words, the average first-language speaker of English has a word-stock only in the low tens of thousands. Yet everyone can improve their English vocabulary by learning the basic principles of word building. Since many English words in common use are made up from one or more Greek and Latin words, the first thing to learn is the way in which words are divided up into their constituent parts. The word **theology,** for instance, consists of two main parts: *theo-* and *-logy*. Each of these parts is derived from an ancient Greek word: *theos*, "god," and *logos*, "word," "explanation," "study." Therefore **theology** is taken to mean the "study of gods" or "the study of religion."

There are many other words in English that end in *-logy* with a variety of different Greek or Latin derived bases in front. A word made up of elements from these different languages is known as a "hybrid," as the word **sociology** in the list below. Almost all words that end in *-logy* mean the "study of" something; the base in front tells us what is being studied. For example:

- **Anthropology** is the study of mankind; from *anthropos*, the Greek word for "person" or "human being."
- **Biology** is the study of life; from *bios*, the Greek word for "life."
- **Graphology** is the study of handwriting; from *graphē*, the Greek word for "writing."
- **Osteology** is the branch of medicine concerned with study of the nature and diseases of the bones; from *osteon*, the Greek word for "bone."
- **Psychology** is the study of the human mind; from *psychē*; the Greek word for "soul" or "mind."
- **Sociology** is the study of society or of groups of people; from *socius*, the Latin word for "companion" (member of a group).
- **Zoology** is the study of animals; from *zoōn*, the Greek word for "animal."

Influence of Greek and Latin upon English

At various stages in the development of the English language, Greek and Latin words have been borrowed by speakers of English. Before about 1500 CE, however, there was very little direct contact between speakers of Greek and speakers of English. Greek was not widely known in Britain, but Greek words did enter English indirectly via Latin. On the other hand, Latin has influenced English directly and indirectly through the languages that have developed from Latin. Languages descended from Latin are known as Romance languages. French, Italian, Spanish, and Portuguese are the most important of these languages insofar as the influence upon English is concerned.

Since Christianity started in the Roman province of Judea in the eastern Mediterranean area, where Greek was widely spoken, a number of Greek words related to religion entered Latin and from there were taken into English. Some examples appear in the table below.

English	Latin	Greek
bishop	*episcopus*	*episkopos* ("overseer")
butter	*butyrum*	*boutyron* ("butter")
deacon	*diaconus*	*diakonos* ("servant," "attendant")
dish	*discus*	*diskos* ("quoit," "disk," "dish")
mint (herb)	*ment(h)a*	*minthē* ("mint")

Word for Word

From 43 CE the Romans occupied most of southeast Britain, but Latin seems to have had little effect on Celtic, which was the language spoken by the inhabitants of this area. An example of one group of borrowings from Latin are the elements *-chester* and *-caster*, which are derived from the Latin word *castra*, which means "military camp." These components form part of many town names in the English-speaking world, for example, **Ro***chester* and **Man***chester*.

In the middle of the fifth century CE the migration of Germanic tribes to Britain began. These people included the Angles, who gave their name to England and to English, the Saxons and the Jutes. Eventually they settled in southern Britain and their Germanic language ousted Celtic in the area that corresponds roughly to England today. This language is now called Old English. Before the invasion of Britain, these tribes had been in contact with the Romans and had already taken some Latin words into their language, for example, **street** from *strata* ("paved road"), **cheese** from *caseus*, and **wine** from *vinum*.

Christian missionaries began to reach Britain from about 600 CE. Latin was the language of the Christian Church in the West and also the language of scholarship, and as a result many more Latin words were brought into Old English. The influence of Latin through the Christian Church and through scholarship lasted for many centuries. Loan words from Old English include the following examples.

English	Latin
altar	*altare*
creed	*credere* ("to believe")
disciple	*discipulus* ("pupil")
master	*magister* ("teacher")
temple	*templum*

Word for Word

The French-speaking Normans defeated the English in 1066 CE and as a result French became the language of government in England for several centuries. Many French speakers settled in England and a flood of new words, most derived ultimately from Latin, entered English. Words adopted or used by a race or culture other than the one that originated them are commonly referred to as "loan words." Examples of loan words from Old French appear in the following table.

English	Old French	Latin
army	*armée*	*armata* ("armed")
beauty	*bealté*	*bellus* ("pretty")
crime	*crimne*	*crimen* ("guilt," "fault," "misdeed")
government	*governement*	*gubernare* ("to steer," "to rule")
medicine	*medecine*	*medicina* ("medicine," "surgery")
parliament	*parlement*	*parabola* ("parable," "speech")
people	*peuple*	*populus* ("people")

With the renewed interest in and knowledge of Classical Greek and Latin that came with the Renaissance, which lasted for several centuries and affected different countries at different times (in England it began in the late fifteenth century), many words were borrowed directly from Greek and Latin and new words were formed using bases from these languages.

The borrowing of Greek and the forming of new words was particularly common in areas in which the ancient Greeks had made important discoveries, for example, in science, medicine, and philosophy. Some examples of Renaissance loan words from Greek appear below.

English	Greek
autograph	*autos* ("self") + *graphē* ("writing")
criterion	*kriterion* ("means for judging," "standard")
encyclopedia	*enkuklios* ("circular," "all-round," "general") + *paideia* ("education")
pneumonia	*pneumonia* ("lung disease")
thermometer	*thermē* ("heat") + *metron* ("measure")
utopia	*ou* ("not") + *topos* ("place")

Word for Word

MANY PEOPLE DREAM OF A **UTOPIA** WHERE EVERYTHING IS IDEAL AND FAULTLESS!

WHEN SIR THOMAS MORE WROTE "UTOPIA" IN 1516 HE WAS MORE REALISTIC!

HIS IMAGINARY ISLAND, UTOPIA, WITH ITS PERFECT SOCIAL AND POLITICAL SYSTEM WAS NAMED FROM THE GREEK - OU···NOT TOPOS···PLACE!

IT MEANT "NOWHERE!"

@ATCHISON

The revival of interest in Classical Latin and the opening up to other cultures and languages that came during the Renaissance brought many new words into English from Latin and from Italian, French, Spanish, and Portuguese. Examples of Renaissance loan words from Latin include the following words.

English	Latin
benefit	*bene factum* ("benefits," "benefactions")
emancipate	*emancipare* ("to declare free")
exact	*exactus* ("a sending off")
excursion	*excursio* ("attack," "a running out")
temperature	*temperatura* ("consistency"; a mixture of substances in proper proportions)
vacuum	*vacuus* ("empty")

The process of borrowing words directly from Greek and Latin and of forming new words from the bases of these languages continues today. The majority of words derived from Greek are used for scientific and technological purposes. The following table contains a few examples of later loan words from Greek.

English	Greek
anesthesia (eighteenth century)	*anaisthesia* ("lack of feeling")
chromosome (late nineteenth century)	*chroma* ("color") + *soma* ("body")
telephone (middle of the nineteenth century)	*telē* ("at a distance," "far off" + *phonē* ("voice," "sound")

Examples of modern loan words from Latin include those in the table below.

English	Latin
penicillin (twentieth century)	*penicillum* ("paint brush)
quantum (early twentieth century in the scientific sense)	*quantus* ("how much")
vitamin (early twentieth century)	*vita* ("life")

Terminology of Word Building

It is not necessary to become too involved in technical terminology and explanations when discussing the principles and mechanics of word building, but the following terms are useful for identifying basic word elements.

- A "base" is part of an English word derived (in terms of this book) from a Greek or Latin word that usually has a constant meaning and a constant form. Although both form and meaning may vary, both must be present in order for a base to be identified. For example, **com*pos*e** and **im*pos*ition** have slightly different variants of the same base (*pos-*) meaning "place." Although the word "possible" has an element with a similar form (*pos-*), it does not share the meaning "place" and therefore does not have the same base. Similarly, **confer** and **collate** both share the meaning "carry" but do not have the same form, while the verbs **position** and **locate** have the same meaning but not the same form.
- A "prefix" is an element that can be added only to the *beginning* of a base or word. Some prefixes can only be used in combination with a base; others can function either as independent words or in combination.
- A "suffix" is an element that can be added only to the *end* of a base or word.

In addition to these basic elements, it is also helpful to make use of the terms "combining form" and "combining vowel."

- The terminological phrase "combining form" is a convenient way of identifying a base and suffix combination that is added to another base without specifying these elements individually. The phrase can also be used to describe a second base without a suffix.
- A "combining vowel" (usually "o" or "i") is sometimes used to link a base with subsequent elements. In the word **osteopathy** the combining vowel "o" links *oste-* ("bone"), the base, with *-pathy* ("disease of"), the combining form.

Structure of Words

The most important elements of which words are built are bases, prefixes, and suffixes. The "base" carries the main meaning of the word. It can be used alone, as in English **duct** (Latin *duct-*, "led"), or in combination with another base, as in **aqueduct** (Latin *aqua*, "water" + *duct-*). A base can also be modified usually by the addition of a prefix, as in **abduct** (prefix *ab-* + base *duct-*), or by a suffix, as in **ductile** (base *duct-* + suffix *-ile*).

A word may contain more than one prefix, as in **asymmetry** (prefix *a-* + prefix *sym-* + Greek combining form *-metry*), or suffix, as in **tyrannical** (Greek base *tyrann-* + suffix *-ic* + suffix *-al*). Some prefixes have meaning, as in **superimpose** ("put on *top of*"), but others have lost their meaning entirely, as in **convert** ("change"). When prefixes are joined to certain bases, sound changes, which are reflected in the spelling of the word, may result, for example, in the word **commute** (*con-* + *mute*).

Some suffixes function linguistically to turn bases into nouns or adjectives, while other suffixes turn bases into verbs. An example of an English base whose derivational suffixes determine its word class and grammatical function in a given sentence is *dramat-* (the extended base of Greek *drama*, "theatrical performance"), to which suffixes commonly beginning with a vowel are joined.

- In **dramatic** the suffix *-ic* is an adjective ending; for example, "The young actor showed great **dramatic** ability."
- In **dramatics** the suffix *-ics* is a noun ending; for example, "I love taking part in amateur **dramatics**."
- In **dramatist** the suffix *-ist* is a noun ending; for example, "Shakespeare was a famous **dramatist**."
- **Dramatize** means "make into a drama," so the suffix *-ize* is a verb ending; for example, "The productions **dramatize** the history, folklore, and social issues of the Americas."

Word for Word

Suffixes may be said traditionally to carry meaning, as in the word **dramatist,** whose suffix *-ist* denotes the person who performs the action that is obviously implied by the meaning of the base *dramat-*. Nouns can be categorized according to the various meanings of their suffixes.

- A "general" noun suffix indicates that the word is a noun such as a thing or a substance.
- An "abstract" noun refers to an abstract concept, quality, or entity that is the result of some action or process.
- An "agent" noun refers to a person or entity that performs an action.
- A "locative" noun refers to a place.
- A "diminutive" suffix indicates that the entity referred to is small. Sometimes this type of suffix refers to something that is young or lovable as the result of its small size.
- A "medical" term often has a suffix that indicates a specific medical condition. (For suffixes of this type, see Chapter 5, "Medicine.")

While some Greek and Latin noun-forming suffixes, especially those that form medical terms, have clearly definable meanings, the meanings of many other suffixes are often unclear and confusing. But even suffixes that lack clear meanings indicate the word classes (noun, adjective, verb, and adverb) to which individual words belong.

Adjectives usually show a relationship with nouns that can be expressed loosely as "being," "having," and "relating to." The use of different adjective-forming suffixes affects the meaning of the resultant compound, for instance, **corporeal** (*corporeus* and *corporealis*, "bodily," from *corpus*, "body"), **corporal** (*corporalis*, "relating to the body," from *corpus*, "body") and **corporate** (*corporatus*, "made into a body," from *corporare*, "to make into a body," which is from *corpus*, "body"). Suffixes that form verbs convey the idea of making and causation.

Coining New Words

Some of the Latin words used in English were made up, or coined, creating a word previously absent in the language. One example of this is the word *essentia* ("essence") that was invented by the Roman orator, Cicero, to express the Greek word *ousia* ("being"). Similarly, the Latin term *quinta essentia* was made up in the Middle Ages for Aristotle's *pemptē ousia* ("fifth element"), ether, an addition to the four known elements of which the universe was thought to be composed. Ether (compare **ethereal,** meaning "heavenly") was considered to be the fine air above the earth that also constituted the material of the soul; hence it was the finest, most perfect matter. Therefore **quintessence** means the "perfect manifestation" of something, as in the sentence, "His behavior was the quintessence of good taste."

Word for Word

EARLY GREEK PHILOSOPHERS BELIEVED THE UNIVERSE WAS COMPOSED OF FOUR ELEMENTS OR ESSENCES! — EARTH! — AIR! — FIRE! — WATER! — LATER THEY ADDED ANOTHER, THE RAREST OF ALL, FROM WHICH, THEY SAID, THE STARS WERE MADE! — THIS WAS CALLED "THE FIFTH ESSENCE". IN LATIN, QUINTA ESSENTIA! — TODAY'S WORD... QUINTESSENCE! — ©ATCHISON

The Latinate Register of English

As a result of extensive borrowings from Latin, English has developed a register that may be called Latinate English. It is this register of English that is commonly used in academic texts, often because appropriate terms do not otherwise exist in English; for example, **digital** (from Latin *digitus*, "finger") is widely used in English to refer to information in numeric form.

Scientific language is particularly Latinate since new inventions are often given Latin names (for example, **radio, television, computer**). Business people often use Latinate terms to enhance the prestige of their products or services (for example, **rodent operatives** for "rat catchers"). Words such as **beef, pork,** and **poultry** are used to hide the fact that such food comes from animals, that is, cows, pigs, and chickens, respectively.

Word for Word

THE WORD RADIO ORIGINATED IN THE UNITED STATES IN 1915! IT IS SHORT FOR RADIOTELEGRAPHY... BASED ON THE LATIN RADIUS - STAFF, STAKE! THIS CAME TO MEAN "THE SPOKE OF A WHEEL" OR A RAY!

THUS RADIOTELEGRAPHY IS THE SENDING OF MESSAGES BY ELECTROMAGNETIC RAYS!

www.red-e2.com

The use of Latinate vocabulary in academic books is often pretentious and unnecessary. Such jargon is often used to make a subject appear more scientific. Politicians often reject this register of the language in order to appear more populist and democratic. Newspapers prefer shorter Anglo-Saxon words to longer, polysyllabic Latin ones; for instance, the word **row** may be used instead of **controversy.**

CHANGES IN WORDS ACROSS LANGUAGES

Greek and Latin words that enter English frequently change in meaning and appearance. These words can extend or narrow in meaning when used in English, while the most obvious changes in appearance involve transliteration (of Greek), spelling, and the form of words.

Changes in Meaning of Greek and Latin Words in English

Most Greek and Latin words are used in English in ways that extend the range of their meanings. Other Greek and Latin words are used unchanged in English or the range of their meanings is narrowed so that they are used mainly in a specialized sense. *Corpus* is good example of a Latin word that is used unchanged in English. A **corpus** ("body"; compare **corpse**), for example, refers to a grouping of texts or writings such as the

Brown Corpus of English Texts. The Latin word *corpus* was used in this sense in antiquity, for example, the *Corpus Iuris Civilis* or the body of civil law codified by Justinian. **Corpus,** however, is only used in this narrow, specialized sense in English. The Latin *corpus*, which was used, for example, of the physical body, originally had a much wider range of meanings that it does in English. The English word "body," however, has a much wider range of meanings as, for example, in "body corporate" and "this wine has plenty of body."

Some examples of the use of unchanged Latin words in English appear in the table below.

Latin/English Word	Latin Meaning	English Meaning
circus	circle, racecourse	travelling show with horses, clowns; "circle" is derived from Latin *circulum*
formula	beauty, mould, pipe, rule	fixed form of words, mathematical or chemical rule, recipe
forum	public place, market	a meeting place or medium for public discussion
radius	a rod, a spoke, shuttle, spur, sting, beam, ray	bone in arm, mathematical line from center to circumference

Other words used differently in English from their original Latin meanings appear in the following table.

Latin Form	Latin Meaning	English Spelling	English Meaning
cursus	a running, passage, racecourse	**course**	movement, layer of stone, medicine, series of classes
pietas	duty to gods, parents, or country	**piety**	devotion, religious observance
potis	able, possible (*potiri*, "to possess")	**power**	ability, energy, government, multiplying factor
sacer, sacra	holy, accursed	**sacred**	devoted, holy

The words *cursus* and *potis* appear to have extended their range of meanings in English, whereas *pietas* and *sacer* have narrowed in meaning.

Many Greek and Latin words are used as technical terms in English. If these terms fall into frequent usage, then they can take on additional meanings and even lose their original meanings. The word **anthology** (from Greek *anthos* + *logia*), for example, which literally means a "collection of flowers," is now used to refer to a collection of choice literary pieces or passages or beautiful works of art or music. It has lost its original, literal meaning through common use in a number of contexts.

Some words are used more abstractly in English than in Greek and Latin. The Greek word *psychē* is an example of such a word. In Greek *psychē* means "breath," "principle of life," "soul," and "spirit," while in English **psyche** is often used to refer to the principle of conscious and unconscious mental, emotional, and behavioral life.

Changes in Spelling of Greek and Latin Words in English

Greek words are not written in the Roman alphabet exactly as they were spelled in Greek due to sound changes in Latin and English. When Greek words were taken into Latin, their spellings changed because the Romans wrote the letters of the alphabet in a different way from the Greeks. The Roman alphabet is based on the letters used by the Etruscans, whose alphabet was modeled on the Greek forms. (See Appendix 1, "Greek and Latin Alphabets," and Appendix 2, "Writing of Greek Words in English.")

Latin words that enter the English language through a third language such as French usually undergo significant changes in spelling, while many English words derived directly from Latin change only a little in spelling from the original Latin. The spelling of some Greek and Latin words change considerably when taken into English. This means that the English derivatives appear to be unrelated to the Greek or Latin words from which they are derived.

Some English words derived from Latin have changed only in their spellings. For example, **chaste** is derived from *castus* (compare **chastity** from Latin *castitas*). This word is used in much the same way as it was in Latin, particularly with regard to women, to mean "morally pure." In many cases the changes in the spelling of words have been slight: often the word endings have simply been dropped or modified; for example, **navigate** from Latin *navigatus*, **navigation** from *navigationis*, and **urbanity** from *urbanitas*. In other cases, however, the changes have made the origin of the word almost unrecognizable, as in **issue** (from Latin *exitus*, "a going out") and **inch**.

Word for Word

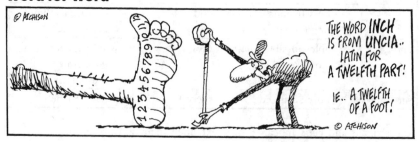

The reason for the great changes in spelling of some English words that are derived from Latin is that they came into English through French. A well-known example of this is **lieutenant,** a deputy officer who takes the place of his superior. This word comes ultimately from Latin *locus* ("place") and *tenent-*, the extended form of *tenens* ("the one holding"). Besides spelling changes, French introduced other words from Latin into English, as discussed in the first section of this chapter. As a result, English has a large number of synonyms that have been derived at different times from Anglo-Saxon, French, and Latin.

Anglo-Saxon	French	Latin
ask	question	interrogate
fast	firm	stable
fear	terror	horror
holy	sacred	pious
kingly	royal	regal
lawful	loyal	legal
rise	mount	ascend

Changes in the Forms of Words

Greek and Latin are inflected languages, which means that their words often change form depending upon how they are used in a sentence.

Nouns, Pronouns, and Adjectives

Nouns (words that refer to a thing, quality, state, action, or concept), pronouns (words used as substitutes for nouns), and adjectives (words that modify nouns) in Greek and Latin change their forms according to their grammatical function. English was once an inflected language and there are still some traces of this system, as in the following examples featuring the use of pronouns and a possessive adjective.

> **He** caught the train to New York.
> I saw **him** at the station.
> Someone stole **his** suitcase.

Most English nouns also change their forms to denote possession.

> The president made a speech.
> The president**'s** speech was reported in all the newspapers.

In Greek and Latin there are many more of these inflected forms. This is one reason several English words that look different can be derived from a single Greek or Latin word. For example, the Greek word *haima/haema* ("blood") has derivatives such as **hemorrhage** and **hematology.** Sometimes a modified form of the base occurs in the subject form of the word; this form is usually the one in which a Greek or Latin word is given when cited on its own.

Subject Form	Meaning
corpus (Latin)	body
eros (Greek)	love
Mars (Latin)	Mars (the god of war)
pais (Greek)	child

The full base is found in the other forms, which can be referred to conveniently as extended forms. Very often English derivatives are based not on the subject form, in which the true base has often been obscured by phonetic development, but rather on the base found in the extended forms.

The following table shows an extended form (the form used to indicate possession) and the base of the words given in the previous table along with an English derivative.

Extended (Possessive) Form	Base	English Derivative
corporis	*corpor-*	**corpor**al
erotos	*erot-*	**erot**ic
Martis	*Mart-*	**mart**ial
paidos	*paid-*	**ped**ophile

Sometimes an English dictionary gives only the subject form; sometimes it gives both the subject and extended (possessive) forms; and sometimes it gives the subject form and the base derived from the extended form. The following examples illustrate how these bases may be listed: **eros,** Greek *eros* (subject form only); **venereal,** Latin *venus, veneris* (subject and extended possessive form); **genus,** Latin *genus, -eris* (subject and extended possessive form abbreviated); and **legal,** Latin *lex, leg-* (subject and base of extended forms).

Verbs

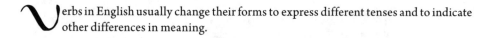erbs in English usually change their forms to express different tenses and to indicate other differences in meaning.

> I **walk** [present] to work each day.
> The boy **walks** [present] to school each day.
> The boy **walked** [past] to school yesterday.
> Having **walked** [past participle] to school, the boy was tired.

In Greek and Latin verbs have several different bases (and endings) to express different tenses (and persons), as in the following examples.

Language/ Meaning	Present Tense	Past (Perfect) Tense	Past Participle
Greek	*graphō*	*egrapsa*	*gegrammenon*
Latin	*scribo*	*scripsi*	*scriptum*
Meaning	I write	I wrote	(having been) written

Sometimes the vowel changes in different forms of the base, for example, in Greek *pempō* ("I send") and *pepompha* ("I have sent"). Such vowel changes occur not only within verbs but also in nouns and other parts of speech derived from the same base. This phenomenon is common in Greek and English, for example, *lego* ("I say"), *logos* ("word") and "drive," "drove," "driven."

There are often English derivatives from more than one part of a verb, for example, **(tele) graph/(tele)gram** and **scribe/script** from the verbs in the table above. These examples illustrate that words derived from the same Greek or Latin verb can look different. Other examples are **convenient, convene,** and **convention,** which are all derived from the Latin verb *convenire* ("to assemble," "to come together").

Sometimes the derivatives reflect the meaning of the particular Greek or Latin form quite closely, as in the above examples, but sometimes only the basic meaning of the verb is reflected, and the precise meaning of the particular part is no longer preserved. For example, **confound** and **confuse,** which both mean "perplex," "cause confusion," are derived respectively from *confundere,* "to pour together," "to mix up," and *confusum,* "(having been) poured together," "mixed up."

Greek and Latin Plural Forms in English

When a Greek or Latin word is taken directly into English, it sometimes retains its original plural form, as in the examples listed below. Other words are "naturalized" and add the English "s" to form their plural.

Greek

- singular ending in *-on*; plural ending in *-a*

Singular Ending	Plural Ending
criterion	criteria
phenomenon	phenomena

- singular ending in *-is*; plural ending in *-es*

Singular Ending	Plural Ending
analysis	analyses
basis	bases
emphasis	emphases
exegesis	exegeses
hypothesis	hypotheses
prognosis	prognoses
synthesis	syntheses

- singular ending in -*ma;* plural ending in -*mata*

Singular Ending	Plural Ending
carcinoma	carcinomata
miasma	miasmata
trauma	traumata

Latin

- singular ending in -*um;* plural ending in -*a*

Singular Ending	Plural Ending
addendum	addenda
atrium	atria
curriculum	curricula
erratum	errata
gymnasium	gymnasia
memorandum	memoranda
millennium	millennia
rostrum	rostra
spectrum	spectra

- singular ending in -*us;* plural ending in -*i*

Singular Ending	Plural Ending
bacillus	bacilli
calculus	calculi
colossus	colossi
fungus	fungi
gladiolus	gladioli
locus	loci
radius	radii
terminus	termini

- singular ending in *-a;* plural ending in *-ae*

Singular Ending	Plural Ending
alga (usually used in the plural)	algae
alumna	alumnae
antenna	antennae
lacuna	lacunae
larva	larvae
nebula	nebulae

- singular ending in *-ex, -ix;* plural ending in *-ices*

Singular Ending	Plural Ending
codex	codices
matrix	matrices
vertex	vertices
vortex	vortices

- singular endings in *-yx, -x;* plural endings in *-yces, -ces*

Singular Ending	Plural Ending
calyx	calyces
crux	cruces

- singular endings in *-us, -ies;* plural endings in *-era/-ora, -ies*

Singular Ending	Plural Ending
corpus	corpora
genus	genera
opus	opera
species	species

BIBLIOGRAPHY AND FURTHER READING

Ayers, D. M., *English Words from Latin and Greek Elements*, 2nd Ed. (Tucson 1986).

Burriss, E. E. and Casson, L., *Latin and Greek in Current Use*, 2nd Ed. (Englewood Cliffs 1949).

Crystal, D., *The English Language*, 2nd Ed. (London 2002) 143–214.

Dunmore, C. W. and Fleischer, R., *Studies in Etymology*, 2nd Ed. (Newburyport 2008).

Denning, K. and Leben, W. R., *English Vocabulary Elements* (Oxford 1995).

Else, G., "The Pronunciation of Classical Names and Words in English," *The Classical Journal* 62.5 (1967) 210–214.

Goodspeed, R. C., *From Greek to Graffiti: English Words that Survive and Thrive* (Hicksville 1981).

Green, T. M., *The Greek and Latin Roots of English*, 4th Ed. (Lanham 2008).

Krill, R. M., *Greek and Latin in English Today*, 3rd Ed. (Wauconda 2003).

Luschnig, J., *Etyma: An Introduction to Vocabulary-Building from Latin and Greek* (Lanham 1982).

O'Reilly, N. J., *Latin, Not Dead: Greek, Alive and Well in Today's Words* (Lima 2005).

Randall, T., "How to Improve Your Vocabulary" (New York n.d.).

Sweet, W. and Knudsvig, G. M., *A Course on Words* (Ann Arbor 1989).

Walker, T. E., *Word Resources*, 3rd Ed. (Indianapolis 1979).

WEB SITES: NAMES AND URLS

"Behind the Name: The Etymology and History of First Names"
    http://www.behindthename.com

"The English Language: Words Borrowed from Other Languages"
    http://www.krysstal.com/borrow.html

"Etymologic: The Toughest Game on the Web"
    http://www.etymologic.com

"Etymologically Speaking"
    http://www.westegg.com/etymology

"Etymology — Roots"
    http://ancienthistory.about.com/cs/roots

"Etymology"
    http://eleaston.com/etymology.html

"Focusing on Words"
    http://www.wordfocus.com

"History of the English Language"
    http://homes.chass.utoronto.ca/~cpercy/hell

"A Little Etymology"
    http://ancient.history.about.com/library/weekly/aa052698.htm

"Loanords: Major Periods of Borrowing in the History of English"
    http://www.ruf.rice.edu/~kemmer/Words/loanwords.html

"Martha Barnette: Buff Up Your Brain"
    http://www.marthabarnette.com

"Merriam-Webster's Collegiate Dictionary"
    http://www.m-w.com/cgi-bin/dictionary

"Merriam-Webster's Word Game of the Day"
    http://www.m-w.com/game/index.html

"Merriam-Webster's Word of the Day"
    http://www.m-w.com/cgi-bin/mwwod.pl

"My Word!"
    http://ablemedia.com/ctcweb/myword.html

"Origin of Phrases"
    http://www.phrases.org.uk

"Oxford English Dictionary Word of the Day"
    http://oed.com

"Roots of English: An Etymological Dictionary"
　　　http://ablemedia.com/ctcweb/showcase/roots.html
"Surnames: What's in a Name?"
　　　http://surnames.behindthename.com
"Take Our Word for It"
　　　http://www.takeourword.com
"What's the Meaning of This?"
　　　http://www.rootsweb.ancestry.com
"The Word Detective"
　　　http://www.word-detective.com
"Word of the Day"
　　　http://dictionary.reference.com/wordoftheday
"Word Wizard"
　　　http://www.wordwizard.com
"World Wide Words: Exploring the English Language"
　　　http://www.worldwidewords.org/index.htm

EXERCISES

1.　Why has Latin influenced English vocabulary much more than Greek has?

2.　From which Latin word is the English word **mile?** Explain the relationship between the two words. Use an English dictionary if necessary.

3.　List five towns in North America or Britain that end in *-chester* or *-caster*. Consult an atlas if necessary.

4.　Give concise definitions of the following terms:
　　a.　base　　　　　　　　　　　c.　suffix
　　b.　combining vowel　　　　　d.　prefix

5.　Give the plural form of each of the following words:
　　a.　**crisis**　　　　　　　　　f.　**hippopotamus**
　　b.　**stimulus**　　　　　　　g.　**formula**
　　c.　**stratum**　　　　　　　　h.　**thesis**
　　d.　**prolegomenon**　　　　i.　**bacterium**
　　e.　**appendix**　　　　　　　j.　**corpus**

6.　Give the singular form of each of the following words:
　　a.　**cacti**　　　　　　　　　f.　**consortia**
　　b.　**alumni**　　　　　　　　g.　**diagnoses**
　　c.　**metamorphoses**　　　h　**indices**
　　d.　**vertebrae**　　　　　　i.　**data**
　　e.　**media**　　　　　　　　j.　**moratoria**

7.   Sort the following words into the appropriate grammatical categories. Be sure to pay
     particular attention to the suffixes. Use an English dictionary if necessary.

     **bigamy, bigamist, demonize, plastic (2), mysticism, Cypriot,
     plagiarize, neologism, aphrodisiac (2), rhythmic, logic, ethics**

Nouns	Adjectives	Verbs

CHAPTER 2

WORD-BUILDING TOOLS:
GREEK COMPONENTS

W. J. Dominik, J. L. Hilton, and A. P. Bevis

THE GREEK ALPHABET

The letters of an alphabet are the most fundamental components of the vocabulary of a language. The Greek alphabet was borrowed from the Greeks at Cumae by the Etruscans, who were an indigenous people of pre-Roman Italy. It is beneficial to be familiar with the Greek alphabet since many scientific, mathematical, and other words in general use in English are derived from original Greek word forms. (For a discussion of the alphabet, see Appendix 1, "Greek and Latin Alphabets.")

GREEK BASES

Nouns

There are numerous Greek nouns that are used in English today. The following tables list some English combining-forms derived from Greek nouns. Other tables listing combining forms appear in Chapter 5 ("Medicine").

Combining Forms

- *-archy, -arch*

Greek Base	English Combining Form	Meaning	English Derivative
-archia	-archy	rule by	gyn**archy**
-archos	-arch	ruler	mon**arch**

- *-cracy, -crat*

Greek Base	English Combining Form	Meaning	English Derivatives
-kratia	-cracy	rule by, ruling body of	demo**cracy**, aristo**cracy**
-kratēs	-crat	supporter of rule by, member of ruling body	demo**crat**, aristo**crat**

- *-graphy, -graph*

Greek Base	English Combining Form	Meaning	English Derivatives
-graphia	-graphy	art or method of writing	calligraphy
		descriptive science	geography, bibliography
-graphos	-graph	something written	photograph
		instrument that writes	seismograph, polygraph

- *-logy*

Greek Base	English Combining Form	Meaning	English Derivative
-logia	-logy	subject of study	theology
		discourse	eulogy

- *-mania*

Greek Base	English Combining Form	Meaning	English Derivatives
-mania	-mania	madness	kleptomania, megalomania
		excessive enthusiasm	bibliomania

- *-metry*

Greek Base	English Combining Form	Meaning	English Derivative
-metria	-metry	art or process of the science of measuring	geometry

- *-nomy*

Greek Base	English Combining Form	Meaning	English Derivative
-nomia	-nomy	law of, arrangement of, science of	antinomy

- *-pathy*

Greek Base	English Combining Form	Meaning	English Derivative
-patheia	-pathy	feeling	telepathy

- *-philia, -phile*

Greek Base	English Combining Form	Meaning	English Derivative
-philia	**-philia**	love of	pedo**philia**
-philos	**-phile**	lover of	biblio**phile**

- *-phobe*

Greek Base	English Combining Form	Meaning	English Derivative
-phobos	**-phobe**	one who fears	xeno**phobe**

- *-skopy, -skope*

Greek Base	English Combining Form	Meaning	English Derivative
-skopia	**-scopy**	observation or examination of or by	colono**scopy**
-skopos	**-scope**	instrument for observing or examining	tele**scope**

Adjectives

Many English words are derived from Greek adjectives. Most English derivatives of Greek adjectives are based on the form of the Greek adjective that describes the subject, but some English words are based on an extended form of the Greek adjective. For example, the Greek adjectives *aristos* ("best") and *monos* ("single," "alone") form English words based on the form of the adjective that describes the subject, whereas the Greek *pas, pantos* ("all") forms English derivatives based on its extended possessive form (**pantheist, pantomime**). A number of examples appear in the tables below.

- *acr-*

Greek Adjective	English Base	Meaning	English Derivatives
akros	**acr-**	high, topmost	**acr**opolis, **acr**onym

- *all-*

Greek Adjective	English Base	Meaning	English Derivative
allos	**all-**	other	**all**ergy

- *arist-*

Greek Adjective	English Base	Meaning	English Derivative
aristos	**arist-**	best	**arist**ocracy

- *aut-*

Greek Adjective	English Base	Meaning	English Derivative
autos	**aut-**	self, one's own	**aut**onomy
		of or by oneself or itself	**aut**omobile

- *cac-*

Greek Adjective	English Base	Meaning	English Derivative
kakos	**cac-**	bad	**cac**ophony

- *heter-*

Greek Adjective	English Base	Meaning	English Derivative
heteros	**heter-**	other	**heter**osexual

- *hier-*

Greek Adjective	English Base	Meaning	English Derivative
hieros	**hier-**	holy	**hier**oglyphics

- *hol-*

Greek Adjective	English Base	Meaning	English Derivative
holos	**hol-**	whole	**hol**ocaust

- *hom-*

Greek Adjective	English Base	Meaning	English Derivative
homos	**hom-**	same	**hom**osexual

- *home-*

Greek Adjective	English Base	Meaning	English Derivative
homoios	**home-**	similar, same	**home**opath

- *idi-*

Greek Adjective	English Base	Meaning	English Derivatives
idios	**idi-**	own, personal	**idi**om, **idi**osyncrasy

- *macr-*

Greek Adjective	English Base	Meaning	English Derivative
makros	**macr-**	long, large	**macr**ocosm
		large-scale	**macr**oeconomics

- *mega-, megal-*

Greek Adjective	English Base	Meaning	English Derivative
megas, megale	**mega-**	great, large, powerful	**mega**phone
	megal-		**megal**omania
	mega-	one million (in the metric system)	**mega**byte

- *mes-*

Greek Adjective	English Base	Meaning	English Derivative
mesos	**mes-**	middle	**Mes**opotamia

- *micr-*

Greek Adjective	English Base	Meaning	English Derivative
mikros	**micr-**	small	**micr**oscope
		(denoting a factor of) one millionth	**micr**ogram

- *mon-*

Greek Adjective	English Base	Meaning	English Derivative
monos	**mon-**	single, one, alone	**mon**otonous

- *neo-*

Greek Adjective	English Base	Meaning	English Derivative
neos	**neo-**	new	**neo**lithic

- *olig-*

Greek Adjective	English Base	Meaning	English Derivative
oligos	**olig-**	few	**olig**archy

- *orth-*

Greek Adjective	English Base	Meaning	English Derivative
orthos	**orth-**	straight, correct	**orth**odontist

- *pale-*

Greek Adjective	English Base	Meaning	English Derivative
palaios	**pale-**	old	**pale**ography

- *pan-, pant-*

Greek Adjective	English Base	Meaning	English Derivative
pas, pan (*pantos*)	**pan-**	all	**pan**theist
	pant-		**pant**omime

- *poly-*

Greek Adjective	English Base	Meaning	English Derivative
polys, poly	**poly-**	many	**poly**chrome

- *pseud-*

Greek Adjective	English Base	Meaning	English Derivative
pseudes	**pseud-**	false	**pseud**onym

- *scler-*

Greek Adjective	English Base	Meaning	English Derivative
skleros	**scler-**	hard	**scler**osis

- *therm-*

Greek Adjective	English Base	Meaning	English Derivative
thermos	**therm-**	hot	**therm**ostat

Adverb

- *eu-*

Greek Adverb	English Base	Meaning	English Derivatives
eu	**eu-**	well, favorable	**eu**logy, **eu**phemism, **eu**phony, **eu**genic

Verbs

The following tables contain some common verbs and the different bases derived from them. Some of these bases were used not only for forming verbs but also for forming nouns and other parts of speech in Greek. (The Greek verb forms given have the meaning of the English infinitive "to" followed by the meaning of their bases; for example, *agein* means "to lead.")

- *agog-*

Greek Verb	English Base	Meaning	English Derivatives
agein	**agog-**	lead	ped**agog**ue, dem**agog**ue, syn**agog**ue

- *acou-*

Greek Verb	English Base	Meaning	English Derivative
akouein	**acou-**	hear	**acou**stic

- *ball-, bol-*

Greek Verb	English Base	Meaning	English Derivatives
ballein	ball-	throw	ballistic
	bol-		metabolism, symbol

- *cri-*

Greek Verb	English Base	Meaning	English Derivatives
krinein	cri-	judge	crisis, critic

- *do-*

Greek Verb	English Base	Meaning	English Derivative
didonai	do-	give	dose

- *gen-*

Greek Verb	English Base	Meaning	English Derivative
gignesthai	gen-	become, be born	genesis

- *gno-*

Greek Verb	English Base	Meaning	English Derivatives
gignoskein	gno-	know	agnostic, diagnosis

- *graph-, gram-*

Greek Verb	English Base	Meaning	English Derivatives
graphein	graph-	write	graphology
	gram-		telegram, program, diagram

- *id-*

Greek Verb	English Base	Meaning	English Derivative
idein	id-	see	idea

- *log-, lect-*

Greek Verb	English Base	Meaning	English Derivative
legein	log-	say	epilogue
	lect-		dialect

- *ora-*

Greek Verb	English Base	Meaning	English Derivative
horan	**ora-**	see	pan**ora**ma

- *opt-*

Greek Verb	English Base	Meaning	English Derivatives
opsesthai	**opt-**	see	**opt**ic, syn**opt**ic

Word for Word

- *path-*

Greek Verb	English Base	Meaning	English Derivative
paschein	**path-**	suffer	a**path**y

Word for Word

- *phen-, phan-, pha-*

Greek Verb	English Base	Meaning	English Derivative
phainein	**phen-**	show	**phen**omenon
	phan-		**phan**tom
	pha-		**pha**se

- *pher-, phor-*

Greek Verb	English Base	Meaning	English Derivative
pherein	**pher-**	carry	**pher**omone
	phor-		phos**phor**escent

- *prag-, prac-*

Greek Verb	English Base	Meaning	English Derivative
prattein/	**prag-**	do	**prag**matic
prassein	**prac-**		**prac**tical

- *rheu-, rh-*

Greek Verb	English Base	Meaning	English Derivative
rheein	**rheu-**	flow	**rheu**matism
	rh-		diar**rhea**

- *skept-*

Greek Verb	English Base	Meaning	English Derivative
skeptesthai	**skept-**	look at	**skept**ical

- *skop-*

Greek Verb	English Base	Meaning	English Derivative
skopein	**scop-**	look at	peri**scop**e

Word for Word

MY RHEUMATISM IS PLAYING UP AGAIN!

RHEUMATISM TAKES ITS NAME FROM THE GREEK RHEUMA... A FLOW OR STREAM!

IT WAS ONCE BELIEVED THAT THE PAINFUL CONDITION WAS CAUSED BY WATERY SECRETIONS FLOWING THROUGH THE AFFECTED PART!

@ATCHISON www.red-e2.com

- *sta-*

Greek Verb	English Base	Meaning	English Derivitave
histanai	**sta-**	set up, cause to stand	**sta**tic
histasthai		stand	

- *tom-*

Greek Verb	English Base		Meaning	English Derivative
temnein	**tom-**	cut		**atom**

- *the-*

Greek Verb	English Base		Meaning	English Derivatives
tithenai	**the-**	place		**the**sis, synthe**tic**

- *trop-*

Greek Verb	English Base		Meaning	English Derivatives
trepein	**trop-**	turn		**trope**, **trop**ics

Word for Word

- *treph-*

Greek Verb	English Base		Meaning	English Derivative
trephein	**troph-**	nourish		a**troph**y

Numerous other Greek bases are mentioned elsewhere in this chapter, particularly in the following sections on Greek prefixes and suffixes, in the exercises at the end of this chapter and other chapters, in the main text of the other chapters of this book, especially Chapter 5 ("Medicine"), and in Appendix 3 ("Numbers and Colors").

GREEK PREFIXES

Understanding the meanings of the Greek prefixes in the following table will aid in the understanding of English words that include them. The variants indicate how the prefix changes if the following syllable starts with certain letters. The changes are natural and allow for easier pronunciation; for instance, the prefix *syn-* combines with the base *bol* as **symbol** because this word is easier to pronounce than "synbol." In the following list the basic form of each prefix is given first and variants are given in the second column.

- *a-, an-,* "not," "without," "un-"

Prefix	English Base	Meaning of Base	English Derivative
a-	**mnes-**	remember	**a**mnesia
an- (before vowels and "h")	**osm-**	smell	**an**osmia

Word for Word

- *amphi-,* "both," "on both sides," "around"

Prefix	English Base	Meaning of Base	English Derivative
amphi-	**bi-**	life	**amphi**bious

- *ana-,* "up," "back," "again"

Prefix	English Base	Meaning of Base	English Derivative
ana-	**chron-**	time	**ana**chronism

- *anti-, ant-,* "instead of," "against," "in opposition to," "opposite"

Prefix	English Base	Meaning of Base	English Derivative
anti-	**path-**	feeling	**anti**pathy
ant- (before vowels and "h")	**agon-**	struggle	**ant**agonism

- *apo-,* "from," "out of," "away," "away from," "off," "utterly," "completely"

Prefix	English Base	Meaning of Base	English Derivative
apo-	**log-**	speech	**apo**logy

- *cata-, cat-,* "down," "against," "completely," "wrongly"

Prefix	English Base	Meaning of Base	English Derivative
cata-	**stroph-**	turn	**cata**strophe
cat- (before vowels and "h")	**hol-**	whole	**cat**holic

- *dia-, di-,* "through," "across," "over," "apart"

Prefix	English Base	Meaning of Base	English Derivative
dia-	**chron-**	time	**dia**chronic
di- (before vowels and "h")	**ora-**	see	**di**orama

- *dys-*

Prefix	English Base	Meaning	English Derivative
dys	**dys-**	bad	**dys**lexia

Word for Word

- *ec-, ex-,* "out," "from," "off"

Prefix	English Base	Meaning of Base	English Derivative
ec-	**stas-**	cause to stand	**ec**stasy
ex- (before vowels and "h")	**od-**	road	**ex**odus

- *en-*, *em-*, "in"

Prefix	English Base	Meaning of Base	English Derivative
en-	**dem-**	people	**en**demic
em- (before "m," "p" and "b")	**path-**	feeling	**em**pathy

- *epi-*, *ep-*, "on," "upon," "above," "over," "at," "near," "in addition"

Prefix	English Base	Meaning of Base	English Derivative
epi-	**taph-**	tomb	**epi**taph
ep- (before vowels and "h")	**hemer-**	day	**ep**hemeral

- *exo-*, *ecto-*, "outside"

Prefix	English Base	Meaning of Base	English Derivative
exo-	**gam-**	marriage	**exo**gamy
ecto- (before vowels and "h")	**plasm-**	mould	**ecto**plasm

- *hyper-*, "over," "above," "beyond," "excessive"

Prefix	English Base	Meaning of Base	English Derivative
hyper-	**therm-**	heat	**hyper**thermia

- *hypo-*, *hyp-*, "under," "below," "insufficient"

Prefix	English Base	Meaning of Base	English Derivative
hypo-	**derm-**	skin	**hypo**dermic
hyp- (before vowels and "h")	**hen-**	one	**hyp**hen

- *meta-*, *met-*, "behind," "beyond"; it often indicates change

Prefix	English Base	Meaning of Base	English Derivative
meta-	**morph-**	form	**meta**morphosis
met- (before vowels and "h")	**hod-**	way	**met**hod

Word for Word

WE'RE ALL FAMILIAR WITH THE WORD PARALLEL. IT IS BASED ON TWO GREEK TERMS... PARA.. BESIDE AND ALLELOS..ONE ANOTHER!

www.red-e2.com   © ATCHISON

- *para-, par-,* "beside," "beyond," "near," "incorrectly"

Prefix	English Base	Meaning of Base	English Derivative
para-	**dox-**	think, seem	**para**dox
par- (before vowels and "h")	**allel-**	other	**par**allel

- *peri-,* "around," "about"

Prefix	English Base	Meaning of Base	English Derivative
peri-	**pher-**	carry	**peri**phery

- *pro-,* "earlier," "in front of," "instead of"

Prefix	English Base	Meaning of Base	English Derivative
pro-	**gno-**	know	**pro**gnosis

- *syn-, sym-, syl-, sy-,* "together," "with"

Prefix	English Base	Meaning of Base	English Derivative
syn-	**chron-**	time	**syn**chronic
sy- (before "s")	**stem-**	cause to stand	**sy**stem
syl- (before "l")	**log-**	word, reckoning	**syl**logism
sym- (before "m," "p," "b")	**path-**	feeling	**sym**pathy

GREEK SUFFIXES

The tables below contain some commonly used suffixes derived from Greek. Some of these suffixes form words that function both as nouns and adjectives and are discussed under the separate headings. For an explanation of the functions (and meanings) of noun-, adjective-, and verb-forming suffixes, refer to the discussion in Chapter 1 ("Word-Building Basics").

Some suffixes not listed here are discussed elsewhere in this book, especially in Chapter 3 ("Word-Building Tools: Latin Components") and Chapter 5 ("Medicine").

Noun-forming Suffixes

General Function

• *-ac*

Suffix	English Base	Meaning of Base	English Derivative
-ac	**mani-**	madness	mani**ac**

• *-ic*

Suffix	English Base	Meaning of Base	English Derivative
-ic	**crit-**	judge	crit**ic**
	mus-	muse	mus**ic**

• *-ite*

Suffix	English Base	Meaning of Base	English Derivative
-ite	**dynam-**	power	dynam**ite**
	dendr-	tree	dendr**ite**
	graph-	writing	graph**ite**

• *-oid*

Suffix	English Base	Meaning of Base	English Derivative
-oid	**anthrop-**	human being	anthrop**oid**

• *-ot*

Suffix	English Base	Meaning of Base	English Derivative
-ot	**idi-**	own, personal	idi**ot**
	patri-	father	patri**ot**

Abstract Function

• *-ics*

Suffix	English Base	Meaning of Base	English Derivative
-ics	**polit-**	citizen	polit**ics**
	phys-	nature	phys**ics**
	athlet-	contestant (for a prize)	athlet**ics**

Word for Word

MANY ATHLETES COMPETE FOR THE PLEASURE OF IT.

HOWEVER, ATHLETE IS BASED ON ATHLON, GREEK FOR PRIZE:

AN ATHLETE IS ONE WHO "COMPETES FOR A PRIZE!"

©ACHISON
www.red-e2.com

- **-is**

Suffix	English Base	Meaning of Base	English Derivative
-is	**cris-**	a separating, decision	cris**is**

- **-ism**

Suffix	English Base	Meaning of Base	English Derivative
-ism	**ostrac-**	potsherd (pottery fragment)	ostrac**ism**
	barbar-	foreign, barbarian	barbar**ism**
	social-	companion, ally, associate	social**ism**

- **-y**

Suffix	English Base	Meaning of Base	English Derivative
-y	**harmon-**	joining, fitting together	harmon**y**
	microscop-	small (prefix) + look at	microscop**y**
	econom-	household management	econom**y**

Agent Function

- **-ist**

Suffix	English Base	Meaning of Base	English Derivative
-ist	**cycl-**	circle	cycl**ist**
	dogmat-	opinion, decree	dogmat**ist**
	hedon-	pleasure	hedon**ist**

Adjective-forming Suffixes

- *-ac*

Suffix	English Base	Meaning of Base	English Derivative
-ac	**cardi-**	heart	cardi**ac**
	Dionysi-	Dionysus/Dionysia	Dionysi**ac**

- *-ic*

Suffix	English Base	Meaning of Base	English Derivative
-ic	**poet-**	poet	poet**ic**
	symbol-	symbol	symbol**ic**

- *-oid*

Suffix	English Base	Meaning of Base	English Derivative
-oid	**aster-**	star	aster**oid**

This adjective suffix almost always conveys the meaning "resembling."

Verb-forming Suffix

- *-ize*

Suffix	English Base	Meaning of Base	English Derivative
-ize	**synchron-**	"together" (prefix)+ "time"	synchron**ize**
	ostrac-	"potsherd" (pottery fragment)	ostrac**ize**
	agon-	struggle	agon**ize**

BIBLIOGRAPHY AND FURTHER READING

Ayers, D. M., *English Words from Latin and Greek Elements*, 2nd Ed. (Tucson 1986).

Borror, D. J., *Dictionary of Word Roots and Combining Forms* (Palo Alto 1960).

Burriss, E. E. and Casson, L., *Latin and Greek in Current Use*, 2nd Ed. (Englewood Cliffs 1949).

Dunmore, C. W. and Fleischer, R., *Studies in Etymology*, 2nd Ed. (Newburyport 2008).

Green, T. M., *The Greek and Latin Roots of English*, 4th Ed. (Lanham 2008).

Krill, R. M., *Greek and Latin in English Today*, 3rd Ed. (Wauconda 2003).

Luschnig, C. A. and Luschnig, J., *Etyma: An Introduction to Vocabulary-Building from Latin and Greek* (Lanham 1982).

Moore, B. and Moore, M., *NTC's Dictionary of Latin and Greek Origins* (Chicago 1997).

O'Reilly, N. J., *Latin, Not Dead: Greek, Alive and Well in Today's Words* (Lima 2005).
Schaeffer, R. F., *Greek-English Derivative Dictionary* (Oxford 1963).
Taylor, B. C., *The Greeks Had a Word for It* (Oxford 1973).
Walker, T. E., *Word Resources*, 3rd Ed. (Indianapolis 1979).

WEB SITES: NAMES AND URLS

Web Sites in Chapter 1 ("Word-Building Basics") plus:
"Maths — Classics Project"
> http://www.users.globalnet.co.uk/~loxias/mathsclassics.htm

"A Selection of Greek and Latin Roots"
> http://abasiccurriculum.com/homeschool/roots

"English Words from Classical Origins"
> http://www.personal.kent.edu/~rlarson/words

"Greek Language Instruction"
> http://ancienthistory.about.com/cs/greekinstructio1

EXERCISES

1. What English word is derived from the first two letters of the Greek alphabet?

2. The Greek letter iota, which is the smallest letter in the Greek alphabet, is used as a word in English. Write a sentence using the word iota and then explain what your sentence means.

3. Jesus is reported to have said, "I am the Alpha and Omega, the Beginning and the End" (Revelation 1:8). What did he mean by this?

4. Write the following Greek words in the Roman alphabet. (See Appendix 1, "Greek and Latin Alphabets," and Appendix 2, "Writing of Greek Words in English.")
    a. ἀγορά
    b. βάθος
    c. μετρικός
    d. δρᾶμα
    e. ἐλευθερία
    f. ῥόμβος
    g. ἱερός
    h. καταράκτης
    i. ἡδονή
    j. γλῶσσα

5. Write the following words in the letters of Greek. Do not worry about the accents. (See Appendices 1 and 2.)
    a. *mythologia*
    b. *logistikos*
    c. *paralysis*
    d. *polymathēs*
    e. *tetrarchēs*
    f. *sardonyx*
    g. *schēma*
    h. *rhētorikos*
    i. *philosophia*
    j. *psychē*

6. The base *Hellen-* means "Greek" or "Greece." Using this base and appropriate Greek suffixes, form
    a. an adjective with the meaning "relating to Greece."
    b. a verb with the meaning "to make Greek."

7. Combine pairs of Greek words in Table 1 to form English words with the given meanings in Table 2. The first line of Table 2 contains a completed example. You may refer to the tables of combining forms, suffixes and prefixes in this chapter and in Chapter 5 ("Medicine"). If necessary, use an English dictionary to check the spelling of the derivatives.

Table 1

Greek Word	Meaning of Greek	Greek Word	Meaning of Greek
bathys	deep	*baros*	weight, pressure
chrōma	color	*glōtta*	tongue, language
gramma	something written	*graphein*	to write, draw
hemi	half	*hippos*	horse
hōra	time, hour	*hydro-*	water
isos	equal	*kenos*	empty
kyklos	wheel	*lithos*	stone
mania	madness	*megas*	big
metron	measure	*monos*	single, alone
nomos	law, melody	*peri*	around
philos	friend	*phobos/-phobia*	fear
phōnē	voice, sound	*phōs, phōtos*	light
poly	much, many	*potamos*	river
pyr	fire	*skopein*	to look at, examine
sophia	wisdom	*stethos*	chest
sphaira	ball	*taphos*	tomb
technē	skill, art	*telē*	at a distance
theos	god	*thermē*	heat
xenos	foreigner, stranger		

Table 2

English Derivative	Definition of English Word
polytheism	belief in many gods
	a large stone
	a single stone
	instrument for carrying a voice a long way
	instrument for looking around
	instrument for measuring heat
	instrument for making sound greater
	a picture made by the action of light
	a vehicle with a single wheel
	a picture made with limestone
	instrument for seeing things at a distance
	instrument for detecting sound under water
	instrument for measuring a liquid's specific gravity
	the measurement around something
	river horse (horse-like animal fond of river water)
	love of wisdom
	half the globe
	fear of foreigners
	a vehicle used to explore deep water
	instrument for measuring the intensity of light
	a person who speaks many tongues
	fear of water
	instrument for examining a person's chest
	instrument for measuring out a regular beat in music
	instrument for measuring atmospheric pressure
	line on map denoting equal atmospheric pressure
	having only one color
	having many colors
	a memorial tomb with no burial
	a written message sent from a distance
	mad enthusiasm for lighting fires
	examination of the heavens at a particular moment
	art of making firework displays
	instrument for producing sound from written discs

8. (a) Using the following list of Greek prefixes and their meanings, complete the list of English words in the table by writing in the appropriate prefix.

ana-, "up," "back"
dia-, "through; "between," "apart"
epi-, "on," "upon," "over"
cata-, "down"
meta-, "with," "after," "across"; it often denotes "change"
syn- (*sym-* before some consonants), "together," "with"
hypo-, "under"

Prefix	Base/Suffix	Meaning of English Word
	-morphosis	"change of shape," for example, from a tadpole to a frog
	-gnosis	"knowing through"; identification of, for example, a disease
	-demic	"upon the people"; widely prevalent disease
	-phony	"sound together"; music for instruments in concert
	-thesis	"placing under"; underlying supposition
	-lysis	"loosening up"; resolution into elements
	-chronize	"bring together," as with watches to the same time
	-scopal	"pertaining to a bishop"; literally, "pertaining to one who oversees"
	-opsis	"a seeing together"; overall view, summary
	-logue	"word upon"; a speech on top (at the end)
	-meter	"measurement across," especially of a circle
	-bolic	"throwing [that is, building] up" of muscles
	-biosis	"life together"; situation in which one species lives with another to mutual advantage
	-lyst	"loosening down," as with a substance, thereby releasing a chemical reaction
	-bolism	"throwing across"; the chemical change and use of nutrition by an organism
	-thermia	"underheat"; lowering of the temperature of the body's inner core as a result of exposure to cold
	-gram	"written backward"; one word made by writing the letters of another backward (or jumbled up)
	-phor	"carrying over"; figure of speech in which a term is transferred to something analogous
	-drome	"running together"; a set of symptoms occurring together

(b) In the list of English words above there are a number of bases derived from Greek verbs. Identify ten bases from the English words and give the Greek verbs and their meanings from which the English words are derived. The first line contains a completed example.

English Word	Base	Greek Verb	Meaning (of Greek Verb)
prologue	log-	legein	to say

9. Choose ten of the words from the list below and for each word write down in the following table the part of speech to which the word belongs; the prefix (if any) and its meaning; the base/bases and its meaning/their meanings; the suffix/suffixes (if any) and its meaning/their meanings; and the literal meaning of the word. Use an English dictionary if necessary. A sample word has been analyzed in the first line of the table.

amnesty, anthropomorphism, antibiotic, antidote, antipathy, apology, bibliophile, catalogue, diabolic, diaphanous, Dionysiac, dystrophy, epidemic, epitaph, eulogy, geography, geology, historiography, homogenize, homonym, homophobia, hypothesize, kaleidoscope, macroeconomics, metamorphosis, metempsychosis, misogyny, monarchist, monarchy, optometrist, paralysis, parapsychology, parataxis, parenthetic, perimeter, pheromone, philology, program, psychosis, rheostat, Stoicism, sympathy, synchronic, telepathy, telephone, trigonometry

English Word	Part of Speech	Prefix	Base/ Bases	Suffix/ Suffixes	Literal Meaning
catastrophe	noun	*cata-*	*-strophe*	_____	down turn

10. Complete the following tables using the suffixes listed in this chapter. Use an English dictionary if necessary to check the meanings.

(a) *pragm-*

English Word	Base	Suffix/ Suffixes	Part of Speech	English Meaning
pragmatic	*prag-* ("do")			
pragmatics				
pragmatist				
pragmatism				

(b) *polit-*

English Word	Base	Suffix/ Suffixes	Part of Speech	English Meaning
politic	*polit-* ("citizen")			
politicize				
politics				
polity				

11. Complete the following table from the table of prefixes given in this chapter. Use an English dictionary if necessary to check the meanings.

English Word	Prefix	Meaning of Prefix	Base	Meaning of Base	English Meaning
analyze			-lyze	loosen	
antithesis			-thesis	place	
atypical			-typical	belonging to a type	
dialogue			-logue	word, speech	
euphony			-phony	sound	
metaphor			-phor	carry	
paragraph			-graph	writing	
periscope			-scope	look	
prologue			-logue	word, speech	
synthesis			-thesis	place	

12. Using the suffixes discussed in this chapter, form three words from each of the following bases and identify their parts of speech. Use an English dictionary if necessary.

Base	English Word (1)	Part of Speech	English Word (2)	Part of Speech	English Word (3)	Part of Speech
atom-						
econom-						
harmon-						
magnet-						
monopol-						

13. Complete the following tables after considering how each of the bases is modified by the prefix at the beginning of the given words, then complete the tables. Use an English dictionary if necessary to check the meanings.

(a) Base: -thesis, "putting," "placing," "proposition"

Word	Prefix	Meaning of Prefix	Meaning of Word
antithesis			
hypothesis			
metathesis			
prosthesis			
synthesis			

(b) Base: *-graph/-gram*, "something written"

Word	Prefix	Meaning of Prefix	Meaning of Word
anagram			
epigraph			
paragraph			
program			

14. After combining each of the following prefixes with the bases provided, given the meaning of the words formed. Use an English dictionary if necessary to check the meanings.

(a) Prefix: *a-, an-*, "not," "without," "un-"

Base	Word	Meaning of Word
-theist		
-mnesia		
-archist		
-ecdote		

(b) Prefix: *anti-, ant-*, "against," "in opposition to," "opposite"

Base	Word	Meaning of Word
-dote		
-oxidant		
-onym		
-podes		

(c) Prefix: *syn-, sym-, syl-*, "with," "together"

Base	Word	Meaning of Word
-agogue		
-chronicity		
-drome		
-posium		
-phony		
-ergy		
-logism		

CHAPTER 3

WORD-BUILDING TOOLS: LATIN COMPONENTS

W. J. Dominik, J. L. Hilton, and A. P. Bevis

THE LATIN ALPHABET

The alphabet used by the Romans reached them via the Etruscans and was derived from a slightly different form of the Greek alphabet. For these reasons and because Latin had some sounds that Greek did not have (and vice versa), the Latin alphabet includes some new letters and omits others, while some letters have a different value. The Latin alphabet became the basis (with some slight modifications) for the alphabets of most European languages. It is helpful to be familiar with the Latin alphabet since most English words are derived from original Latin word forms. (For a discussion of the alphabet, see Appendix 1, "Greek and Latin Alphabets.")

LATIN BASES

A countless number of Latin bases are used in English today. The following tables list some of these bases and provide examples of English derivatives. Simple and compound forms (that is, forms that have prefixes and suffixes) of these derivatives have been used.

Nouns

- *aqu-*

Latin Noun	English Base	Meaning	English Derivative
aqua	**aqu-**	water	**aqu**arium, **aqu**educt

Word for Word

• *gener-*

Latin Noun	English Base	Meaning	English Derivatives
genus, generis	**gener-**	race, kind	**gener**ality, **gener**osity

• *grad-*

Latin Noun	English Base	Meaning	English Derivatives
gradus	**grad-**	step	**grad**ualism, **grad**ation

• *jur-*

Latin Noun	English Base	Meaning	English Derivatives
ius, iuris	**jur-**	right, law	**jur**ist, **jur**isprudent

• *patr-*

Latin Noun	English Base	Meaning	English Derivatives
pater, patris	**patr-**	father	**patr**ician, **patr**ilineal

• *sen-*

Latin Noun	English Base	Meaning	English Derivatives
senex, senis	**sen-**	old man	**sen**ility, **sen**escent

• *serv-*

Latin Noun	English Base	Meaning	English Derivatives
servus	**serv-**	slave	**serv**itude, **serv**iceable

• *tempor-*

Latin Noun	English Base	Meaning	English Derivatives
tempus, temporis	**tempor-**	time	**tempor**ary, **tempor**ization

• *verb-*

Latin Noun	English Base	Meaning	English Derivatives
verbum	**verb-**	word	**verb**al, **verb**iage

• *vir-*

Latin Noun	English Base	Meaning	English Derivatives
vir	**vir-**	man	**vir**ile, **vir**ilization

Verbs

- *ag-, act-, ig-*

Latin Verb	English Base	Meaning	English Derivative
agere	**ag-**	do, act, drive	**ag**ent
	act-		**act**ion
	ig-		ex**ig**ent

- *capt-, cept-, -ceive*

Latin Verb	English Base	Meaning	English Derivative
capere	**capt-**	take	**capt**ive
	cept-		de**cept**ion
	-ceive		re**ceive**

- *-ced, -ceed, cess-*

Latin Verb	English Base	Meaning	English Derivative
cedere	**-ced**	go	inter**ced**e
	-ceed		pro**ceed**
	cess-		re**cess**ion

- *-cid, cis-*

Latin Verb	English Base	Meaning	English Derivative
caedere	**-cid**	cut, kill	homi**cid**e
	cis-		in**cis**ion

- *dat-, dit-*

Latin Verb	English Base	Meaning	English Derivative
dare	**dat-**	give	**dat**a
	dit-		tra**dit**ion

- *fac-, fact-, fect-*

Latin Verb	English Base	Meaning	English Derivative
facere	**fac-**	make, do	**fac**ile
	fact-		**fact**ory
	fect-		de**fect**ion

- *leg-, lect-*

Latin Verb	English Base	Meaning	English Derivative
legere	**leg-**	read	**leg**ible
	lect-		**lect**ure

- *-mit, mitt-, miss-*

Latin Verb	English Base	Meaning	English Derivative
mittere	**-mit**	send	re**mit**
	mitt-		inter**mitt**ent
	miss-		**miss**ile

Word for Word

BY THE WAY, DID YOU KNOW THAT THE WORD **MISSILE** IS FROM THE LATIN **MITTERE** ·· TO SEND?

- *pon-, pos-, posi-*

Latin Verb	English Base	Meaning	English Derivative
ponere	**pon-**	place, put	op**pon**ent
	pos-		**pos**ture
	posit-		**posit**ion

- *ven-, vent-*

Latin Verb	English Base	Meaning	English Derivative
venire	**ven-**	come	inter**ven**e
	vent-		con**vent**ion

Numerous other Latin bases are mentioned elsewhere in this chapter, particularly in the following sections on Latin prefixes and suffixes, in the exercises at the end of this chapter and other chapters, in the main body of the other chapters in this book, and in Appendix 3 ("Numbers and Colors").

LATIN PREFIXES

The prefixes derived from Latin normally occur only in ⸤ as independent words. A prefix makes the meaning of a ba⸥ ple, *-vene*, the last English base discussed in the previous section, m⸤ *venire*, "to come"), so **intervene** means "come between" and **convene** m⸤

Many words in English are formed by adding Latin prefixes to bases, below. The basic form is given with variants (due to sound changes) giv⸤ following list does not include all the prefixes derived from Latin; nor do⸤ possible meaning of each prefix.

- **ab-, a-, abs-**, "away," "from"

Latin Prefix	English Base	Meaning	English Derivati⸤
ab-	**ject-**	throw	**ab**ject
a-	**vert-**	turn	**a**vert
abs-	**tract-**	drag	**abs**tract

- **ad-, a-, ac-, af-, ag-, al-, an-, ap-, ar-, as-, at-**, "to," "toward"

Latin Prefix	English Base	Meaning	English Derivative
ad-	**-mit**	send	**ad**mit
a-	**spir-**	breathe	**a**spire
ac-	**cept-**	take	**ac**cept
af-	**fix-**	fix, fasten	**af**fix
ag-	**greg-**	flock	**ag**gregate
al-	**loc-**	place	**al**locate
an-	**nounc-**	report	**an**nounce
ap-	**prehend-**	seize	**ap**prehend
ar-	**rog-**	ask	**ar**rogant
as-	**sent-**	feel	**as**sent
at-	**tract-**	drag	**at**tract

Word for Word

bi-, "both," "on both sides"

Latin Prefix	English Base	Meaning	English Derivative
mbi-	**dextr-**	right (-handed)	**ambi**dextrous

ante-, "before"

Latin Prefix	English Base	Meaning	English Derivative
ante-	**ced-**	go	**ante**cedent

- *circum-,* "around," "about"

Latin Prefix	English Base	Meaning	English Derivative
circum-	**navig-**	sail	**circum**navigate

- *com-, co-, col-, con-, cor-,* "with," "together," "thoroughly"

Latin Prefix	English Base	Meaning	English Derivative
com-	**par-**	equal	**com**pare
co-	**opt-**	choose	**co**-opt
col-	**loq-**	speak	**col**loquium
con-	**sci-**	know	**con**scious
cor-	**rupt-**	break into pieces	**cor**rupt

The prefix *co-* is frequently used with bases beginning with vowels (for example, *co-ed, co-operate, co-opt, co-ordinate*). It has been greatly extended in English, however, and often appears hyphenated before consonants (for example, *co-star, co-worker*).

- *contra-,* "against"

Latin Prefix	English Base	Meaning	English Derivative
contra-	**dict-**	say	**contra**dict

Counter- is derived from *contra* ("against") and is used productively in English in a number of ways: to indicate opposition, as in *counterclaim;* opposite direction, as in *countercurrent;* correspondence, as in *countersign;* and duplicate, as in *countershaft.* Compare *counterpoint,* a melody added as accompaniment to another melody in music.

- *de-,* "down," "away from"

Latin Prefix	English Base	Meaning	English Derivative
de-	**ject-**	throw	**de**jected

This prefix is used frequently in English with bases that are not derived from Latin for example, *de-bus, de-clutch.*

- **dis-, di-, dif-,** "apart," "not"

Latin Prefix	English Base	Meaning	English Derivative
dis-	**cern-**	separate	**dis**cern
di-	**gest-**	carry	**di**gest
dif	**fer-**	carry	**dif**ferent

- **equi-, equa-,** "equal"

Latin Prefix	English Base	Meaning	English Derivative
equi-	**val-**	strong	**equi**valent
equa-	**anim-**	mind	**equa**nimity

- **ex-, e-, ef-,** "out of," "from," "away from"

Latin Prefix	English Base	Meaning	English Derivative
ex-	**pos-**	place	**ex**pose
e-	**ject-**	throw	**e**ject
ef-	**flu-**	flow	**ef**fluent

- **extra-,** "outside," "beyond"

Latin Prefix	English Base	Meaning	English Derivative
extra-	**mur-**	wall	**extra**mural

- **in-, il-, im-, ir-,** "in," "into," "on"

Latin Prefix	English Base	Meaning	English Derivative
in-	**ject-**	throw	**in**ject
il-	**lumin-**	light	**il**luminate
im-	**migr-**	depart	**im**migrate
ir-	**rig-**	water, moisten	**ir**rigate

- **in-, il-, im-, ir-,** "not," "without"

Latin Prefix	English Base	Meaning	English Derivative
in-	**act-**	do, act	**in**active
il-	**leg-**	law	**il**legal
im-	**med-**	middle	**im**mediate
ir-	**resist-**	stand back	**ir**resistible

The prefix *in-* ("not") is used usually with words derived from Latin, whereas *un-* is used with other English words (compare Latinate **in**felicitous, English **un**happy).

- *infra-*, "below"

Latin Prefix	English Base	Meaning	English Derivative
infra-	**struct-**	build	**infra**structure

- *inter-*, "between," "among"

Latin Prefix	English Base	Meaning	English Derivative
inter-	**ject-**	throw	**inter**ject

- *intra-*, "inside," "within"

Latin Prefix	English Base	Meaning	English Derivative
intra-	**-net**	net	**intra**net (compare **inter**net)

- *multi-*, "many"

Latin Prefix	English Base	Meaning	English Derivative
multi-	**plic-**	fold	**multi**plication

- *non-*, "not"

Latin Prefix	English Base	Meaning	English Derivative
non-	**sens-**	feel	**non**sensical

This prefix, which is derived from Latin *non* ("not"), is one of the most common prefixes in English. It can be added to English words very freely either in an exclusive sense, for example, **non**believer (compare **unbeliever, disbelief**), **nonverbal, nonviolent, nonwhite**, and **nonplussed**, or with a pejorative meaning, for instance, **nonevent** and **nonsense**. There is also a dissimulative meaning of *non* in which the word carries two mutually contradictory meanings, for example, **nonprofit** and **noncandidate**, and also a class of words in which an adjective is created from a verb, for instance, **nonslip**. Occasionally compounds with *non* are hyphenated, especially when the base words begin with a capital letter (for example, **non-American**).

Word for Word

- *ob-, oc-, of-, op-,* "toward," "against, "across"

Latin Prefix	English Base	Meaning	English Derivative
ob-	**ject-**	throw	**ob**ject
oc-	**cur-**	run	**oc**cur
of-	**fer-**	carry	**of**fer
op-	**pos-**	place	**op**posite

- *per-,* "through," "by," "completely," "to the bad"

Latin Prefix	English Base	Meaning	English Derivative
per-	**-mit**	send	**per**mit

- *post-,* "after," "behind"

Latin Prefix	English Base	Meaning	English Derivative
post-	**pone**	place	**post**pone

- *pre-,* "before," "in front of"

Latin Prefix	English Base	Meaning	English Derivative
pre-	**pos-**	place	**pre**position

Word for Word

- *pro-,* "forward," "for," "on behalf of"

Latin Prefix	English Base	Meaning	English Derivative
pro-	**ject-**	throw	**pro**ject

- *re-, red-,* "back," "again"

Latin Prefix	English Base	Meaning	English Derivative
re-	**ject-**	throw	**re**ject
red-	**empt-**	buy back	**red**emption

- *retro-*, "backward"

Latin Prefix	English Base	Meaning	English Derivative
retro-	**spect-**	view	**retro**spect

- *se-, sed-*, "apart, "without," "aside"

Latin Prefix	English Base	Meaning	English Derivative
se-	**duct-**	lead	**se**duction
sed-	**it-**	go	**sed**ition

- *semi-*, "half," "partly"

Latin Prefix	English Base	Meaning	English Derivative
semi-	**ann-**	year	**semi**annual

- *sub-, suc-, suf-, sug-, sup-, sus-*, "under," "beneath," "secret"

Latin Prefix	English Base	Meaning	English Derivative
sub-	**ject-**	throw	**sub**ject
suc-	**cinct-**	surround	**suc**cinct
suf-	**fer-**	carry	**suf**fer
sug-	**gest-**	carry	**sug**gest
sup-	**port-**	carry	**sup**port
sus-	**spect-**	look	**sus**pect

Word for Word

- *super-*, "over," "above," "beyond"

Latin Prefix	English Base	Meaning	English Derivative
super-	**vis-**	see	**super**vise

This prefix is used extensively in English with bases that are not derived from Latin, for example, *super*heat and *super*glue.

- *trans-, tra-, tran-,* "across," "over"

Latin Prefix	English Base	Meaning	English Derivative
trans-	**-mit**	send	**trans**mit
tra-	**duc-**	lead	**tra**duce
tran-	**qui-**	rest, calm	**tran**quil

- *ultra-,* "beyond"

Latin Prefix	English Base	Meaning	English Derivative
ultra-	**-violet**	violet	**ultra**violet

LATIN SUFFIXES

The tables below contain some commonly used suffixes derived from Latin. Some of these suffixes form words that function both as nouns and adjectives and are discussed under the separate headings. For an explanation of the functions (and meanings) of noun-, adjective-, and verb-forming suffixes, refer to the discussion in Chapter 1 ("Word-Building Basics").

Some suffixes not listed here are discussed elsewhere in this book, especially in Chapter 2 ("Word-Building Tools: Greek Components") and Chapter 5 ("Medicine").

Noun-forming Suffixes

General Function

- *-ane, -ine*

Suffix	English Base	Meaning	English Derivative
-ane	**meth-**	wine	meth**ane**
-ine	**can-**	dog	can**ine**

- *-ite*

Suffix	English Base	Meaning	English Derivative
-ite	**nitr-**	natron	nitr**ite**

- *-ment*

Suffix	English Base	Meaning	English Derivative
-ment	**frag-**	break	frag**ment**

This suffix forms nouns from verbs (for example, **abridgement**) and nouns from adjectives (for example, **merriment**).

- *-ose*

Suffix	English Base	Meaning	English Derivative
-ose	**gluc-**	sugar	gluc**ose**

- *-ure*

Suffix	English Base	Meaning	English Derivative
-ure	**pict-**	paint	pict**ure**

This suffix is used not only for nouns of action (for example, **seizure**, **agriculture**) and result (for example, **picture**, **creature**, **fracture**, **rupture**, **puncture**) but also for collective nouns (for example, **nature**).

Abstract Function

- *-acy, -acity, -y*

Suffix	English Base	Meaning	English Derivative
-acy	**fall-**	deceive	fall**acy**
-acity	**ten-**	hold fast	ten**acity**
-y	**custod-**	guard	custod**y**

- *-al*

Suffix	English Base	Meaning	English Derivative
-al	**remov-**	set aside, take away	remov**al**

- *-ance, -ancy, -ence, -ency*

Suffix	English Base	Meaning	English Derivative
-ance	**repent-**	regret	repent**ance**
-ancy	**hesit-**	stick fast, hesitate	hesit**ancy**
-ence	**depend-**	hang from	depend**ence**
-ency	**flu-**	flow	flu**ency**

- *-ation, -ion, -tion*

Suffix	English Base	Meaning	English Derivative
-ation	**declar-**	explain, reveal	declar**ation**
-ion	**un-**	one	un**ion**
-tion	**erup-**	burst forth	erup**tion**

These suffixes denote action (for example, **intermission,** "sending between"; **gestation,** "carrying"; **suggestion,** "putting forward"); or a resulting state (for example, **vexation, concoction**).

- *-ety, -ity, -ty*

Suffix	English Base	Meaning	English Derivative
-ety (after "i")	**vari-**	various	vari**ety**
-ity	**humil-**	low, humble	humil**ity**
-ty	**novel-**	new	novel**ty**

- *-ice*

Suffix	English Base	Meaning	English Derivative
-ice	**mal-**	bad	mal**ice**

- *-ile*

Suffix	English Base	Meaning	English Derivative
-ile	**miss-**	throw, send	miss**ile**

- *-itude*

Suffix	English Base	Meaning	English Derivative
-itude	**sol-**	alone	sol**itude**

- *-ive*

Suffix	English Base	Meaning	English Derivative
-ive	**adhes-**	stick to	adhes**ive**

- *-mony*

Suffix	English Base	Meaning	English Derivative
-mony	**matri-**	mother, matron	matri**mony**

- *-or*

Suffix	English Base	Meaning	English Derivative
-or	**val-**	strong	val**or**

Agent Function

- *-ain, -an*

Suffix	English Base	Meaning	English Derivative
-ain	**capt-**	head	capt**ain**
-an	**veter-**	old	veter**an**

- *-and, -end*

Suffix	English Base	Meaning	English Derivative
-and	**gradu-**	step, degree	gradu**and**
-end	**rever-**	respect	rever**end**

These suffixes are derived from the Latin gerundive ending *-ndus, -nda, -ndum* ("to be done"), but they have never been a living suffix since they have not existed separately from the Latin gerundive form from which they are derived. The gerundive endings are sometimes retained in their Latin (neuter) form (with plural *-a*), as in **add*endum*, ag*endum*, corrig*endum*, refer*endum*,** and **memor*andum*.** The meaning of these words is passive; therefore **agenda** literally means "things to be done."

- *-ant, -ent*

Suffix	English Base	Meaning	English Derivative
-ant	**litig-**	plead a case	litig**ant**
-ent	**respond-**	reply	respond**ent**

- *-ar*

Suffix	English Base	Meaning	English Derivative
-ar	**schol-**	school	schol**ar**

- *-arian, -ian*

Suffix	English Base	Meaning	English Derivative
-arian	**veget-**	grow, be fresh	veget**arian**
-ian	**phonetic-**	sound	phonetic**ian**

- *-ate*

Suffix	English Base	Meaning	English Derivative
-ate	**magistr-**	teacher	magistr**ate**

- *-or*

Suffix	English Base	Meaning	English Derivative
-or	**creat-**	make	creat**or**

Locative Function

- *-arium, -orium*

Suffix	English Base	Meaning	English Derivative
-arium	**terr-**	earth	terr**arium**
-orium	**audit-**	hear	audit**orium**

- *-ary, -ory*

Suffix	English Base	Meaning	English Derivative
-ary	**libr-**	book	libr**ary**
-ory	**dormit-**	sleep	dormit**ory**

Word for Word

Diminutive Function

- *-cle, -cule, -icle*

Suffix	English Base	Meaning	English Derivative
-cle	**mus-**	mouse	mus**cle**
-cule	**mole-**	mass	mole**cule**
-icle	**part-**	part	part**icle**

- *-el, -le*

Suffix	English Base	Meaning	English Derivative
-el	**mors-**	bite	mors**el**
-le	**scrup-**	stone	scrup**le**

Word for Word

- **-il**

Suffix	English Base	Meaning	English Derivative
-il	**penc-**	brush	penc**il**

- **-ule, -ole**

Suffix	English Base	Meaning	English Derivative
-ule	**caps-**	box	caps**ule**
-ole	**aure-**	gold	aure**ole**

These Latinate diminutive suffixes correspond to the English noun suffixes *-kin* (for example, **mani*kin***), *-let* (for example, **book*let***), and *-ling* (for example, **duck*ling***).

Adjective-forming Suffixes

- **-able, -ble, -ible**

Suffix	English Base	Meaning	English Derivative
-able	**dur-**	hard	dur**able**
-ble	**volu-**	roll, wrap	volu**ble**
-ible	**leg-**	read	leg**ible**

Adjectives with these suffixes convey the meaning of "able to." By far the most numerous of the -ble words are those in -able.

- **-ain, -an, -ane, -ine**

Suffix	English Base	Meaning	English Derivative
-ain	**cert-**	certain	cert**ain**
-an	**Anglic-**	English	Anglic**an**
-ane	**mund-**	world	mund**ane**
-ine	**bov-**	cow	bov**ine**

- *-ant, -ent*

Suffix	English Base	Meaning	English Derivative
-ant	**radi-**	beaming	radi**ant**
-ent	**insist-**	stand upon	insist**ent**

- *-ar, -al, -ary*

Suffix	English Base	Meaning	English Derivative
-ar	**lun-**	moon	lun**ar**
-al	**arbore-**	tree	arbore**al**
-ary	**milit-**	soldier	milit**ary**

Word for Word

The suffix *-ar* (from Latin *-aris*) is a variant of Latin *-al* (from Latin *-alis*), which also means "pertaining to." It is usually used where "l" in the base precedes it, for example, as in **stellar;** hence it is found with diminutive adjectives with *-ul-, -ell-*, as in **globular** and **cerebellar**.

- *-arian, -ian*

Suffix	English Base	Meaning	English Derivative
-arian	**agr-**	field	agr**arian**
-ian	**Mart-**	Mars	Mart**ian**

- *-ate, -ite*

Suffix	English Base	Meaning	English Derivative
-ate	**liter-**	letter	liter**ate**
-ite	**favor-**	favor	favor**ite**

- *-ic*

Suffix	English Base	Meaning	English Derivative
-ic	**civ-**	citizen	civ**ic**

- *-id*

Suffix	English Base	Meaning	English Derivative
-id	frig-	cold	frigid

- *-ific*

Suffix	English Base	Meaning	English Derivative
-ific	horr-	bristling, shivering	horrific

- *-il, -ile*

Suffix	English Base	Meaning	English Derivative
-il	civ-	citizen	civil
-ile	volat-	fly	volatile

- *-ilent, -olent, -ulent*

Suffix	English Base	Meaning	English Derivative
-ilent	pesti-	plague	pestilent
-olent	vi-	strength	violent
-ulent	op-	wealth	opulent

- *-ious, -ose, -ous*

Suffix	English Base	Meaning	English Derivative
-ious	loquac-	speech	loquacious
-ose	bellic-	war	bellicose
-ous	vitre-	glass	vitreous

- *-ive*

Suffix	English Base	Meaning	English Derivative
-ive	impuls-	impel	impulsive

- *-ory*

Suffix	English Base	Meaning	English Derivative
-ory	amat-	love	amatory

Verb-forming Suffixes

- *-ate*

Suffix	English Base	Meaning	English Derivative
-ate	**navig-**	sail	navig**ate**

- *-efy, -ify*

Suffix	English Base	Meaning	English Derivative
-efy	**liqu-**	fluid	lique**fy**
-ify	**pac-**	peace	pac**ify**

- *-esce*

Suffix	English Base	Meaning	English Derivative
-esce	**conval-**	thoroughly be well	conval**esce**

This verb suffix conveys the idea of change or mutation and often conveys the meaning of "to become."

LATIN EXPRESSIONS

Abbreviations

The following Latin abbreviations are some of the more commonly used abbreviations in the English language:

Abbreviation	Latin	English Meaning
A.D.	*anno domini*	in the year of the Lord
a.m.	*ante meridiem*	before noon
c.	*circa*	about
c.v.	*curriculum vitae*	course of life; career achievements
cf.	*confer*	compare
e.g.	*exempli gratia*	for the sake of an example
etc.	*et cetera*	and other things
i.e.	*id est*	that is
ibid.	*ibidem*	in the same place
n.b.	*nota bene*	note well
p.m.	*post meridiem*	after midday
p.s.	*post scriptum*	written after
v.	*versus*	against

Phrases

L atin phrases are used in English usually to express a complex idea in a few words. (For Latin legal phrases, see Chapter 6, "Politics and Law.")

Latin Phrase	English Meaning and Usage
a fortiori	"from the stronger argument" (with even greater reason)
a priori	"from the earlier argument" (self-evident)
ad hoc	"for this purpose" (a short-term, unplanned provision)
ad hominem	"against the person" (an argument against a particular person rather than the principle involved)
ad nauseam	"to the point of sickness"
alumnus/alumna	"a male/female foster child" (a male/female graduate student of a university)
cum laude	"with praise"
deus ex machina	"a god from the machine"
ex gratia	"out of goodwill" (a payment made out of favor rather than obligation)
ex officio	"as a result of being in office"
ex tempore	"out of time" (improvised)
in camera	"in a room" (in a judge's chambers)
in toto	"in total"
inter alia	"among other things"
mutatis mutandis	"with the various factors changed that need to be changed"
non sequitur	"it does not follow" (an argument that does not follow logically from what has gone before)
quorum	"of whom" (the minimum number of members of a body required for a meeting)
sine die	"without a date" (without setting a date)
terminus ante quem	"the limit before which" (the time before which something occurred; the finishing point of a period)
terminus post quem	"the limit after which" (the time after which something occurred; the starting point of a period)
vice versa	"in turn"

Quotations

Many quotations from literary, philosophical and medical writers have entered English from Latin. When they are used, they provide a kind of intellectual shorthand. What saves these expressions from being mere clichés is the fact that they articulate ideas whose wisdom is widely acknowledged and that are quite closely related to proverbs.

Latin Quotation	English Meaning
Ars longa, vita brevis est.	Art is long; life is short.
Carpe diem.	Seize the day.
Dulce et decorum est pro patria mori.	It is sweet and fitting to die for one's country
Mens sana in corpore sano.	A sound mind in a sound body.
Quis custodiet ipsos custodes?	Who will guard the guards themselves?
Quot homines, tot sententiae.	So many men, so many opinions.

BIBLIOGRAPHY AND FURTHER READING

Ayers, D. M., *English Words from Latin and Greek Elements*, 2nd Ed. (Tucson 1986).

Borror, D. J., *Dictionary of Word Roots and Combining Forms* (Palo Alto 1960).

Burriss, E. E. and Casson, L., *Latin and Greek in Current Use*, 2nd Ed. (Englewood Cliffs 1949).

Conway, R. S., *The Making of Latin: An Introduction to Latin, Greek and English Etymology* (New York 1923).

Dunmore, C. W. and Fleischer, R., *Studies in Etymology*, 2nd Ed. (Newburyport 2008).

Green, T. M., *The Greek and Latin Roots of English*, 4th Ed. (Lanham 2008).

Krill, R. M., *Greek and Latin in English Today*, 3rd Ed. (Wauconda 2003).

Los Angeles Unified School District, *Look for the Latin Word* (Los Angeles 1972).

Luschnig, C. A. and Luschnig, J., *Etyma: An Introduction to Vocabulary-Building from Latin and Greek* (Lanham 1982).

Moore, B. and Moore, M., *NTC's Dictionary of Latin and Greek Origins* (Chicago 1997).

O'Reilly, N. J., *Latin, Not Dead: Greek, Alive and Well in Today's Words* (Lima 2005).

Regenos, G. W., *Latin Words in Current English* (Oxford 1981).

Schaeffer, R. F., *Latin-English Derivative Dictionary* (Oxford 1960).

Walker, T. E., *Word Resources*, 3rd Ed. (Indianapolis 1979).

WEB SITES: NAMES AND URLS

Web sites in Chapter 1 ("Word Building Basics") plus:
"English Words from Classical Origins"
        http://www.personal.kent.edu/~rlarson/words
"Latin — Abbreviations"
        http://ancienthistory.about.com/od/abbreviations/Latin_Abbreviations.htm
"Maths — Classics Project"
        http://www.users.globalnet.co.uk/~loxias/mathsclassics.htm
"Quotes/Expressions, Terminology, Mottoes"
        http://ancienthistory.about.com/cs/quotesexpressions
"Rome — Roman Numerals"
        http://ancienthistory.about.com/od/romannumerals/Rome_Roman_Numerals.htm
"A Selection of Greek and Latin Roots"
        http://abasiccurriculum.com/homeschool/roots

EXERCISES

1.   (a) What is the reason for the name of the group of South American guerillas referred to as the **Contras?**
    (b) What is the meaning of **preposterous** in terms of the prefixes given in this chapter?
    (c) What is the reason for the names of the last four months of the modern calendar? (Note that March was the first month of the Roman year.)

2.   Give five English words (other than months of the year) that are derived from the Latin numeral system and explain their meanings. If necessary, refer to Appendix 3, "Colours and Numbers".

Latin Number	English Derivative

3. Write down two words that share the same bases as each of the words in the first column. Use an English dictionary if necessary.

English Word and Italicized Base	English Word (1)	English Word (2)
*consul*ate		
*corpor*al		
in*fer*		
*manu*al		
*miss*ile		
op*pose*		
re*ject*		
se*cede*		

4. Complete the following table by supplying an English word appropriate to the base and meaning given. Use an English dictionary if necessary. A sample word has been analyzed in the first line of the table.

Base 1	English	Base 2	English	Meaning of Base
ag-	agent	act-	action	do, act, drive
capt-		cept-		take
-ceed		cess-		go

5. In the following table match the words from the list that are derived from the same Latin verbs and write down the Latin verb (and its meaning) from which each pair is derived. The bases are in bold type. Refer to the Latin verbs given in this chapter and use an English dictionary to assist you if necessary. The first row has been completed as an example.

in**quire**, pro**vis**ion, pro**pel**ler, **miss**ionary, e**volut**ion, pre**requis**ite, e**locut**ion, e**vid**ent, con**scrip**tion, re**volve**, pro**posit**ion, ex**clude**, **scrib**ble, con**vinc**e, re**cess**ion, post**pon**e, col**loqu**ium, pro**ced**ure, trans**mit**, con**clus**ion, im**puls**e, **vict**ory

Words from Same Latin Verb	Latin Verb	Meaning of Latin Verb
victory, convince	vincere	conquer, defeat

6. Complete as much of the following table as is possible with combinations of the prefixes and bases supplied. The forms of the prefixes and bases may need to be changed slightly. Use an English dictionary if necessary. The first line of the table has been completed as a guide.

Prefix	port-, "carry"	spir-, "breathe"	vent-, "come"	vert-, "turn"
ad-	apportion	aspire	advent	avert
con-				
ex-				
in-				
per-	_____		_____	
re-			_____	
trans-			_____	

7. Explain the English meanings of the following groups of words on the basis of their prefixes and bases. Use an English dictionary if necessary to check the meanings. A sample word has been analyzed in the first line of the table.

Prefix	Base	Meaning of Base	English Derivative	Meaning of English Derivative
ad-	duc-	lead	adduce	to offer as example, reason, or proof
con-			conducive	
in-			induce	
re-			reduce	
se-			seduce	
tra-			traduce	
ab-	duct-		abduct	
de-			deduct	
de-	pos-	place	depose	
im-			impose	
re-			repose	
sup-			suppose	
trans-			transpose	
ab-	rog-	ask, demand	abrogate	
ar-			arrogant	
de-			derogatory	
sur-			surrogate	

8. Choose ten of the words from the list below and for each word write down in the table the part of speech to which the word belongs; the prefix (if any) and its meaning; the base/bases and its meaning/their meanings; the suffix/suffixes (if any) and its meaning/their meanings; and the literal meaning of the word. Use an English dictionary if necessary. A sample word has been analyzed in the first line of the table.

   abstract, conducive, confirmation, convention, defoliate, imposition, inject, oppose, perversion, procession, reduction, seduction, surrogate

English Word	Parts of Speech	Prefix	Base/Bases	Suffix/ Suffixes	Literal Meaning
abstract	noun/ adjective	abs-	tract-	_____	drag away

9. Compose sentences of your own to show the differences between the following pairs of words.
   a. **corporal/corporeal**
   b. **seducible/seductive**
   c. **consumable/consumptive**
   d. **adjacent/adjective**

10. Complete the following table with appropriate suffixes and supply the meanings of the words formed. Refer to the suffixes in this chapter and use an English dictionary if necessary.

Base	Suffix	Meaning
angul-		
crustace-		
deleg-		
differentia-		
effemin-		
efferv-		
evas-		
fraud-		
incred-		
independ-		
lique-		
magn-		
minu-		
nod-		
orna-		
plen-		
presid-		
rapt-		
sensation-		
sucr-		
superior-		
trem-		

11. For each of the following suffixes write down two English words that contain these suffixes.

Suffix	English Word (1)	English Word (2)
-ate		
-ent		
-ify		
-ity		
-tion		
-ule		

12. Write down and define two English words for each of the following adjectival suffixes. The first line contains an example.

Suffix	First Word	Meaning	Second Word	Meaning
-ary	military	relating to soldiers		
-ble				
-ic				
-ile				
-ive				

13. Give the meaning of each of the following Latin abbreviations used in English.
    a. a.m.   c. ibid.
    b. cf.   d. i. e.

14. Give the meaning of each of the following Latin quotations and explain how you could use each quotation in a sentence of your own.
    a. *Quis custodiet ipsos custodes?*
    b. *Quot homines, tot sententiae.*

15. Give the meaning of each of the following Latin phrases in English and for each phrase write a sentence of your own in which you incorporate the phrase.
    a. *in camera*   d. *ex officio*
    b. *vice versa*   e. *mutatis mutandis*
    c. *bona fide*   f. *persona non grata*

16. For each of the following words check (✓) the definition that comes closest to its literal meaning.
    a. missile
        (1) □ a prayer book
        (2) □ a young woman of marriageable age
        (3) □ an object that can be thrown
        (4) □ a nuclear weapon
    b. aquatic
        (1) □ marine
        (2) □ to do with water
        (3) □ mineral
        (4) □ to do with etching copper with acid
    c. corporal
        (1) □ bodily
        (2) □ a senior rank in the army
        (3) □ to do with business
        (4) □ a beating

d. gestation
- (1) ☐ pregnancy
- (2) ☐ bodily motion
- (3) ☐ spurt of activity
- (4) ☐ period of quiet

e. crescent
- (1) ☐ Arabic
- (2) ☐ an avenue
- (3) ☐ growing
- (4) ☐ lunar

f. intermission
- (1) ☐ religious endeavor
- (2) ☐ interval
- (3) ☐ deep sleep
- (4) ☐ disturbed sleep

g. verbose
- (1) ☐ flattering
- (2) ☐ the scrupulous use of words
- (3) ☐ in exactly the same words
- (4) ☐ wordy

h. virile
- (1) ☐ potent
- (2) ☐ sexually promiscuous
- (3) ☐ manly
- (4) ☐ heroic

i. superlative
- (1) ☐ better than everything else
- (2) ☐ powerful
- (3) ☐ legendary
- (4) ☐ necessary

j. manual
- (1) ☐ book
- (2) ☐ worked by hand
- (3) ☐ virile
- (4) ☐ gear system

CHAPTER 4

MYTHOLOGY

ed. W. J. Dominik

WHAT IS MYTHOLOGY?

*L*ong before the ancient Greeks learned to write, they used to tell traditional stories about their heroes, their gods, and the phenomena of nature. A story that has these features is called a myth, which is derived from the Greek word *mythos*, meaning "story" or "tale." Since mythology is derived from *mythos* and *logos*, which means "word," "explanation," or "study," **mythology** therefore means the study of traditional stories within a culture.

BEGINNINGS

The Creation of the World

> Before anything else existed, there was just something that had no particular shape and could not be described as it was empty; this was called *Chaos*. Then the mother-goddess Earth, whom the Greeks called *Ge* or *Gaia*, arose from Chaos and gave birth to *Uranus*, who became the sky-god and her husband. His rain fertilized the earth and made things grow; therefore the world came into existence. Since the world was an orderly place compared with the primordial Chaos, the Greeks referred to it as *kosmos*, which means "order," "world," and "universe."

*C*haos has come directly into English as **chaos,** meaning confusion and disorder; it has given rise to the adjective **chaotic**. The English word **cosmos** (for Greek *kosmos*) can mean the world or the entire universe, which also seems to be an ordered entity.

Generations of the Gods

> Uranus and Ge had several groups of children, most notably the Titans who were a race of colossal size and strength. Uranus was jealous of his children and so banished them and imprisoned them under the earth. Ge (who *was* the earth), however, released the youngest of the Titans, *Kronos*, who castrated Uranus and ruled in his place. Kronos married his sister, a goddess called *Rhea*, and they in turn produced children. Kronos knew of a prophecy that he, like his father Uranus before him,

would be supplanted by one of his children; in order to prevent this from happening he swallowed each child in turn as it was born. Rhea grew tired of this and after she gave birth to *Zeus*, she gave Kronos a stone wrapped up in baby clothes to swallow and secretly hid him in Crete to be brought up. When Zeus grew up, he challenged Kronos and, as had been predicted, he deposed him. He became the new ruler of the cosmos.

Word Study

Many of the words and names above have connections with English words. The Greek loan-word *kosmos* is an obvious example. English **cosmos** has given rise to the adjective **cosmic,** which means literally "of the universe," and a number of other words in combination with different bases:

- a **cosmetic** is a preparation for external use, especially on the face, for beautifying purposes; from Greek *kosmein*, "to arrange," "to adorn," derived in turn from *kosmos*.
- **cosmogony** is the (theory of the) "origin of the universe"; from *gonē*, the Greek word for "offspring," "family." Compare **theogony,** the (account of the) "birth of the gods"; from *theos*, the Greek word for "god."
- **cosmography** is the "description of (the features of the) universe," from *graphē*, the Greek word for "writing." Compare **biography,** the "writing of (someone's) life story"; from *bios*, the Greek word for "life."
- **cosmology** is the "study of the universe"; from the Greek word *logos* (see above).
- a **cosmonaut** is a person who travels the universe; from *nautēs*, the Greek word for "sailor." Compare **astronaut,** "someone who 'sails' (travels) among the stars"; from *astron*, the Greek word for "star."
- **cosmopolitan** describes a person who belongs to all parts of the world ("universe" is a little exaggerated here); from *politēs*, the Greek word for "citizen." Compare **metropolitan** from *mētēr*, the Greek word for "mother," via *metropolis*, the Greek word for a "mother-city," that is, a major city; **metropolitan** describes a person or thing that is connected with a major city.

The Greek noun *gē* has given rise to a large number of words in English connected with the earth.

- **geography** is literally the "written description of the earth"; from *gē* and *graphē*, the Greek word for "writing."
- **geology** is the "study of the earth," specifically of the rocks and minerals within it; from *gē* and *logos* (see above).

- **geometry** is derived from the Greek word *geometria*, which meant much the same as geometry does today as the branch of mathematics concerned with measurement; however, it was originally the measurement of the earth; from *gē* and *metrein*, a Greek verb that means "to measure."
- the name **George** is derived from the Greek word *georgos*, "farmer", which is composed of the words *gē* and the verb *ergein*, "to work."
- **geothermal** means having to do with the earth's internal heat and is derived from the Greek word *thermē*, meaning "heat."

The Romans called *gē* by a different name, *terra*, which also means "earth" or "land". Several English words are derived from this word:

- **terrain,** an area of ground, is derived from the Latin word *terrenus*, meaning "belonging to the earth," which is in turn in Latin derived from *terra*.
- **terrestrial,** which means "belonging to the ground" (in contrast to **celestial,** "belonging to the sky") is from the Latin adjective *terrestris*, which also means "belonging to the ground" and is derived from *terra*.
- **terrier,** a small dog able to pursue its prey into the earth.
- **territory,** meaning a large "expanse of land," is from the Latin word *territorium*, meaning the "land around a town," "district," and is derived from Latin *terra*.

It is important to recognize that another group of words in English that may look as if they have the same derivation in fact come from a different Latin word. For example, **terrify, terrorize, terrorist, terrific,** and **terrible** are derived from Latin *terrere*, which means "to frighten."

GODS AND GODDESSES

*A*lthough *Kronos* does not appear in any English words, the Romans worshipped the same god by a different name, *Saturn*, which gives rise to **Saturday**, the day of *Saturn*. **Saturn** and **Uranus** are the names of planets in our solar system, as is **Jupiter** or **Jove**, the names by which the Romans knew Zeus.

Word for Word

From the *Titans* comes the adjective **titanic,** which means "gigantic" and therefore very strong (the ship named the **Titanic** earlier this century was supposed to be so strongly built that it was unsinkable), and also the metallic element **titanium,** which in its pure form is the strongest metal.

The Greek word for a god is *theos,* which gives us words like **theology,** the study of religion (literally, "study of gods"), and **theogony,** the (account of the) genealogy or order of birth of the gods, from *gonē,* the Greek word for "offspring," "family." The Latin word for "god" is *deus,* which gives us words like **deity,** a divine being, and **deify,** which means literally "to make into a god."

> In his struggle with Kronos, Zeus released his brothers and sisters who had been swallowed and set himself up as the king of the gods, ruling over them. He married his sister *Hera* and they produced children who were also worshipped as gods and goddesses. The whole family of gods was believed by the ancient Greeks to live amid the clouds on the top of Mount Olympus, a very high mountain in the north of Greece, and from this they were known as the "Olympian Gods."

The following list first gives the names of the twelve main Olympian gods and some of their lesser associates; the names by which the Romans called them appear in the second column. In general, the Romans worshipped the same gods as the Greeks but used other names for most of them. The third column gives the activity or natural force associated with each god by the ancients.

Greek Deity	Roman Deity	Significance
Zeus	Jupiter	King of the gods; god of lightning and thunder
Hera	Juno	Wife of the king of the gods; goddess of marriage and the home
Poseidon	Neptune	God of the sea and of earthquakes
Aphrodite	Venus	Goddess of love and sexuality
Eros	Cupid	Son of Aphrodite, the child-god responsible for making people fall in love by shooting them with his bow and arrows
Ares	Mars	God of war, strife, and dissension
Athena/Athene	Minerva	Goddess of wisdom and skill, especially skill at warfare, handwork, and artistry
Hephaestus/ Hephaistos	Vulcan	God of metalwork: the smith-god
Artemis	Diana	Goddess of hunting and of chastity; sister of Apollo
Apollo	Apollo	God of music, prophecy, intellect, and archery; brother of Artemis
Muses	Muses	Nine minor goddesses associated with Apollo in bringing inspiration to poets
Hermes	Mercury	Messenger god, god of travelers, and of thieves; also god of merchants and traders; noted for quick-wittedness and eloquence
Iris	Iris	Messenger of the gods; also the rainbow
Demeter	Ceres	Goddess of agriculture, especially grain crops
Dionysus/ Dionysos	Bacchus	God of wine; also represents the power of nature
Hades	Pluto	God of the Underworld; Hades is also the place inhabited by the souls of the dead

Word Study

Some of the names of these gods are used directly in English or have given rise to derivatives.

- The largest planet in our solar system is appropriately named **Jupiter.**

Word for Word

THE GREATEST ROMAN GOD WAS JUPITER. NOT ONLY DOES HE HAVE A PLANET NAMED AFTER HIM BUT, ALSO, A MONTH.

THE MONTH OF MAY TAKES ITS NAME FROM THE LATIN MAGNUS... GREAT!

JUPITER IS THE LARGEST OF THE PLANETS... 1250 TIMES THE SIZE OF EARTH!

©ATCHISON

- **Mars, Mercury, Pluto,** and **Venus** are similarly the names of planets. **Mars** is a fiery red planet. **Mercury,** the planet that bustles around the shortest orbit in the solar system, seems to travel more quickly than any of the others. **Pluto** is the furthest away, inhabiting cold regions that are beyond the reach of most living mortals. **Venus** is wreathed in cloud just as a beautiful woman might appear partly shrouded by haze or mist in a photograph.
- The word **aphrodisiac,** which is derived from *Aphrodite*, is a substance that arouses sexual desire.
- An **Apollo** is a young man of great beauty, as *Apollo* was always thought of as being particularly youthful and handsome among the gods.
- A **Bacchanalia** is a term used today to refer to a very drunken party. It was originally a Latin word that meant a festival of *Bacchus*.
- **Cereal** means grain, especially in the form of human food, and is derived from *Ceres*.
- **Cupidity** means greed, desire (now in a greedy rather than a sexual way); from *Cupid*, god of desire.
- **Erotic** things are connected with sexuality and arouse physical desire; from *Eros*.
- **Iridescence** indicates that something shines with the colors of the rainbow (*Iris*) or glitters as the light moves over its surface.
- **March** is the month named after *Mars*. It is also a verb meaning "to march," which is what soldiers do, and the name of a form of western music with a strict beat (four to the bar) suitable for soldiers marching in time. The adjective **martial** means warlike and is derived from *Mart-*, the extended form of *Mars*.
- A **mercurial** person is lively, likely to change moods quickly, and quick-witted. The metallic element mercury, which is a silver-white liquid, is difficult to hold since it slides away from one's grasp; hence its name "quicksilver."

Word for Word

- **Venereal** is an adjective that refers to sexual intercourse, as when it describes the diseases spread through sexual contact. It is derived from the extended form (*Vener-*) of Venus' name.
- **Vulcanology** is the study of volcanoes. The Roman god *Vulcan* (and his Greek equivalent *Hephaestus*) was supposed to have had his metal-working headquarters under Etna, a volcano on the island of Sicily. **Volcano** is derived from an Italian word, which in turn is derived from *Vulcan*.

Some of the gods have important associations. The goddess *Athena* almost always wore a strange, protective garment called the "aegis" over her shoulders and breast. It was given to her by Zeus and was scaly with a fringe of small snakes around the edge.

- **Under the aegis** of someone means to be under that person's protection. The phrase originates from the fact that when Athena wanted to shield someone from trouble she would often stretch it out on her arm and hold it over the person. The word **aegis** is derived directly from the Latin, which in turn comes from Greek *aigis*, "goatskin," which was the material from which the protective shield was fashioned.

The illustration on the right, which is from a Greek vase painting of *circa* 480 BCE, shows the goddess Athena with her attributes as she was typically represented by vase painters: she is dressed in long, flowing garments, holds her spear, and wears her helmet and the aegis, which she holds out over her left arm as if to offer protection.

Apollo was the god of prophecy. The Greeks believed that he controlled the famous oracle at Delphi in Greece, giving prophecies through the mouth of a priestess called the *Pythia*. She would go into a trance and utter strange sounds that would then be interpreted by a priest. The Delphic oracle had a great deal of prestige, giving apparently helpful answers to individuals as

Athena with spear, helmet, and aegis

well as to states. Many of the answers were ambiguous, however, and were unable to be understood at the time; only later, after the events foretold had occurred, could the oracle be shown to have been correct. **Delphic,** therefore, is used in English to describe something obscure, ambiguous, and enigmatic.

- A **python,** any one of various large constricting snakes, is so named after the monstrous serpent that Apollo killed at the site of Delphi. Snakes also guarded the *Pythia* ("priestess of the Python") who uttered her prophecies.

Apollo was also the god of music and culture. He was often represented by the Greeks as playing a stringed instrument, the lyre. He was believed to have nine female associates known as the *Muses,* who were regarded as the source of inspiration for poets, dramatists, and other writers as well as musicians. From their collective name a number of English words are derived.

- To **muse** is a verb that means "to ponder," "to think" about something in a meditative way as, for instance, when seeking inspiration.
- A **museum** is a place for storing and displaying precious or interesting things; it is where people can go to muse and to seek inspiration.
- **Music, musical,** and **musician** should need no explanation; they all are derived from an ancient Greek adjective *mousikos,* which means "connected with the Muses."

THE UNDERWORLD

When a mortal died, the soul (*psychē*) went down to Hades. This was regarded as a cold, dark, cheerless place under the earth. To reach Hades, the souls had to cross the River *Styx.* They were ferried across by the boatman *Charon.* In classical times the dead were always buried with a coin in their mouths to pay their boat fare.

The Greeks believed that after spending some time in Hades, the souls would be reincarnated into the world; before being reborn, they would have to pass over another river, the *Lethe,* and drink a little of the water from it. This would cause them to forget their previous life and their time in the underworld so that they would come fresh into their new life experience.

Word Study

- **Hades** was the name of the underworld as well as of the god in charge of it.
- The noun **lethargy** (and the associated adjective **lethargic**) is derived from Greek *lēthē,* which means "forgetfulness"; it is a sluggish condition when one is indifferent to the world—as if one had forgotten it all.
- The **waters of Lethe** in English are used to mean forgetfulness; to "drink of the waters of Lethe" means to become forgetful.

- **Stygian,** which is derived from *Styg-*, the extended form of *Styx*, is an adjective used in English to describe gloomy darkness.

Divine Punishments

The deepest part of Hades, called *Tartarus*, was reserved for the eternal punishment of those who had committed serious crimes (usually against the gods) when they were alive. Two characters in Tartarus were infamous for their unusual punishments.

Sisyphus

Sisyphus saw Zeus carrying off a young girl to rape her and told her father where to find them. Zeus was naturally very angry with Sisyphus and punished him by sending *Thanatos* (the god of death) to take him to Hades. Sisyphus managed to trick Thanatos and tied him up in a dungeon, which meant that mortals ceased to die. Worried by this, the Olympian gods searched for Thanatos and released him, whereupon Thanatos found Sisyphus again and killed him in revenge. Sisyphus, however, had expected this and had told his wife what to do when it happened; she left his body unburied and made none of the usual offerings to the dead. Sisyphus then persuaded Hades to let him return temporarily to the upper world to punish his wife and make her bury his body. When he was allowed to return to the land of the living, he resumed his life and lived to a great age in defiance of the god of the Underworld. For this impiety, as well as for telling tales about Zeus, Sisyphus was punished in Tartarus after his eventual death by being eternally forced to roll a great stone up a hill; when he had nearly reached the top, it always rolled back to the bottom and he had to begin again.

The story above gives rise to the phrase in English, **Sisyphean task,** which means a task that is endless, laborious, and frustrating.

Tantalus

Tantalus also offended the gods, according to one version of the myth, by stealing their special divine food and drink, ambrosia and nectar, and telling the secrets of the gods to mortals. Another version tells that his crime was to test the omniscience of the gods by inviting them to dinner and serving up his own son in a pie. All the gods knew the truth and refrained from eating except for Demeter, who was so distraught at the loss of her daughter *Persephone* [see story below] that she did not notice what she was eating. The gods reconstituted the boy except for the shoulder that Demeter had eaten, which they made up out of ivory. Tantalus was punished in Tartarus with everlasting hunger and thirst, by being made to stand up to his neck in water, with fruit hanging on branches just over his head; whenever he bent his head to drink, the water-level dropped away from him, and whenever he tried to pick the fruit, the wind tossed it out of his reach.

This is the origin of the English word **tantalize,** which means to torment someone with the sight or promise of a desired thing that is then held out of reach.

Persephone and Demeter

Also associated with Hades and the underworld is the story of Persephone.

Demeter, the goddess of agriculture and the fertility of growing things, had a beautiful daughter named *Persephone* (*Proserpina* in Latin). One day Persephone went with her friends to gather flowers. She had wandered away from them in search of the biggest and prettiest blooms, when suddenly the earth broke open to reveal Hades himself speeding towards her in his chariot. He snatched up the girl, who, though she screamed, could do nothing against him, and he carried her away into the Underworld. No one knew where she had gone and poor Demeter wandered all over the world trying to find out where she was. She was so distraught that she neglected her divine duties; for the many months that she searched for her lost Persephone, not a single plant grew. Mortals were starving to death, with no crops to eat. Eventually Demeter came to a place called Eleusis, which was not far from Athens, where she heard the truth from a small child who had happened to witness the kidnapping. She went to Zeus and begged for his help in getting her daughter back; Zeus subsequently ordered Hades to let Persephone return to the upper world. Hades released her, but gave her some pomegranate seeds to eat as she left. The girl, unaware of the risk, ate six and so was obliged to spend six months of every year thereafter down in the realm of Hades.

Persephone is usually regarded as the embodiment of spring, for when she returns to the earth from Hades, her mother Demeter rejoices and the crops begin to grow. The six months of Persephone's stay in Hades every year are autumn and winter, when Demeter mourns again for the loss of her daughter.

HEROES

The Greeks had myths not only about the gods but also about many heroes, who were usually the semi-divine offspring of gods' love affairs with mortals.

Heracles

Heracles (Latin *Hercules*) was the best-known hero, a very strong man who was able to defeat any enemy and to kill any monster. There are many stories about his adventures. Although most of his activities were to the benefit of other people, on one occasion he suffered from a fit of madness in which he killed his own children unawares. As a punishment for this he was sentenced by the gods to become a servant for a certain period of time of King *Eurystheus,* who imposed upon him a series of twelve exceptionally difficult tasks.

The Twelve Labors of Heracles

The stories about Heracles' twelve undertakings became the most popular of all the stories about Heracles; they are known as the *Twelve Labors of Heracles.*

1. *The Nemean Lion:* His first labor was to kill a monstrous and magical lion that was terrorizing the people of Nemea; its hide could not be harmed by weapons, so Heracles could kill it only by strangling it with his bare hands. He skinned it by using its own claws to cut the hide and afterwards always wore the skin as a protective garment.

The following illustration based on a Greek vase painting of *circa* 520 BCE shows Heracles wrestling with the Nemean Lion.

Heracles and the Nemean lion

On some of his subsequent adventures Heracles was accompanied by his nephew *Iolaus;* he usually had the advice and help of Athena and sometimes also of Hermes.

2. *The Hydra of Lerna:* Another monster encountered by Heracles was the snake-like Hydra, a creature with many heads: every time Heracles cut one off, two more grew in its place. Its ally, a monstrous crab, also attacked Heracles. Eventually, with the help of his nephew Iolaus, he killed the crab and with a flaming branch burned the stumps as he cut them off so that no more heads could grow; and so the Hydra was defeated.

3. *The Deer of Keryneia:* Eurystheus sent him to hunt the beautiful deer of Keryneia, famous for its golden horns. This animal was sacred to the goddess Artemis, so Heracles had to track it for a full year before he could catch it and take it alive back to his master. After that, because it was a holy animal, he had to release it.

4. *The Erymanthian Boar:* A wild boar of gigantic size was ravaging the crops grown by the people near Mount Erymanthos and Heracles was sent by Eurystheus to dispose of it. This time, mischievously, Heracles captured the boar alive and brought it, tied up but kicking ferociously, back to King Eurystheus, who was such a coward that he hid in fear in a large storage container.

5. *The Augean Stables:* Heracles was then set an almost impossible task: to clean out the stables of King *Augeas* in a single day. These stables had never been cleaned before and were so deep in dung that they were unusable. Heracles achieved the near-impossible by making a hole in the stable wall and diverting a river through the building, following the suggestion of Athena.

6. *The Stymphalian Birds:* Lake Stymphalis in central Greece was plagued by monstrous, supernatural birds, bronze-beaked and man-eating; they used their metal feathers as arrows. Heracles first scared them into the air (this he did by frightening them with a bronze rattle given to him by Athena) and, as they flew up, he shot them with his own arrows.

7. *The Cretan Bull:* Heracles had to travel to the island of Crete and capture alive the fire-breathing bull that was running wild there. He brought it successfully back to King Eurystheus, but it then escaped. It was eventually killed near Marathon by *Theseus,* another famous hero.

8. *The Horses of Diomedes:* Heracles was sent to Thrace to fetch the horses owned by King *Diomedes,* a difficult task as the horses were man-eating creatures. Nevertheless, Heracles overcame them and, keeping them quiet by feeding their savage owner to them, he duly harnessed them to his chariot and drove them back to King Eurystheus.

9. *The Belt of the Amazon:* The Amazons were a mythical race of women who lived alone without men. They were famous for their prowess as warriors. Heracles had to fetch the belt of their queen, *Hippolyta,* the best fighter of them all. He succeeded.

10. *Geryon:* He was sent against the three-bodied giant, *Geryon,* whose marvelous cattle he had to steal and take back to Greece for King Eurystheus. He first encountered Geryon's herdsman, *Eurytion,* and his monstrous dog, *Orthros;* he killed them both. He was driving off the cattle when Geryon himself came to investigate; Heracles killed him too, disposing of one body at a time—one with an arrow, one with his spear, and the third with his sword.

11. *The Apples of the Hesperides:* Heracles' next labor was to fetch the golden apples from the Garden of the Hesperides, which was guarded by a fierce dragon that was too much even for Heracles; he asked the Titan *Atlas* to do the job for him. Long before this, Atlas had been condemned to hold up the sky on his shoulders; while he was away fetching the apples, Heracles had to hold up the sky instead. When Atlas came back with the apples, unwilling to take back his burden, he announced that he would take the apples to Eurystheus and Heracles could continue to hold up the sky forever. Heracles pretended to accept this, but asked Atlas to take back the sky just for a minute while he adjusted his position for greater comfort. Atlas foolishly agreed, whereupon Heracles picked up the apples and took them back to Eurystheus.

12. *Cerberus* (Greek *Kerberos*) was the ferocious dog that guarded the entrance to the Underworld. He was an excellent watch-dog as he had three heads. Heracles had to tame him, put a leash on him, and lead him up to the mortal world. Hades allowed him to do so provided he brought the animal straight back afterwards.

After these and many other adventures, when Heracles eventually was due to die, he was taken up from his funeral pyre and became a god.

Word Study

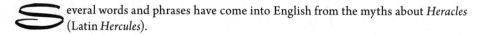

Several words and phrases have come into English from the myths about *Heracles* (Latin *Hercules*).

- The **labors of Heracles** are used metaphorically to refer to a series of very difficult undertakings.
- The word **herculean** can describe either a person, meaning as strong as Heracles, or tasks and undertakings, meaning as difficult as Heracles' labors.
- The phrase **apples of the Hesperides** is used to refer to something very desirable that is difficult to get.
- An **atlas** is now a book of maps, but the English word derives from the giant *Atlas,* whom the ancient Greeks believed held up the sky. Later the story changed and he was thought to hold up not the sky but the whole world. Early books of maps were published with a picture on the front cover of Atlas as a muscled giant holding the world on his shoulders, so they came to be known by the name of **atlases.**
- **Augean** means filthy. The phrase **Augean stables** is used metaphorically to describe a near-impossible (and rather dirty) job.
- A **hydra-headed** problem presents a new difficulty as soon as one is resolved.

Theseus

Theseus was a hero particularly revered by the Athenians, because, according to the myth, he was Athenian by birth. His most famous achievement was to defeat the *Minotaur*, a man-eating monster that was half-man, half-bull. At that time, the Athenians, like many other peoples, were under the domination of King *Minos* of Crete, who compelled them every year to send to him a tribute of seven young girls and seven youths. These young people were condemned to be eaten by the Minotaur who lived in the labyrinth, a maze of winding, confusing passages from which no one had ever found his way out.

Theseus, the son of the King of Athens, was determined to put a stop to this cruel system and one year he volunteered to go as one of the tribute group. On his arrival on Crete, he caught the eye of Minos' daughter, *Ariadne*, who was immediately attracted to his good looks. Before Theseus went into the labyrinth, she gave him a ball of string. She stood at the entrance holding one end of the string and, as he went more deeply into the labyrinth in search of the Minotaur, he unwound the ball; when he had succeeded in killing the monster, he was able to find his way out by following the thread back. When he left Crete to return triumphantly to Athens, he took Ariadne with him on his boat, but apparently tiring of her on the journey back, he abandoned her on the beach of the island of Naxos. She eventually became the bride of the god Dionysus.

Theseus had many other adventures, among them his encounter with *Sinis*, a notorious robber of travelers. He would kill his victim by bending the tops of two tall pine trees to the ground and after tying the man's feet to one and his arms to the other, he would release the trees, which would then spring apart and tear the poor man apart. Theseus used this same method to dispose of Sinis. Another unpleasant character Theseus encountered was *Procrustes*, who would force his victims to lie on an iron bed. If they were too big for the bed, he would cut off the parts that did not fit; if they were too small, he would stretch them until they fitted. They did not survive this hospitality. As with Sinis, however, Theseus forced him to undergo his own treatment and so the world was rid of another predatory outlaw.

Theseus also finished off one of Heracles' monsters. The Cretan Bull, which Heracles had brought to Greece in fulfillment of one of his labors for Eurystheus, subsequently escaped and became a nuisance in the region north of Athens around Marathon. Theseus went out and caught the monstrous bull; he then led it back to Athens, where he sacrificed it to Apollo.

Word Study

The stories about Theseus have given rise to some words and phrases in English.

- The noun **labyrinth** and the related adjective **labyrinthine** are used in English to refer to a maze or any structure with many passages through which it is difficult to find one's way without guidance.
- **Ariadne's thread** is often used metaphorically of something that helps a person to find a way through a complex situation.
- The **bed of Procrustes** is a way of describing an attempt to reduce people to one standard, one way of thinking, or one way of acting that does not suit them all.

THE TROJAN WAR

The best-known of all Greek myths are the stories about the Trojan War.

This was a war in which an army of heroes from all over Greece besieged the city of Troy (a powerful city in northern Asia Minor) for ten years before finally destroying it. The reason for the war lay in the past: a quarrel arose on Mount Olympus over a golden apple upon which had been written "for the most beautiful goddess." Athena, Hera, and Aphrodite laid claim to it. Zeus commanded Hermes to lead the three to Troy, where *Paris,* one of the sons of *Priam,* the king of Troy, was selected to be judge of the beauty contest. Each of the three goddesses tried to bribe Paris: Athena offered him perpetual victory in battle; Hera promised to make him ruler of the whole world; and Aphrodite said she would give him the most beautiful woman in the world to be his wife. Aphrodite won and Paris set out for Greece to fetch home *Helen,* his prize, as she was regarded at the time as the most beautiful woman in the world.

Unfortunately, Helen was already married to *Menelaus,* who was very angry when his wife went off with the Trojan prince. Menelaus organized all the Greek heroes to make up an army to go to Troy and bring her back to Greece. The Trojans were not willing to give her back and so the Greeks laid siege. After ten long years they eventually captured the city by a trick: they built a huge wooden horse, which was made hollow so that Greek warriors could hide inside; they then left it outside the walls of Troy and pretended to give up the siege and to go away. *Sinon,* a Greek who claimed to be a deserter, told the Trojans that if they dragged the horse into the city it would bring them victory. After the Trojans pulled it within the walls of the city, the Greek warriors emerged from inside the horse and opened the gates for the rest of the Greek army that had come back quietly. The Greek warriors then defeated the Trojans and plundered the city.

Word Study

- The **judgment of Paris** has become a term for a decision that brings about a great deal of trouble.
- To liken a woman to **Helen of Troy** is to say that she is a very beautiful woman. This Greek woman is famous for having "the face that launch'd a thousand ships."
- **Trojan horse** is used in English to mean something treacherous, an object that is apparently attractive but which has serious disadvantages hidden within it.

Greek Heroes of the War

Some famous heroes fought on the Greek side and others on the Trojan side. The massed Greek army was led by Menelaus' elder brother *Agamemnon*; he fought well at Troy and survived, but on his return home he was assassinated in his bath by his treacherous wife *Clytemnestra* and her paramour *Aegisthus*. *Achilles* of the swift feet was the most famous of the Greek heroes who fought at Troy. The son of *Peleus*, a mortal, and *Thetis*, a sea-nymph, he was invulnerable (unable to be wounded), except for a small spot on the heel of his foot; he was eventually killed in the last year of the war by being hit in that one vulnerable place. *Ajax* of the mighty shield was the best fighter for the Greeks after Achilles. After Achilles' death at Troy there was great rivalry for his armor because it had been made for him by Hephaestus; the two main contenders were strong *Ajax*, the best warrior, and wily *Odysseus*, noted for his brains rather than his muscles. Agamemnon and Menelaus were the arbitrators and awarded the armor to Odysseus, whereupon Ajax became insane and eventually killed himself in his humiliation. The oldest of the Greek heroes at Troy was *Nestor*, king of Pylos, who was always a source of wise (if sometimes long-winded) advice. The ancient Greeks did not have a public address system, so public announcements had to be made by a herald; the most famous Greek herald who served at Troy was *Stentor*, whose voice was said to be as loud as that of fifty men combined.

Word Study

- The **Achilles' heel** is used metaphorically for the single, small vulnerable point in an otherwise unassailable person or thing.
- To refer to someone as a **Stentor** (or the associated adjective **stentorian**) is to suggest that he or she has a voice that can be heard from a considerable distance.

Word for Word

- To call someone a **Nestor** in English means that he is a wise old man, an "elder statesman."
- The name of **Odysseus** has become a way of referring to someone who is ingenious and clever at finding his or her way out of trouble. There is an added implication that luck in the form of the gods is always on this person's side.

Trojan Heroes of the War

On the Trojan side, *Hector* was the best warrior (he was another son of King Priam and a brother of Paris). All the stories about him indicate that as well as being a great fighter he was a courteous and considerate man. He was finally killed by Achilles shortly before the sack of Troy. *Aeneas* was another of the foremost Trojan warriors; he survived the fall of Troy and was ordered by the gods to take up the images of the gods of the city and to lead his family and a few other survivors to a land far away where he would found a new Troy (the Romans claimed that Rome was that city founded by Aeneas). Aeneas obeyed the gods and left Troy even as it was being sacked by the Greeks, carrying his aged father *Anchises* on his back as the old man was too frail to walk. Another notable figure from Troy was *Cassandra,* one of King Priam's daughters. She was a prophetess, able to predict the future. The god Apollo had fallen in love with Cassandra and bribed her to have intercourse with him by offering her the gift of prophecy. Cassandra accepted his offer, but when it was time to fulfil her part of the bargain she changed her mind. Apollo could not take back his gift, but changed it so that no one would believe anything Cassandra prophesied. Cassandra in fact foretold the whole doom of Troy, but the Trojans just laughed at her.

Word Study

- To **hector** a person is to harass or bully her or him. This usage is at odds with the traditionally courteous character of Hector, but it seems to arise from his being such a persistent and fierce fighter who was always urging his fellow Trojans to fight harder.
- To **work like a Trojan** is to work very hard, often at something that is not very enjoyable. The Trojans were notable for their courage and determined perseverance.
- To call someone a **Cassandra** implies that she or he often foresees doom and gloom yet nobody believes these predictions.
- The name of **Aeneas** has come to stand for someone who reveres his parents and his country more than most people do.

Some of these stories about the Trojan War are known to us from one of the very earliest Greek poems, a traditional epic poem called the *Iliad*, said to have been composed by a poet known as Homer. The English word "epic" is derived from the Greek word *epos* (the ancient Greek word for traditional heroic poetry) and means first of all a very long poem telling of heroic achievements or of historical events. From this it has come to describe a film of the same kind, while the adjective "epic" now generally means "on a grand scale."

THE WANDERINGS OF ODYSSEUS

nother traditional epic poem called the *Odyssey*, attributed to the same poet Homer, tells what happened to Odysseus, one of the Greek warriors, on his way home from the Trojan War.

> It took *Odysseus* ten years to return to his wife *Penelope* after Troy had fallen because of all the adventures he had on the way. He was captured along with his men by the *Cyclops*, a man-eating giant called *Polyphemus* who had only one large round eye in the center of his forehead. Odysseus, who had told the giant his name was "Nobody," managed to make the Cyclops drunk and then blinded his one eye with a sharpened stick; when the giant's screams attracted the attention of his neighbors and they asked who was hurting him, he yelled out, "Nobody is hurting me!", so the neighbors went away again. Odysseus and his men escaped by hanging on under the Cyclops' sheep as they went out to graze the next morning; the blinded giant felt the sheeps' backs but forgot about their undersides. Odysseus had numerous other adventures on his long trip home to Troy. The witch *Circe* fell in love with him and kept him captive on her island for a year until the gods forced her to let him go. Odysseus was forewarned about encountering one particularly dangerous group of creatures during his voyage. These were the Sirens, who were mythical creatures: half woman, half bird, who sang so sweetly that any sailor who heard them was compelled to stay and listen entranced for ever; the ground around them was white with bleached bones. Odysseus was curious to hear them, but as he did not want to be trapped, he ordered his men to bind him securely to the mast of his ship and then to fill their own ears with wax. In this way he heard the magic song but was carried away to safety by his men.

The following illustration from a Greek vase painting of *circa* 450 BCE depicts Odysseus tied to the mast of his ship.

Odysseus and the Sirens

In this illustration he is listening to the Sirens' song while his men (with their ears blocked) row him to safety. The Siren dive-bombing the ship apparently is doing so in frustration.

Odysseus also encountered a people known as the Lotus-eaters, who were addicted to eating a plant (not the flower now known as the lotus) that made them forget who they were and what they were supposed to be doing: they lived in a state of blissful apathy. Some of his men tried the plant and Odysseus had to leave them behind.

Another dangerous hazard that Odysseus met at sea was a narrow channel through which he had to pass, with a man-eating sea-monster called *Scylla* on the shore of one side while near the other side was a huge whirlpool called *Charybdis*, strong enough to suck in and wreck any ship that went too close. Odysseus had to sail very carefully to avoid both of them.

Odysseus finally made his way back home, but his troubles were not yet over: he had been away so long that everyone except his wife, Penelope, thought he must be dead. Penelope was a beautiful and clever woman whom everyone wanted to marry, so her whole house was filled with suitors who ate all her food and drank all her wine and generally made her life miserable. They kept trying to force her to choose one of them to marry and did not accept her refusals. Finally in desperation she said that she would marry one of them just as soon as she had finished weaving a large and complicated piece of cloth. They were pleased to see her working at it every day, but they did not know that every night she unpicked her day's work. Odysseus' young son *Telemachus* had grown up during his father's absence: he had been left in the care of Penelope and an old family friend named *Mentor,* who did his best to protect him and saw to his upbringing and education. When Odysseus came home, he found his wife still faithfully waiting for him. With the help of Telemachus he killed all the suitors.

Word Study

- **Circe** has now come to mean a woman who bewitches men and makes them almost like slaves.
- The adjective **Cyclopean** is used by archaeologists to describe walls made of such huge blocks of stone that only a giant such as the Cyclops could have constructed them.
- The phrase **lotus-eaters** is used in English to refer to people who enjoy a life of lazy luxury.
- A **mentor** in English is a trusted adviser, usually rather older than the person receiving the advice.
- To call a woman a **Penelope** in English means that she is a faithful and ingenious person.
- The English word **siren** has several meanings, all connected with the creatures of the myth: a sweet singer, a dangerously fascinating woman, and a device that makes a loud, prolonged sound as an alarm signal.
- The phrase **Scylla and Charybdis** in English means two related dangers such that avoiding one increases the risk from the other.

OEDIPUS AND HIS FAMILY

Another set of stories, entirely unrelated to the Trojan War, concerned the city of Thebes. Oedipus was the extreme example of an undeserving victim of Fate.

Oedipus

The story of Oedipus is based on an oracle, which in ancient Greece was a foretelling of the future or a revealing of hidden truth normally by a priestess inspired by one of the gods. In the ancient world Delphi was one of the most famous oracular places; it was controlled by Apollo who prophesied through a priestess called the *Pythia.* She sat behind a screen in the temple on a tripod (a three-legged cooking stand) and answered questions in a trance, uttering strange sounds that had to be interpreted by the priests behind the screen. These priestesses 'translated' them into verse in the dactylic hexameter meter, which was the same meter used by Homer in his famous epic poems known as the *Iliad* and the *Odyssey,* whereupon these oracles acquired a sacred connotation.

Laius, the King of Thebes, was told by an oracle that if he had a son that his son would kill him. When his wife gave birth to a baby boy, therefore, he ordered the baby to be exposed on a faraway hillside on Mount Cithaeron. The Theban shepherd who was to dispose of the baby felt sorry for it, however, and gave it to another shepherd whom he met on the mountain, who came from Corinth. The baby was therefore taken back to Corinth and was adopted by the rulers of that city, King *Polybus* and his wife, *Merope,* who regarded him as their own child.

When *Oedipus* was almost grown up, he was taunted about his birth by people who said he was adopted; disturbed by this claim, he set off for Delphi, hoping to find out the truth from Apollo's oracle there; however, when he put his question to the oracle, he did not receive a straight answer from the *Pythia* but rather the prophecy that he was destined to marry his mother and kill his father. Stricken by horror, Oedipus decided never to return to Corinth (for he still thought that Polybus and Merope were indeed his father and mother). As he left Delphi, wondering where to head for, he came to a place where three roads meet and at a spot where the road became narrow a chariot came towards him; the driver, a middle-aged man, ordered him out of the way and attacked him with his whip. Oedipus defended himself with vigor and ended up by killing the man and all of the people with him, apart from one man who ran away, and in order to protect himself, claimed that they had been set upon by a whole gang of robbers.

Oedipus, meanwhile, continued along the road which happened to lead towards the city of Thebes, until, on the outskirts of the city, he came to a place where a monster called the *Sphinx* lived. The Sphinx had come to Thebes some time before and had terrorized the inhabitants by continually asking anyone who walked by to answer a riddle: "What is it that goes on four legs in the morning, on two legs in the middle of the day, and on three legs in the evening?" If the person was unable to answer (and nobody could), she would kill them. Oedipus was duly asked the riddle and after some deep thought, he answered, "Human beings: they crawl on four legs in their infancy; they walk proudly in their prime; and they resort to a walking-stick when they are old." The Sphinx was so upset that she threw herself over a cliff and died on the rocks below.

The drawing on the right, which is based on a Greek vase painting of *circa* 470 BCE, depicts Oedipus sitting on a rock before the Sphinx. In this illustration Oedipus is pondering what the answer may be to the Sphinx's riddle, as suggested by the resting of his chin on his hand. The Sphinx, who is perched on the top of a column, has a woman's head, eagle's wings, and the body of a lion.

Oedipus and the Sphinx

Oedipus then went into Thebes where he was welcomed as a savior for killing the Sphinx. He married the Queen of Thebes, a woman called *Jocasta* who had recently lost her husband, and lived as king for many years, producing a family of two sons and two daughters.

After quite a long time, a plague fell upon Thebes, affecting the crops, which did not ripen, the cattle, which did not breed, and the women, who were unable to give birth to live babies. Oedipus sent a messenger to Delphi to ask the oracle what has caused the plague: the answer came back that he must find the killer of Laius. Oedipus, eager to see the plague ended, proclaimed a curse on the unknown murderer and declared that he must be turned away by all the citizens and go into exile to spend the rest of his life a wretched outcast.

Oedipus then proceeded to try to discover the murderer only to find out after much inquiry that it was himself: the man in the chariot at the place where three roads meet was none other than Laius, who was the first husband of Jocasta. He found, worse, that he had indeed fulfilled the prophecy he had received long before from Delphi: he had killed Laius, who was his father, and had married Jocasta, his mother. Laius' original oracle had also been fulfilled, for he had been killed by his son. Both Oedipus and Jocasta were overcome with horror at what they found out: she committed suicide and he blinded himself (he thought that death would be too easy) so that he could no longer see the awfulness of his life. Oedipus then fulfilled his own curses by going into exile as a blind beggar.

The story of Oedipus has always fascinated people. There is the temptation to wonder what would have happened if, for example, he had not stayed away from Corinth or if Laius had not ordered him to be killed after his birth. One of the main points of the myth is that you cannot escape your destiny no matter how hard you try. Another discussion point that emerges from the story is the blamelessness of Oedipus: it seems very unfair that he suffered so much for what was not at all his fault. The "father of modern psychology," Sigmund Freud, was inspired by the Oedipus myth to postulate his famous theory of the **Oedipus complex.** In psychological terms the myth of Oedipus and his children can be seen as an expression of the dread of and taboo against incestuous marriage.

Eteocles and Polynices

The story continues into the next generation, for his children, born into a wrongful, incestuous marriage between Oedipus and his mother, Jocasta, also come to grief.

> Oedipus had two sons, *Eteocles* and *Polynices.* Soon after their father went into exile, they quarreled about which of them should rule. With the intervention of their uncle, *Creon* (Jocasta's brother), it was decided that they should rule in alternation, with Eteocles taking the first turn. But Polynices was not satisfied and, having sought the help of the citizens of Argos as his allies, he attacked Thebes, his own city. Each of the seven gates was attacked by a leader of the allied army, who were thereafter known as the Seven Against Thebes. Polynices and Eteocles met on the battlefield, fought, and each simultaneously killed the other. With that the battle was over, the Argive army driven away.

Eteocles and Polynices were the ancient Greeks' prime examples of civil war, where brother fights against brother.

Antigone and Ismene

> Creon, who now ruled Thebes, arranged for Eteocles to be buried with full military honors, but ordered that Polynices, as a traitor to his people, should be left to rot where he lay on the battlefield; he even commanded that anyone trying to give the body burial would in turn be regarded as a traitor and sentenced to death. This was very disturbing to Oedipus' two daughters, *Antigone* and *Ismene.*
>
> Antigone, the stronger of the two girls, was determined to do her best to bury her brother despite Creon's decree. She was caught in the act, brought before Creon, tried, and sentenced to death. Her fiancé *Haemon,* the son of Creon, tried to plead for her life, but was ignored by his father. She was taken to be walled up in a cave. Haemon went to rescue her, but found that she had already committed suicide in despair.

He then in grief killed himself. His mother, *Eurydice,* also committed suicide when she heard the news, leaving Creon to live on in suffering, wondering where he went wrong when all he meant to do was to ensure that a traitor to the state of Thebes was made an example of.

The story of Antigone has been told and retold not just by ancient Greeks and Romans but down the ages by many nations. Antigone is usually seen as a heroine for whom blood ties are more important than the law of the land since she was prepared to sacrifice her life for what she believed in. This is just one of the numerous stories told by the ancient Greeks about heroes and heroic events that afford some insight into their view of their society and the relationship of the individual to it.

BIBLIOGRAPHY AND FURTHER READING

Asimov, I., *Words from the Myths* (London 1963).
Burkert, W. (tr. J. Raffan), *Greek Religion* (Oxford 1985).
Dibbley, D. C., *From Achilles' Heel to Zeus's Shield: A Lively, Informative Guide to More than 300 Words and Phrases Born of Mythology* (New York 1993).
Dodds, E. R., *The Greeks and the Irrational* (Boston 1957).
Grant, M., *Myths of the Greeks and Romans* (New York 1995).
Grant, M. and Hazel, J., *Gods and Mortals in Classical Mythology: A Dictionary* (New York 1979).
Graves, R., *The Greek Myths* (Mt. Kisco 1988).
Grimal, P. (tr. A. R. Maxwell-Hyslop), *The Dictionary of Classical Mythology* (Oxford 1996).
Kerényi, C., *The Gods of the Greeks* (London 1951).
Kerényi, C., *The Heroes of the Greeks* (London 1974).
Parker, R., *On Greek Religion* (Ithaca 2011).
Pinsent, J., *Greek Mythology* (London 1983).
Powell, B. B., *Classical Myth*, 7th Ed. (Upper Saddle River 2011).
Room, A., *Room's Classical Dictionary* (London 1983).
Rose, H. J., *Handbook of Greek Mythology*, 6th Ed. (London 1990).

WEB SITES: NAMES AND URLS

"Ancient Greek and Roman Myths Index"
        http://www.abcgallery.com/mythindex.html
"Classical Myth: The Ancient Sources"
        http://web.uvic.ca/grs/department_files/classical_myth/index.html
"Encyclopedia Mythica"
        http://www.pantheon.org/mythica.html
"An Etymological Dictionary of Classical Mythology"
        http://library.oakland.edu/information/people/personal/kraemer/edcm/contents.html

"Etymology: Ideas in Words and Medical Terminology"
      http://www.consultos.com/pandora.sample.htm
"Greek Mythology"
      http://classiclit.about.com/msub-grmyth.htm
"Greek Mythology"
      http://www.desy.de/gna/interpedia/greek_myth/greek_myth.html
"Greek Mythology"
      http://eawc.evansville.edu/quizzes/greekmyth.htm
"Greek Mythology and Religion Photo Gallery"
      http://atheism.about.com/library/FAQS/religion/blgrk_religion.htm
"Greek Mythology for Educators"
      http://www.hipark.austin.isd.tenet.edu/mythology/introduction.html
"Greek Mythology from the Iliad to the Fall of the Last Tyrant"
      http://www.messagenet.com/myths/index.html
"Greek Mythology Today and the Myth of the Month"
      http://greekmythology.com
"Hercules or Heracles"
      http://ancienthistory.about.com/od/hercules/Hercules_Heracles_Herakles.htm
"MythNET: Where Togas are Still Hip"
      http://www.classicsunveiled.com/mythnet/html/index.html
"Mythology — Religion"
      http://ancienthistory.about.com/od/godsmyth/Gods_and_Goddesses.htm
"Mythology in Art"
      http://www.artcyclopedia.com/feature-2000-05.html
"Mythology Links — Gods, Goddesses, Greek, Roman"
      http://www.theoi.com
"Mythography"
      http://www.mythography.com/myth
"Olympian Individual Gods and Goddesses"
      http://ancienthistory.about.com/od/religionmythology/Beliefs_Mythology_Religion.htm
"Pandora's Word Box"
      http://www.pandorawordbox.com
"Perseus Project"
      http://www.perseus.tufts.edu
"Roman Mythology"
      http://classiclit.about.com/od/romanmythology/Roman_Mythology.htm
"Roman Mythology"
      http://www.pantheon.org/areas/mythology/europe
"Wordsmyth: The Educational Dictionary-Thesaurus"
      http://www.wordsmyth.net

EXERCISES

1. Complete the following table of Greek and Roman gods and goddesses and their functions.

Greek Name	Roman Name	Function
Aphrodite		
	Apollo	
		chief god; god of lightning and the thunderbolt
	Ceres	
Dionysus		
		goddess of hunting and chastity

2. From what ancient Greek mythological figures and places are the following English terms derived? Explain the meaning of the words with reference to their derivations.

    a. **titanium**
    b. **erotic**
    c. **cereal**
    d. **martial**
    e. **iridescent**
    f. **lethargic**
    g. **mentor**
    h. **Delphic**

3. Divide the following words into their bases and give the usual meaning of each base in English, then give the Greek or Latin word from which each base is derived and the meaning of these ancient words.

    Example: **cosmopolitan**
    Base 1: *cosmo-*
    Meaning: *world*
    Greek word: *kosmos*
    Meaning: *order (in the world)*

    Base 2: *-politan*
    Meaning: *citizen*
    Greek word: *politēs*
    Meaning: *citizen*

    a. **geothermal**
    b. **mythology**
    c. **vulcanology**
    d. **theology**
    e. **theogony**
    f. **thanatology**
    g. **geography**
    h. **mythography**

4. In the following sentences a word or phrase is highlighted. For each sentence, briefly explain its origin with reference to ancient myth and then explain what it means in the sentence in the modern context.

Example:
*Any woman entering politics today has to be an **Amazon** to succeed.*
Origin:
The Amazons were a mythical race of women warriors who fought in the Trojan War.
Meaning:
In order to be successful in politics a woman has to be strong and aggressive.

(a) The young woman started her political career under the **aegis** of the prime minister.
(b) The burglars took all my valuables, leaving **chaos** throughout my house.
(c) Unable to find the light switch, the detective hesitated to enter the **Stygian** darkness of the basement.
(d) Cleaning his bedroom proved to be an **Augean** task.
(e) The adventurer described his overland journey as an **odyssey.**
(f) The government attempted to impose its will upon the populace in a **Procrustean** manner.
(g) A successful professional person often has a **mercurial** character.
(h) Some people regard the attractive female pop star as a **siren.**
(i) Doctors refer to the inner ear as the **labyrinth.**
(j) When he first set his eyes on the woman, he felt **Cupid's arrow** strike his heart.
(k) Some people regard modern politicians as a bunch of **lotus-eaters.**
(l) Achieving both democratic freedom and law and order in a country is like sailing between **Scylla and Charybdis.**

5. Write a sentence exemplifying the modern English use of the following words and phrases, then explain the ancient origin of the word.

Example:
stentorian
Sentence:
The man next door has a stentorian voice: you can hear everything he says right down the street!
Explanation:
Stentor was the name of a herald (public announcement-maker) in the Trojan War.

a. Hercules   d. tantalize
b. Apples of the Hesperides   e. epic
c. to muse   f. titanic

6. Answer the following general knowledge questions on Greek myth.
   (a) Who was Zeus? Why was he described as an Olympian god?
   (b) What was the Hydra and what happened to it?
   (c) Tell the story of the Judgment of Paris up to the judgment itself. What major conflict resulted from the judgment and who was the woman involved?
   (d) Why do you think Oedipus is described as an extreme example of an undeserving victim of Fate?
   (e) Give an account of the story Theseus and Ariadne. What may it have meant or represented in reality?
   (f) Relate the events surrounding the bringing of the Trojan Horse into the city of Troy. What were the consequences of the Horse for Troy and her inhabitants?

CHAPTER 5

MEDICINE
W. J. Dominik

GREEK MEDICINE

Beginnings

In the fifth century BCE medicine began to emerge as a scientific discipline among the Greeks, moving away from its beginnings in religion and magic. Previously various ailments had been considered as caused by the gods; for example, gastritis was regarded as the curse of the god *Apollo*, since it recalls the liquid droppings of swallows, the birds of the god. Apollo was associated with healing in Greek mythology and his son *Asklepios* (Roman *Aesculapius*) was the god of medicine. Apollo entrusted the upbringing of his son to the wise Centaur *Chiron*, who taught him the art of medicine. The most famous temple of Asklepios' cult was at Epidaurus, where patients seeking a cure slept in the temple, where the cure was effected in the night, or information about the method of the cure was received in dreams. The snake was associated with Asklepios, since it was felt to have the power of rejuvenation in the shedding of its skin; and therefore, sacred snakes were kept in the precincts of the temples of Asklepios. They were believed to heal the sick by licking them. The statue below shows Asklepios holding a staff with a snake entwined around it and a *patera*, a broad, flat dish used in offerings to deities. The short figure to the right is Telesphoros, a healing deity associated with Asklepios.

*Marble statue of Aesculapius
(Greek Asklepios)*

Hippocrates and Rational Medicine

The beginnings of Greek rational medicine are attributed to *Hippocrates*, who lived around 430 BCE. He founded a medical school on the island of Cos, off the coast of Asia Minor, and traveled widely in Greece and Asia Minor, teaching and practicing his art. A large collection of treatises on a variety of medical subjects, including anatomy, physiology, prognosis, surgery, gynecology, obstetrics, pediatrics, treatment through diet and drugs, medical ethics and etiquette, was attributed to Hippocrates in antiquity.

There is also the famous Hippocratic oath, a modified version of which many doctors still take upon graduation today, and in which the doctor swore by Apollo and Asklepios. The following extracts are from the ancient form of the oath.

> I will apply dietetics for the benefit of the sick according to my ability and judgment; I will keep them from harm and injustice. Neither will I give a deadly drug to anyone, though asked to do so; nor will I suggest such a course of action. Similarly I will not give to a woman an abortive remedy. I will keep both my life and my art in purity and holiness. . . Whatever I see or hear concerning the life of men while treating the sick or apart from such treatment, which one ought not to spread abroad, I will not divulge and will regard such things to be sacred secrets.
>
> (Hippocratic Oath)

The oath illustrates the ethical principles to which ancient Greek doctors, or at least those trained under the influence of Hippocrates, adhered. In the sections dealing with behavior towards colleagues, the oath shows how the medical schools were organized.

> To look upon him who has taught me this art as equal to my own parents and to share my life with him . . . and to regard his offspring as equal to my own brothers and to teach them this art—if they want to learn it— without fee or contract; to give a share of the precepts, oral instruction and all the other learning to my sons, to the sons of my teacher, and to pupils bound by the covenant and oath according to medical law, but to no one else.
>
> (Hippocratic Oath)

This system of learning from older established practitioners, partly through oral instruction, generally at the bedside of the patient, is prevalent today in the years of clinical study for a medical degree. In the ancient Greek world, however, there was no formal course of study nor any examination the aspiring young doctor had to pass in order to qualify. He learned by watching older practitioners and could set up in business for himself when he felt he knew enough. A Greek doctor often traveled widely, either from town to town, attending to patients in the rural areas on his way, or setting up a surgery in the big cities.

Hippocrates' "rational" attitude to medicine was in direct opposition to the religious and mystical outlook of the temple doctors who believed that all illness was caused by the gods. Hippocrates rejected this belief

Hippocrates

and preferred instead to observe the course of an illness, recording the successive stages, so that when the same illness was encountered on a subsequent occasion, it could be recognized and its development predicted. This is called "prognosis," the prediction of the outcome of a disease. The Greek doctors were, however, weak in the field of "diagnosis," the identification of disease, since they lacked a good knowledge of how the body worked. They believed that the body was composed of elements that had to be in a proper balance for good health and their treatment consisted largely of diet, exercise, blood-letting, purgative drugs, and some surgery.

Word Study

- **Prognosis** is a Greek noun cognate with the verb *progignoskein* ("to know beforehand") and therefore indicates the prior knowledge of the course of a disease that is gained from close observation of many similar cases.
- **Diagnosis** comes from the Greek verb *diagignoskein*, which means "to distinguish" or "to discern."
- **Carcinoma,** which originated in ancient times when the nature of malignant growth was little understood, is made up of the Greek base *karkinos* ("crab") + the suffix *-oma* ("tumor"). One explanation of its origin is that the swollen veins surrounding the diseased area resembled the claws of a crab. The Latin word for "crab" is *cancer.*

Medical Treatment

Drugs

One of the treatments offered by Greek doctors included medicinal therapy (the use of drugs). Drugs consisted of vegetable or mineral remedies that were supplied to the doctors by traditional traders or collectors. They were used for their known effects with little or no explanatory theory being found in the treatises. Wine was regarded in ancient medicine as a disinfectant. The leaves of fig and olive trees were said to have a cleansing effect when boiled. If after cleansing the wound tried to inflame the neighboring parts, the doctor was advised to apply a plaster of lentils pounded with wine and oil and cover this with a bandage. Minerals of various kinds were used for drying and disinfecting ulcers and wounds. Oxides of copper and lead and sulfate of lead were reduced to powders and sprinkled on; these are the forerunners of the powders modern medicine uses on wounds and sores.

Surgery

Surgery was the other main form of treatment in medicine. Ancient Greek surgery was generally concerned with bones and the accompanying tissues. There are two treatises in the Hippocratic corpus entitled *Fractures* and *Joints* that describe the treatments recommended in such cases. *Fractures* deals with the arm, the foot, the leg, thigh, and shoulder and gives details about how to set the various fractures by using splints and bandages.

Joints deals with dislocations and gives instructions for treatment using powerful leverage. There is also a treatise on *Head Wounds,* presumably written because of the author's experience in warfare, where these injuries would have been extremely common whenever metal helmets were not worn.

Word Study

- The Greek word for "drug," *pharmakon,* has given rise to many modern words; for example, **pharmacist** comes from *pharmakon* + the noun suffix *-ist* and denotes a person qualified to prepare and dispense drugs; **pharmacology** is derived from Greek *pharmakon* + suffix *-logy* ("study of") and means the branch of medicine that deals with the uses, effects and modes of action of drugs; and **pharmacy** denotes not only the shop where drugs can be bought but also the actual preparation and dispensing of drugs.

Word for Word

- **Surgery** comes (through Middle French *cirugie, surgerie*) from Greek *cheir* ("hand") + *ergein* ("to work"). It denotes the act of healing by manual operation.

The Theory of Humors

Much Greek medical thought was based on the theory of humors, in which the balance of the four humors in a person's body determined his physical health. The four humors, or elemental fluids, were said to be blood, phlegm, black bile, and yellow bile. Physical illness was attributed to a disturbance in the natural balance of these humors in the body.

The theory of humors was also applied to mental states, since it was believed that the state of mind and character of an individual depended upon a balance among the four elemental fluids. The four basic human temperaments (sanguine, phlegmatic, melancholic, and choleric) were each thought to be the result of a predominance in one of the four humors. **Sanguine** (from Latin *sanguinis,* an extended form of *sanguis,* "blood") personalities were cheerful and lively as a result of the dominance of blood. People with a **phlegmatic** (from Greek *phlegmatos,* "abounding in phlegm") character were calm and tough due to an excess of phlegm, which was thought to be cold and moist. **Melancholic** (from Greek *melan-,* "black" + *cholē,* "bile") individuals were gloomy and anxious owing to a surplus of black bile; and those with a **choleric** (from Greek *cholerikos,* "full of cholera") disposition were lively and sometimes irascible because they had too much yellow bile in their bodies. The perfect temperament resulted when these humors balanced each other.

The balance of the four humors was thought to be affected by diet and climate. This belief in the effect of climate led Greek doctors to observe the weather at various seasons of the year in various places. One of the treatises in the Hippocratic corpus is entitled *Airs, Waters, Places* and the following extract illustrates that the Greeks thought it important for a doctor to pay attention to the environment in which his patients lived. This was especially important when the doctor traveled from place to place since different environments caused different problems.

> Therefore, when a doctor arrives at a city with which he is unfamiliar, he should consider its position and how it lies both with regard to the winds and the rising of the sun. For a northern, southern, eastern, or western aspect each has its own individual effects. He must reflect on these things very carefully as well as what water they have, whether they use marshy soft water or hard water from high and rocky ground, or brackish and harsh. The soil too may be barren and dry or wooded and well watered, hollow and stiflingly hot or dry and cold. [He must take into consideration] what sort of life-style the inhabitants enjoy, whether they are heavy drinkers, take lunch and are inactive, or fond of exercise and exertion, eat well and drink little.
>
> (Hippocrates, *Airs, Waters, Places* 1)

The balance of the humors within the body was thought to be affected by the environment, particularly the climate, and domination of one humor over the others caused the various diseases that the Greek doctors had to treat. It was believed that the inhabitants of cities exposed to hot winds and sheltered from northerly ones would have heads full of phlegm. Among those living in cities exposed to west winds, many different diseases were thought to occur because the weather was like autumn, being very changeable, and this supposedly led to an unhealthy alternation of dominant humors. For those living in cities exposed to the east wind, it was believed that the prospects for good health were improved since this situation seemed to favor a balance of the humors, while the inhabitants of cities exposed to the north wind were considered to be bilious rather then phlegmatic, sinewy, spare and with hard, healthy heads, but the cold waters supposedly made their women barren.

Medical Ethics and Etiquette

There are treatises in the Hippocratic corpus that deal with medical ethics, etiquette, and the appropriate manner of dealing with patients. *The Physician* advises the doctor to keep himself in good physical condition, for a doctor who is unable to take care of himself would hardly inspire confidence in his patients. He should be clean about his person, well-dressed, and sweet-smelling. His demeanor should be quiet, grave, and humane, since too much harshness and too much bonhomie alike would cause problems among his patients. The practice of doctors in keeping information from the patient seems to date from antiquity as the following extract from the treatise entitled *Decorum* shows.

> Carry out your treatment calmly and courteously, concealing most things from the patient during treatment. Give necessary orders cheerfully and calmly, turning a deaf ear to his comments. Rebuke your patient sharply and emphatically at times and at others encourage him with concern and attention. Do not reveal anything about his future or present condition, for many have suffered a setback on account of this cause...
>
> (Hippocrates, *Decorum* 16)

Nevertheless, good advice is given in the same treatise about maintaining confidentiality and a sober way of life; it also includes a warning about patients' inclination to lie about taking the medicine prescribed if they found it unpleasant. Sometimes they died as a result and the doctor was blamed.

Patients consulted the doctor in his surgery, which would be open to the street and arranged so as to best utilize the available daylight for carrying out examinations and surgical procedures while at the same time protecting patients from the sun's glare. Other necessities in the surgery would be an adequate supply of clean bandages and pure water. The use of surgical knives and cupping vessels is described. In the vase drawings below (*circa* 470 BCE) are two scenes from a doctor's consulting room, one depicting the waiting patients and the other the doctor treating a patient.

Some clients wait to see the doctor while he treats another patient

Ancient doctors did make house calls on occasion and for this purpose they were advised in *Decorum* to have prepared a portable doctor's case having compartments for readily accessible drugs and instruments. In the treatise on *Precepts* the doctor is advised not to discuss fees during the course of the patient's illness, since that might suggest that he would leave the patient or neglect to propose immediate treatment if no agreement is reached. The effect of worry on the patient might well be harmful, particularly if the disease is acute. It was also easier to ask for payment from a patient who had been cured, while it would be dishonorable to extort money from a mortally ill patient. Young doctors were advised to give their services for nothing on occasion and especially to assist a stranger if he was short of money. Apparent here is the emergence of medical ethics in which medical practitioners were expected to subscribe to high ideals and to be more than skilled craftsmen.

Word Study

- **Ethics** is derived from the Greek word *ethos*, which means "nature" or "disposition," hence the characteristic spirit or attitudes of a community, people or system. **Ethics** now means a set of moral principles; medical **ethics** are those to which the medical profession subscribes.

Anatomy and Physiology

Since ancient Greek doctors did not learn about anatomy from the dissection of the human body as modern medical students do, their knowledge of the systems of the body was necessarily limited. They did, however, gain some insights from serving as military doctors when they had to treat wounds received on the battlefield or from treating injuries incurred on the *palaistra* ("wrestling ground") when they had to deal with strains, dislocations, and broken bones. Dissection of human bodies was forbidden on religious grounds, largely because of the Hippocratic respect for the dead, and the acquisition of knowledge by analogy from the dissection of animals was of limited value.

In treatises dealing with anatomy Hippocratic knowledge of the skeleton (from the Greek word *skeletos*, "dried up") is fairly accurate, but there was no knowledge of the circulatory system or of the heart as a pump although they were aware of the vascular system. The Hippocratics erroneously used this system to explain the neurological processes of the body since it was the only system they knew of with channels to all parts of the body.

Word Study

- **Anatomy** is derived from Greek *anatomē,* which was formed from two Greek words: *ana* ("up") + *temnein* ("to cut"). It means the science of bodily structure, which was learnt later from the dissection of cadavers.
- **Physiology** comes from two Greek words: *phusis* ("nature") + *-logy* ("study of"). At first the word meant natural science, but now it denotes the science of the functions of living organisms and their parts.
- **Neurology** is derived from the Greek base *neuron* ("nerve") + suffix *-logy* ("study of"). It means the scientific study of nerve systems. **Neuralgia** is made up of the Greek bases *neuron* ("nerve") + *algia* ("pain") and means intense intermittent pain along the course of a nerve. **Neuroma,** which is made up of the Greek base *neuron* ("nerve") + suffix *-oma* ("tumor"), is a tumor on a nerve or in nerve tissue.

Gynecology

Not a great deal is mentioned in the Hippocratic corpus on the subject of female anatomy and physiology, but given the absence of dissection of cadavers, this is not surprising. Many of the female reproductive organs are too far within the body to be seen, so Hippocratic doctors were unaware of the existence of the ovaries and Fallopian tubes and therefore of the causes and cycle of menstruation. There are treatises, however, dealing with women in the clinical context, that is, detailing observations made and treatments prescribed.

Greek doctors knew enough about the normal position of the womb to note any deviations, but there were beliefs that the right side of the womb was warmer than the left and so produced male embryos, which matured more quickly than female. The sex of the infant was thought to be determined by the greater strength of the male or female seed at the time of conception. Familial likeness was explained by this mingling of seed from all parts of both parents' bodies.

The birth of twins was believed to be the result of a variety of folds and recesses in the womb, which received and nurtured separate parcels of seed into distinct individuals. Childbirth was thought to be brought on when the fetus had exhausted its food supply, whereupon it agitated and broke the membranes surrounding it. Nonetheless, the Greeks did appreciate the role of the **placenta** in maintaining the life and growth of the fetus.

Word Study

- **Gynecology** is from *gynaikos*, an extended form of *gynē* ("woman"), + *-logy* ("study of"). The modern meaning is the science of the physiological functions and diseases of women.
- **Pediatrics** and its cognate noun **pediatrician** come from Greek *paidos*, an extended form of *pais* ("child") + *iatros* ("physician"). The noun has the noun suffix *-ician* added. Today **pediatrics** is the branch of medicine dealing with children and their diseases; a doctor who specializes in **pediatrics** is called a **pediatrician.**
- **Placenta** comes from an extended form *plakountos* of the Greek word *plakous*, which means "a flat cake." It describes the flattened circular organ in the womb that nourishes and maintains the fetus through the umbilical cord.

ROMAN MEDICINE

Beginnings

By tradition, the first Greek doctor to come to Rome was Archagathus of Sparta, who settled there in 219 BCE. A century later, in the second century BCE, Asclepiades of Bithynia came to Rome and became a self-taught physician. There was at that time a strong prejudice against Greek doctors, so he moderated Greek medical thought with a sound practical approach more attuned to the Roman character; this led to a gradual acceptance of Greek doctors and medicine in the Roman world.

Word Study

- **Medicine** is a word of Latin derivation and comes from *medicina*, the physician's art, from *medicus*, "a physician." **Medicine** has several meanings in English: it denotes the science or practice of diagnosis, treatment and prevention of disease, especially as distinct from surgery; it also means a drug for the treatment or prevention of disease. There are many cognate words such as **medical, medicate** (treat with drugs), **medication** (treatment with drugs), and **medicinal** (when used of a substance, healing).

The Training of Doctors

As in Greece, the training of doctors in the Roman world was a haphazard affair. Anyone could set up in practice as a doctor, since there was no formal system of teaching or testing of proficiency. It was not necessary to pass any exams before opening a practice and many unscrupulous "quacks" proclaimed themselves to be doctors without any previous experience. This lack of training and experience on the part of many doctors in antiquity is reflected in the following comment of the Greek writer Athenaeus.

> If it were not for doctors, there would not be anyone more stupid than professors!
>
> (Athenaeus 666a)

The following epigram of the Roman poet Martial illustrates the poor public image of doctors in certain quarters of society.

> Recently Diaulus was a doctor; now he is an undertaker.
> What he does as an undertaker he used to do as a doctor!
> (Martial, *Epigrams* 1.47)

More scrupulous doctors joined an established physician and learned from him while assisting him in his work. This apprentice system was prevalent in Roman society for all arts and crafts, from carpentry to medicine, but there was no legal requirement for trainee doctors to do this. The system gave the physician extra help in dealing with his patients and the apprentice in turn gained knowledge from the more experienced practitioner.

Doctors

Independent and Public Doctors

M ost doctors set up their own private practices in the Roman world. There were also public doctors who were paid by the civic authorities to provide medical care for all who required it. Part of their remuneration could include exemption from taxation and, although they were not permitted to charge their patients, they might receive a gift of money from a grateful patient. Premises for their consulting rooms might be provided by the civic authority, perhaps the same sort of small shop *(taberna medica)* occupied by other traders or craftsmen, or the doctor might consult in a room in his own home. It seems that competition for these posts of public doctors was lively, since in 160 CE the emperor Antoninus Pius introduced a law restricting their number: ten for capital cities, seven for large towns, and five for small towns.

Galen

O ne of the most renowned doctors in the Roman world was Galen, who was born in Pergamum in the province of Asia Minor (modern Turkey) in 129 CE, the son of a wealthy architect, Nikon. He studied Greek, rhetoric, and philosophy before beginning his medical studies at the age of sixteen. He studied in Pergamum under the physician Satyros and then went to Smyrna to study anatomy. He then furthered his studies in Corinth and Alexandria (Egypt), which was an important medical center and had a well-known medical school. After twelve years of study, he returned to Pergamum where he was appointed surgeon to a school of gladiators. This would have given him not only much experience in the treatment of wounds and fractures but also the opportunity to expand his knowledge of anatomy as well as to experiment with diet and exercise.

In 162 CE Galen went to Rome, where his skill and connections gave him access to the highest circles of Roman society. He made himself unpopular by criticizing other physicians who failed to meet his exacting standards and this may have contributed to his flight to Pergamum in 166 CE, although an outbreak of plague in Rome at the time may have had something to do with his decision to leave the city. He returned to Rome three years later at the request of the co-emperors Marcus Aurelius and Lucius Verus, who appointed him a court physician. He wrote many medical treatises, twenty-one volumes of which are still extant and which alone are twice as long as the entire Hippocratic corpus.

Galen made considerable advances in anatomy and physiology. Although it is unclear whether he practiced human dissection, he did conduct experiments on animals such as Barbary apes, dogs, and pigs, which he regarded as "near to man." By his discovery of the recurrent laryngeal nerve, which runs from the spinal cord to the chest and then to the larynx, he was able to prove that the brain is the controlling organism of speech, refuting the followers of Aristotle, who believed that the heart fulfilled this function, since the voice issues from the chest. Galen died around 210 CE, a rich and respected physician, leaving behind a vast collection of writings on medical topics that influenced medical thought in Europe for many hundreds of years.

Female Doctors

Medicine was one of the few activities open to Roman women as well as to men, in contrast to their exclusion from other such male preserves as politics and business. Such women were called *medicae* and, from the surviving references to them, it seems that women doctors were not so unusual in the Roman world. Women had long been associated with folk medicine and sorcery, and this may be the reason for their acceptance as practitioners of more scientific medicine.

Women doctors may have concerned themselves mainly with the diseases and conditions of women, though men, notably Soranus of Ephesus, also dealt with gynecological complaints.

A midwife performing a delivery

There were also *obstetrices* ("midwives") who not only dealt with childbirth but also with other ailments peculiar to women, often under the direction of a male physician.

The relief on the left shows a midwife delivering a baby; her assistant holds the patient who grasps the handles of the special obstetrical chair. The midwife played an important role in the health care of women. She not only dealt with obstetric cases but also with gynecological problems. Soranus expected a good midwife to possess many qualities as the following extract shows.

A suitable person will be literate, quick-witted, have a good memory, be diligent, respectable, generally not too handicapped in respect of her senses, sound of limb, vigorous and, according to some people, will have long slender fingers and trimmed nails on her fingertips... We call the "best midwife" someone who goes further and in addition to her experience in case management is very knowledgeable about theory. More particularly, we say that someone is the "best midwife" if she has received training in all areas of therapy (some cases require dietetic therapy, others surgery, and others need to be treated with drugs) and can prescribe rules of hygiene, observe general and specific symptoms, and ascertain from them what needs to be done... She will be calm and undaunted in crises, able to explain clearly her treatments, provide encouragement to her patients, and be sympathetic... She will be self-controlled and always sober because it is unclear when she may be called to women in danger. She will have a reserved disposition, since she will be likely to share in many secrets of life. She will not be fond of money, lest she wickedly administer an abortive for pay. She will disbelieve superstitions so as not to overlook something beneficial on account of a dream or omen or some customary ritual or vulgar superstition.

(Soranus, *Gynecology* 1.2–4)

Military Doctors

Surgeons in the army would have had much opportunity to practice their surgical skills, since they would have had to deal with men wounded in battle. Although abdominal surgery would probably have been avoided in civilian life, an army doctor would have had no choice but to try to treat a severely wounded soldier through surgery. Plutarch tells us of a military doctor, Cleanthes, who performed a complex but successful operation that involved replacing the intestines that had spilled out of a lower chest wound, stopping the bleeding, and stitching and bandaging the wound. Less serious flesh wounds received in battle from swords, lances, daggers, or projectiles could be treated with a reasonable hope of success, although infection would have been a constant worry and, if gangrene set in, amputation would have become necessary.

Military hospitals formed part of the legionary camp or fort in many parts of the Roman world and even in the forts of auxiliary troops, from which it can be seen that the health of the soldier was of concern to the authorities. It is also possible that local inhabitants may also have been treated on an informal basis by the military doctors. These doctors would also have had the opportunity to learn about local cures, particularly in the field of pharmacology, which would have broadened their knowledge of curative plants and herbs. As its name implies, an effective styptic (a drug that checks bleeding) called *barbarum* was discovered across the frontiers, probably during military operations.

Surgery

The practice of surgery in ancient medicine was very different from its modern counterpart, largely because of the lack of knowledge about anatomy and because of the absence of anesthesia. Although the practice of dissection flourished briefly in Alexandria, it had died out almost entirely by the first century CE, leaving many gaps in the knowledge of ancient doctors. Despite the fact that preparations from the opium poppy and henbane were used as sedatives and painkillers during surgery, the lack of true anesthesia meant that the surgeon's main concern was to complete a surgical procedure as quickly as possible. Likewise, the lack of antiseptic agents meant that infection was a major hazard of ancient surgery, although some medical writers do mention the antiseptic properties of pitch and turpentine.

Medical and Surgical Instruments

Sets of medical instruments, bottles and jars, some of which still contained the residue of the medicines they had contained, have been found at archaeological sites such as Pompeii and Herculaneum. The quality of the surgical instruments is excellent and they were obviously precision tools made for specific tasks. The sets include scalpels, forceps, hooks, probes, and needles. Often a set of instruments was kept in a custom-made, hinged wooden case and examples of these have been found depicted in relief on tombstones.

Bloodletting was a common practice in ancient medicine and examples of bronze cups used in this procedure have been found in many places. The cup was a bell-shaped object, with a carefully rolled rim to ensure a good contact with the skin, and on the other end was a hook that enabled it to be hung on a stand when not in use.

Word Study

- **Doctor** is derived from *doctus*, a form of the Latin verb *docere*. *Doctus* means "having been taught," "learned," and **doctors,** like teachers, were regarded as learned men. This explains the fact that the highest university degree is called a **doctorate.**

Word for Word

- **Obstetrics** is derived from Latin *obstetrices* ("midwives"), an extended form of *obstetrix* ("midwife"), which is made of up of the words *ob* ("before," "in the way") + *stare* ("to stand"). The Latin word *obstetrix* therefore describes the action of standing or kneeling before a woman when delivering a baby (as in the relief above under the heading "Female Doctors"). In modern terms **obstetrics** is the branch of medicine and surgery that deals with childbirth and midwifery.
- **Infection** comes from the Latin verb *inficere* ("to taint"). The modern meaning is to affect a person with harmful organisms, for example, a **virus** (from the Latin *virus*, meaning "a slimy liquid" or "poison") or by bacteria.
- **Bacteria** (singular **bacterium**) is a Latin word that comes from the Greek word *bakterion*, which refers to the appearance of these micro-organisms under the microscope. It is akin to the Latin *bacillus*, which is the diminutive form of *baculus* ("stick").

Word for Word

- **Amputate** is derived from two Latin words *ambi* ("around") + *putare* ("to prune," "to trim") and means to cut off by surgical operation a part of the body, particularly a limb, because of injury or disease.
- **Scalpel** is derived from the diminutive form, *scalpellum*, of the Latin word *scalprum*, a sharp, cutting instrument, for example, "a knife" or "a chisel." **Forceps** has come down to English unchanged from the Latin word and means "an instrument for grasping (or holding)."

Gynecology

Soranus and Gynecology

S oranus was born in Ephesus, a city in Asia Minor, in the second half of the first century CE. He studied at Alexandria, which at the time was the great center of scientific medicine. He eventually went to Rome where he practiced medicine during the reigns of Trajan (98–117 CE) and Hadrian (117–138 CE). Of his extant works the *Gynecology* is the most important, but he also wrote about internal medicine, surgery, hygiene, ophthalmology, and embryology. Some of the passages in his *Gynecology* reflect the general Roman belief that the function of marriage was to produce a family. Girls were married in their early teens and newlyweds were encouraged to have children as soon as possible. Women who did not conceive quickly or easily might seek help from a doctor. The following extract contains Soranus' views on the best timing for conception.

> Since many women become married for the sake of children and succession and not for mere enjoyment, it is utterly absurd to inquire about their ancestry and nobility of birth and the abundance of their money but fail to inquire into whether they are able to conceive or not and whether they are physically endowed for childbirth or not.
>
> (Soranus, *Gynecology* 1.34.1)

> Just as not every season is suitable for sowing seed on the ground in order to produce fruit, so too for people not every season is suitable for the conception of seed released in intercourse. Therefore it is useful to talk about the critical time in order that the desired result may be attained through the employment of the favorable timing of sexual activity. The most favorable time for intercourse leading to conception is when menstruation is coming to an end and waning; when the urge and appetite for intercourse are present and the body is neither hungry nor too full and heavy from drunkenness and indigestion; and when after a massage and the consumption of a light meal, the body finds itself in a every respect in a pleasant state.
>
> (Soranus, *Gynecology* 1.36.1–2)

When conception has been successfully achieved, nature takes its course, and Soranus' description of the morning sickness and unusual cravings that often occur in pregnancy is as applicable today as when he wrote it.

> In most pregnant women morning sickness comes on around the fortieth day and keeps on for the most part until the fourth month. In some women, however, it comes on sooner or later and in some cases it lasts for a shorter time, in others again for a longer time, and in some rare cases it lasts until childbirth, but in others it does not manifest itself at all. Those women suffering from this condition experience the following: a stomach upset, indeed full of fluid; nausea and lack of appetite, sometimes for all foods, sometimes for certain foods; an appetite for unusual things such as earth, charcoal, tendrils of the vine, and unripe and acid fruit; bad color, discomfort, heartburn, slow digestion, and rapid decomposition of food. Some women suffer from vomiting at intervals or at every meal and from a feeling of heaviness.
>
> (Soranus, *Gynecology* 1.48)

Soranus' advice on the care of pregnant women recognized the need to avoid any excess and physical stress, particularly in the first trimester. He advocated the avoidance of too vigorous physical exercise, including lifting heavy objects, and recognized the harmful effects of drunkenness, diarrhea, malnutrition; blood letting and certain drugs. He did not subscribe to the belief that the pregnant woman must eat for two.

Childbirth

Childbirth was a risky business in the ancient world and, even if the mother and child both survived, there was always a chance that the child would not live to adulthood, since infant mortality was high, as is evidenced by the following epitaph.

> Quintus Haterius Ephebus and Julia Zosime furnished this epitaph for their hapless daughter Hateria Superba who lived one year, six months, twenty-five days.
>
> (*Corpus Inscriptionum Latinarum* 6.19159)

If the child did survive, a wet nurse was often employed, particularly by the wealthy, or if anything prevented the mother from feeding the child herself. Like the midwife, a good wet nurse had to fulfil many requirements, including several physical ones: she should be healthy, have given birth herself on two or three occasions, be of good habits, large frame, and good color. She should also be self-controlled, sympathetic, and not ill-tempered. She in turn would receive payment for her services and either be accommodated in the family home or be provided with the wherewithal to ensure that she would be able to nurse the child appropriately in her own home. Since her health would directly affect the health of the child, care was taken to provide her with a good diet.

Contraception

In contrast to those women who wished to have a child, there were those who did not wish to do so and who took measures either to prevent conception, to abort a pregnancy, or to dispose of an unwanted child. Contraceptive measures mentioned by Soranus included smearing the entrance to the uterus with olive oil or honey or sap from a cedar or a balsam tree, alone or mixed with white lead, as well as drinking the juice of the silphium plant, but there were other superstitions such as the following one given by the elder Pliny.

> There is a third kind of spider, called the hairy spider, which has an enormous head. When this is dissected, it is said that within are found two little worms, which when tied on women with deerskin before sunrise prevent conception, or so Caecilius has written in his notebooks. Its effectiveness lasts for a year. It would be proper for me to mention this contraceptive only because the fertility of some women results in so many children that they are in need of a respite.
>
> (Pliny, *Natural History* 29.27.85)

Abortion

Abortion was also used as a method of birth control and the physician generally suggested those measures that were not recommended for women wishing to carry a child to term. They included violent exercise, the lifting of heavy weights, and being jolted and shaken up during carriage rides. If these measures were not successful, protracted baths in various substances were recommended, as well as abstention from food and drinking the juice of the silphium plant. As a last resort:

> She then has a vein opened and much blood is taken from her. . . After the bleeding she should be shaken by draught animals. . . . After these things an abortive suppository is inserted . . . such as equal quantities of myrtle, the seed of the snowflake, and bitter lupines mixed with water. . . One must take care not to use substances that are too overpowering and not to loosen the embryo with a sharp instrument, for there is a danger that some of the adjacent areas could be injured. After the abortion the patient should be treated for inflammation.
>
> (Soranus, *Gynecology* 1.65.1–7)

Exposure

Disposing of an unwanted child once born was the final resort for those for whom none of the above remedies worked. Some of the earliest Roman laws dealt with the problem of infanticide and exposure. Parents were legally obliged to rear all male children and the first-born female child, while infanticide was only permitted in the case of deformed or crippled babies. Exposure and infanticide, however, remained the most effective means of disposing of an unwanted child. Exposure entailed the abandonment of a child to starve to death and continued particularly among the poor right through the period of the Republic and the Empire. Baby girls were exposed more often than boys because they represented a financial burden to the family; they could not work to support themselves and the parents were expected to provide them with dowries on marriage. Boys might be exposed if the family could not afford to rear them or to prevent the subdivision of the family property.

Word Study

- **Conception** comes from the Latin noun *conceptio* ("conception").
- **Contraception** comes from Latin *contra* ("against") + *conceptio* ("conception") and denotes measures taken to avoid pregnancy.
- **Abortion** comes from the Latin noun *abortio*, which is cognate with the verb *aboriri* ("to miscarry"). **Infanticide** is derived from two Latin words *infans* ("infant") + *caedere* ("to kill").
- **Expose** comes directly from the Latin verb *exponere*, *expositum* and means "to put out" or "to turn out."

Hysteria

There was, in antiquity, a very strange belief that the uterus was a mobile organ that moved around within the abdomen or even further, causing pain through displacement and distortion. This mobility of the uterus (*hystera* in Greek) was said to account for the symptoms of hysteria that were considered to be peculiar to women. Men who exhibited the symptoms of hysteria were thought to be suffering from some other disease such as epilepsy since they did not have a uterus. Both Soranus and Galen rejected the view of the mobility of the uterus, but other doctors sought to return the uterus to its proper position by the use of repellent or pleasant smelling vapors applied to the nose or the vagina. Aretaeus explains the causes and symptoms of hysteria in the following way.

> In the middle of the flanks of women lies the womb, a female internal organ closely resembling an animal. For it moves of its own accord . . . and is entirely erratic. It also delights in fragrant smells and moves toward them, but it is annoyed by foul smells and flees from them. . . When it suddenly moves upwards and remains there for a long time and compresses the intestines, the woman chokes in an epileptic manner but without the convulsions. For the liver, diaphragm, lungs, and heart are suddenly squeezed in a narrow space. Therefore she seems to be breathless and voiceless. In addition, the carotid arteries are compressed in sympathy with the heart; consequently heaviness of the head, loss of senses and deep sleep occur. Foul smells and also the application of fragrances to the vagina cure disorders caused by the womb.
>
> (Aretaeus, *Medical Writings* 2.11.1–3)

Soranus was outspoken in his view of these practices.

> We, however, censure all those who straightaway hurt the inflamed parts and bring about torpor through the noxious outflow of ill-smelling substances. For the womb does not creep forth like a wild animal from its den, delighted by fragrant odors and fleeing from ill-smelling substances; rather, it is drawn together through the constriction of the inflammation.
>
> (Soranus, *Gynecology* 3.29.5)

Word Study

- The two meanings of the Greek word *hysterikos*, "suffering in the uterus" and "hysterical," arise from the ancient belief that, since women seemed to be more **hysterical** than men, it must be related to disturbances of the uterus. The psychiatric condition is known as **hysteria**, which is characterized *inter alia* by emotional excitability and extreme anxiety.

Ophthalmology

Eye diseases were common in the ancient world and although many were treated with ointments and salves, surgery was also undertaken. One of the most frequent operations was the one performed to remove ingrown eyelashes that sometimes resulted from granular **ophthalmia.** The eyelashes were removed with a special forceps and the root was cauterized with a fine iron needle. The upper half of the funerary stele below shows a doctor examining a woman's eye, while in the lower half of the stele mourners pay their respects to the deceased. The eye specialist was known as a *medicus ocularius.* He had to be very dexterous and needed an assistant to hold the patient still during such fine surgery. Cataracts were also dealt with surgically but were generally moved rather than extracted, although instruments for the breaking up and removal of cataracts by suction have been found in France.

Word Study

- **Ophthalmologist** and its cognates come from the Greek word *ophthalmos* ("eye"). An **ophthalmologist** specializes in the eye and its diseases.
- **Optometrist** is derived from Greek *optos* (literally, "visible") + *metrein* ("to measure"). An **optometrist** measures the refraction of the eyes and prescribes correctional lenses. **Optician** is derived from Greek *optikos* ("of sight"). An **optician** fills prescriptions for eyeglasses.

Upper: A doctor examining a patient's eye
Lower: Mourners paying their respects

- **Oculist** and its cognates come from *oculus*, the Latin word meaning "eye." An **oculist** is a person who specializes in the medical treatment of eye disorders or defects. Therefore **binocular** is derived from two Latin words, *bi* ("two") + *oculus* ("eye"), and means using both eyes; hence **binocular** vision.

Medical Treatments

Folk Treatments

Alongside the more scientific medicine there are records of suggested cures for various conditions that may seem strange to modern sensibilities. The elder Pliny, who was not a doctor but was interested in natural science, has preserved some of these in his writings.

> The following remedies cure jaundice within three days: the ashes of a deer's antlers; the blood of a donkey in wine; likewise, the first dung passed by a donkey's foal after birth, of the size of a pea, taken in wine. The first dung of a horse's foal has the same effect.
>
> An instant remedy for broken bones: the ashes of the jawbone of a wild boar or a pig; likewise, bacon fat boiled and tied around the fracture heals it with wonderful rapidity. For fractured ribs, however, goat's dung in old wine is highly recommended.
>
> (Pliny, *Natural History* 28.64–65.227)

Superstitious practices existed as well and were also recorded by the elder Pliny.

> Cutting the hair on the seventeenth or twenty-ninth day of the month prevents baldness as well as headaches... Marcus Servilius Nonianus, a prominent citizen, who not so long ago was afraid of inflammation of the eyes, before mentioning it himself or someone speaking of it to him, used to tie around his neck with a linen thread a piece of papyrus, on which were written two Greek letters, P (rho) and A (alpha). Mucianus, who has been consul three times, followed the same practice but used a living fly in a little piece of white linen cloth. Both men declared that they were free of inflammation of the eyes by means of these remedies.
>
> (Pliny, *Natural History* 28.5.28–29)

Those suffering from illness also had recourse to the gods and may indeed have turned to them for the restoration of bodily health in preference to a doctor. The cult of Asklepios spread to Rome where it was readily accepted by a society that looked to the gods for good health. An Asklepion, or temple of Asklepios, was built on Tiber Island and miraculous cures were recorded here.

To Lucius, who suffered from pleurisy and whose condition all men had considered to be hopeless, the god revealed that he should proceed and take ashes from the triplex altar and mix them completely and place them on his side. He was saved and gave his thanks publicly to the god, whereupon the people celebrated with him.

To Julian, who was coughing up blood and whose condition all men had considered to be hopeless, the god revealed that he should proceed and take the seeds of a pine cone from the triplex altar and ingest them with honey for three days. He was saved and gave his thanks publicly before the people.

(*Inscriptiones Graecae* 14.966)

Divine Healing

The devotees of Asklepios left testimony to their practices in the anatomical ex-votos, which are stone carvings or bronze plaques that depict ears, eyes, limbs, or other body parts for which suppliants were requesting healing or giving thanks for healing received. The following relief shows divine healing taking place under the auspices of Asklepios (Roman Aesculapius).

Divine healing under the auspices of Asklepios, god of medicine

Unfortunately, the ex-votos very rarely depicted the condition for which healing was needed. Their distribution at various shrines has led to the belief that perhaps certain shrines specialized in certain disorders. The preponderance of hand, foot, and limb votives at a rural shrine suggests that injuries or diseases to these parts of the body were of special concern to farmers and agricultural laborers.

Preventive Medicine

In the ancient world preventive medicine was very important, since there was little understanding of the causes and transmission of diseases, particularly those caused by micro-organisms and through poor hygiene and sanitation. Preventive medicine in the Roman world, as in the Greek, concentrated on dietetics and **regimen** (a prescribed course of exercise, way of life or diet; from the Latin *regere*, "to rule"). Asclepiades of Bithynia advocated this type of medicine when he came to Rome; he advocated five basic principles of general application: fasting from food, or abstinence from wine, massage, walking, and various kinds of carriage rides.

Celsus, who lived in the reign of Tiberius (14–37 CE), believed that most people could regulate their own lives in such a way as to remain healthy, provided that they followed a certain kind of lifestyle that not only included a reasonable diet but also an occasional massage and exercise. Massage was recommended for the toning of the body. The curative value of massage was also recognized, particularly for those convalescing from fever and for those suffering from recurrent headaches or from partial paralysis of the limbs.

Celsus favored walking as a form of exercise, but also felt that the vigorous man should gain his exercise from his lifestyle, which should include time spent both in the town and in the country and should include such pastimes as sailing and hunting as well as ball games and running. Exercise, which should produce sweating, or at any rate fatigue, should be followed by a bath and a short rest before eating.

MEDICAL HUMOR

Just as jokes circulate about doctors and their clients today, the Greeks and Romans had their own humorous stories about the medical profession. The anonymous author known as the "The Laughter-lover" (*Philogelos*) records some of the jokes and anecdotes that circulated in antiquity. The brand of humor is surprisingly modern in that many of the jokes are based on witticisms and puns for their effect, contain elements of what can be described as "sick humor," and poke fun at various nationalities and professions. Other jokes reflect prevailing social attitudes and values to infanticide and slavery that are disagreeable to some modern sensibilities.

Jokes and anecdotes about doctors and their patients feature prominently in the *Philogelos*, perhaps a reflection of Hippocrates' belief that "the doctor should have at his disposal a certain ready wit since a gloomy disposition is repugnant to the healthy and the sick" (*Decorum* 7). Only a few of the medical jokes in the *Philogelos* are obscene or scatological by some modern standards, while the tone of others can be described as skeptical, cynical, or disrespectful, which may be attributable to the lack of confidence that some patients had in the medical profession. The following jokes and anecdotes from the *Philogelos* deal with doctors and their patients.

> A man consulted his knucklehead doctor and said, "Doctor, whenever I wake up after sleeping, I'm groggy for half an hour, then I'm fine."
>
> The doctor recommended, "Then wait to get up until a half hour later!"
>
> (*Philogelos* 3)

> When he saw his family doctor approaching, the knucklehead carefully avoided being seen. When his friend asked why he was doing so, he replied, "Because it has been such a long time since I've been sick that I am embarrassed to meet him..."
>
> (6)

> A knucklehead who was sick promised to pay his doctor if he should be cured. Later when his wife was scolding him for drinking while he had a fever, he said, "Do you want me to get well and have to pay the doctor his fee?"
>
> (27)

> When the knucklehead had a child by a slave girl, his father suggested that he kill it. But he responded, "After you kill your own children first, then we can discuss me killing my children!"
>
> (57)

> A Sidonian doctor was left 1,000 drachmas in a will by a man who had been his patient. He attended the funeral and complained about the paltry bequest. When he was later called to treat the dead man's son who had become sick, he said, "Leave me 5,000 drachmas in your will and I'll be sure to cure you the way that I cured your father!"
>
> (139)

> A man from Kyme was so sick that his doctor lost hope; however, he recovered. Afterward, the man studiously avoided meeting the doctor. The doctor eventually managed to confront him and ask why. The man replied, "I'm ashamed to be seen alive after you said I was going to die!"
>
> (174)

There was a doctor from Kyme who switched to using a blunt surgical knife because the patient he was operating on was yelling so much from the pain...

(177)

While operating on a patient with a head wound, a doctor from Kyme turned the patient over on to his back and poured water into his mouth to see if it would come out of the hole in his head...

(182)

A patient came to an ill-natured doctor and complained, "Doctor, I can't lie down, stand up, or even sit down."
"Then the only cure is to hang yourself!"

(183)

An ill-natured doctor with only one eye asked his patient how he was feeling.
"I am as you can see me."
"Well, as far as I can see, you are half dead!"

(185)

A doctor made a house call to an ill-tempered patient, checked his condition, and said, "You're sweating badly."
The patient replied, "If you can sweat better, there's the bed; lie down and sweat!"

(186)

A doctor prescribed bread pieces and swallow-soapwort for a bad-tempered patient. "Take only a swallow," the doctor said.
"A swallow?" replied the patient. "How do you think I'm going to climb up to a nest to get a swallow?"

(189)

MEDICAL TERMINOLOGY

Medicine is such an important discipline in the modern world that everyone at some time or other encounters terms used in this scientific field in the course of their daily life. Many of the words are extremely specialized and complex and this has led to the impression in some quarters that the use of medical language is intentionally pretentious and designed to impress rather than to serve a useful function.

Importance of Medical Terminology

lthough the use of medical language may sometimes appear to be pretentious in some specific circumstances, the fact is that medical terminology is necessary. For it would be a serious impediment to medical practice and advancement if there were not a common language of knowledge and understanding among doctors and scientists.

Role of Greek and Latin

he universal language of medicine generally consists of terms derived from Greek and to a lesser extent Latin. Because of the technical and complex terms doctors and scientists use, they are sometimes said to "speak Greek" when they are not always understood; in a real sense they are speaking Greek, since the vast majority of words used in the medical profession are Greek. Together Latin and Greek form over ninety per cent of the terms used in medicine, with the balance derived from other languages. Sometimes a term is derived not just from one language but from two, such as **tonsillectomy,** whose base (*tonsill-*) is Latin and whose combining form (*-ectomy*) is derived from Greek.

Concision and Simplicity of Medical Terms

here are a number of compelling reasons for the use of technical terms in the medical field. Perhaps the most immediately apparent is that an entire concept or condition can be described through the use of single word. For example, an **electroencephalograph,** "a medical instrument used for measuring brain waves," contains four bases derived from Greek (*electro + en + cephal + graph*) and the combining vowel *o*. So the use of such a word actually helps to simplify the medical language rather than to obfuscate it.

Precision and Extension of Medical Terms

nother reason is that the use of such terms ensures precision of meaning. Words in everyday use usually have a number of definitions and nuances of meaning. While these words may enrich the language and cultural context by offering numerous opportunities for ambiguities and shades of meaning beyond their surface meanings, they often work against understanding in contexts that require precise and economic language for accurate communication. Many medical terms are restricted to specific uses that ensure their precise application and understanding by medical practitioners and scientists worldwide.

Since many medical terms are extremely technical and are not widely used in the general community, they have a limited number of applications and therefore doctors and scientists immediately understand the terms and the concepts behind them without the need for detailed explanation and comment; medical practitioners and scientists who use the terms themselves can be reasonably confident that the use of a particular term in a specific context will be understood by a colleague in the medical profession elsewhere in the world. Many terms have only one specific application, which makes them more precise and therefore more useful in terms of expressing specific medical conditions and concepts.

In some cases technical terms come into common usage and when this happens these terms have a tendency to become less precise and even lose their original meanings. Medical and scientific words such as **complex, phobia,** and **allergy** are examples of words that have gradually broadened or lost their original, literal meanings through frequent use that seem to lend themselves naturally to a wide variety of applications and contexts.

Formation of Medical Terms

From a single base or suffix dozens and sometimes hundreds of medical words can be formed, while combinations of bases and suffixes are responsible for the formation of tens of thousands of such words. Combinations of the bases and suffixes presented in the tables below form hundreds of medical and scientific words. While some of these words are mentioned and discussed in the text and tables in this chapter, it is not possible to mention all of the words that can be formed with these bases and suffixes; nor is it necessary to do so, since with a knowledge of the meaning of these word components, it is possible to figure out the literal meaning—and in many cases the current meanings—of these other words as they are encountered elsewhere. Some bases, suffixes, and English derivatives not listed below are commonly understood and used, for instance, *hypo,* "under" + *derm-,* "skin" (+ adjective ending *-ic*) = **hypodermic,** which means literally "(relating to) under the skin." The list includes some scientific forms and terms that are not strictly medical but that a student can expect to encounter at some point in a medical career.

KEY WORDS DERIVED FROM GREEK

Suffixes and Combining Forms

- *-ectomy,* "surgical removal of"

Base	Combining Form	Word
append- ("appendix")	*-ectomy*	*append**ectomy***
tonsill- ("tonsil")		*tonsill**ectomy***

- *-emia,* "condition of the blood"; occasionally, "congestion of blood in"

Base	Combining Form	Word
leuk- ("white")	*-emia*	*leuk**emia***
septic- ("decay")		*septic**emia***

- **-in, -ine,** "chemical substance"

Prefix	Bases	Suffix	Word
anti- ("against")	**tox-** ("poison")	*-in*	*anti*tox**in**
	melan- ("black," "dark")		*anti*melan**in**
epi- ("upon")	**nephr-** ("kidney")	*-ine*	*epi*nephr**ine**

- **-itis,** "inflammation of," "inflammatory disease of"

Base	Suffix	Word
appendic- ("appendix")	*-itis*	*appendic***itis**
arthr- ("joint")		*arthr***itis**
osteo- ("bone") + *-arthr-* ("joint")		*osteoarthr***itis**
tonsill- ("tonsil")		*tonsill***itis**

Word for Word

- **-meter,** "a device for measuring"

Base	Combining Form	Word
therm- ("heat")	*-meter*	*thermo***meter**

- **-logist,** "one who studies"

Base	Combining Form	Word
cardi- ("heart")	*-logist*	*cardio***logist**

- **-logy,** "study of," "science of"; rarely "collection of"

Base	Combining Form	Word
psych- ("mind")	*-logy*	*psycho***logy**

- **-oma,** usually "tumor arising in or composed of"; sometimes "swelling containing"; rarely "diseased condition," "result of"

Base	Suffix	Word	Meaning
melan- ("black," "dark")	-oma	melan**oma**	highly malignant tumor composed of dark pigment-bearing cells
oste- ("bone")		oste**oma**	benign tumor composed of bone tissue
haemat- ("blood")		hemat**oma**	swelling containing blood, blood blister
trach- ("rough")		trach**oma**	an infectious disease of the eyes in which granulation forms on the inside of the eyelid

- **-osis,** "diseased condition of"; sometimes "act of," "process of"; like **-sis,** of which this is a form

Base	Suffix	Word
psych- ("mind")	-osis	psych**osis**
tubercul- ("nodule")		tubercul**osis**
hypn- ("sleep")		hypn**osis**

- **-path,** "one who suffers from a disease of," "one who treats a disease"

Base	Combining Form	Word
psych- ("mind")	-path	psycho**path**
oste- ("bone")		osteo**path**

- **-pathy,** "disease of," "treatment of disease of or by"

Base	Combining Form	Word
neur- ("nerve")	-pathy	neuro**pathy**
hydr- ("water")		hydro**pathy**
oste- ("bone")		osteo**pathy**

- **-rrhea,** "abnormal discharge of," "flow"

Base	Combining Form	Word
dia- ("through," "across")	-rrhea	dia**rrhea**
log- ("word")		logo**rrhea**

- *-therapy,* "treatment of or by"

Base	Combining Form	Word
chem- ("chemical")	*-therapy*	*chem*o**therapy**
heli- ("sun")		*heli*o**therapy**
psych- ("mind")		*psych*o**therapy**

- *-tomy,* "surgical operation on," "surgical cutting of"

Base	Combining Form	Word
gloss- ("tongue")	*-tomy*	*gloss*o**tomy**
gastr- ("stomach")		*gastr*o**tomy**
trache- ("windpipe")		*trache*o**tomy**
lob- ("lobe [of the brain]")		*lob*o**tomy**

Bases

- *arthr-,* "joint," "articulation"

Base	Word	Meaning
arthr-	**arthr**itis	inflammation of joint
	arthrectomy	excision of a joint

- *cardi-,* "heart"

Base	Word	Meaning
cardi-	**cardi**ograph	instrument for recording the movements of the heart
	cardiology	the science concerned with the heart
	electro**cardi**ogram	record of the heart's electrical activity
	peri**cardi**um	membranous sac enclosing the heart

- *cephal-*, "head," "skull," "brain"

Base	Word	Meaning
cephal-	microcephalic	having an abnormally small head
	cephalopod	class of mollusks, for example, squid, octopus, having tentacles (literally, "feet") around the front of the head
	cephalitis	an inflammation of the brain
en- + cephal-	electroencephalograph	instrument for measuring brain waves

- *chlor-*, "light green," "yellowish-green"

Base	Word	Meaning
chlor-	chlorine	yellowish-green gas
	chlorophyll	green coloring matter in plants
	chloroma	a greenish tumor

- *cirrh-*, "yellow," "tawny"

Base	Word	Meaning
cirrh-	cirrhosis	chronic disease of the liver as the result of alcoholism or hepatitis; literally, "diseased condition of yellowness"

- *dendr-*, "tree," "tree-like structure"

Base	Word	Meaning
dendr-	dendrologist	one who studies trees
	dendroid	shaped like or resembling a tree
	philodendron	ornamental climbing plant that clings to trees

- *enter-*, "intestine"

Base	Word	Meaning
enter-	dysentery	infectious disease of the intestines
	enterectomy	surgical removal of part of the intestine

- *hydr-*, "water"

Base	Word	Meaning
hydr-	de**hydr**ate	make the body deficient in water
	hydrocephalus	accumulation of fluid on the brain that makes the head enlarge and can cause mental handicap

- *hyster-*, "uterus"

Base	Word	Meaning
hyster-	**hyster**otomy	surgical incision into the uterus
	hysterectomy	surgical removal of the uterus
	hysterogenic	producing hysteria

- *leuc-*, *leuk-*, "white"

Base	Word	Meaning
leuc-, *leuk-*	**leuc**ocyte	white blood cell
	leucoderma	abnormal whiteness of the skin occurring in patches due to the absence of skin pigmentation
	leucoma	whitish cloudiness in the cornea of the eye owing to an injury or ulcer
	leukemia	disease characterized by an abnormal increase in the number of white blood cells

- *mast-*, "breast"

Base	Word	Meaning
mast-	**mast**ectomy	surgical removal of the breast
	mastitis	inflammation of the breast or udder
	mastoid	nipple-shaped projection of the temporal bone behind the ear
	mastodon	a large, extinct animal named from the nipple-like projection on its molar teeth

- *melan-*, "black," "dark"

Base	Word	Meaning
melan-	**melan**in	dark pigment found in skin, hair
	melanosis	abnormal presence of dark pigment in the body tissue, often of a malignant character
	melancholy	literally, "black bile," an excess of which, according to the physiological theory of humors, produced a condition of sadness and depression
	melanoderma	abnormal black coloring of the skin

- *my-, mus-, myos-*, "muscle"

Base	Word	Meaning
my-	**my**ograph	instrument for recording muscular action
	myology	the branch of the science of anatomy that deals with muscles
	myalgia	muscular pain
mus-	**mus**cle	"muscle"; literally, "a little mouse"
myos-	**myos**itis	inflammation of a muscle

- *myc-, mycet-*, "fungus," "mould"

Base	Word	Meaning
myc-	**myc**ology	study of fungi
	mycosis	a condition of fungal infestation
	strepto**myc**in	an antibiotic drug obtained from mould
mycet-	**mycet**oma	a tumor caused by a fungus

- *nephr-*, "kidney"

Base	Word	Meaning
nephr-	**nephr**itis	inflammation of the kidneys
	nephrolith	kidney stone

• *neur-,* "nerve"

Base	Word	Meaning
neur-	**neur**algia	pain along the course of a nerve
	neurosis	emotional or mental disorder accompanied by obsessive behavior
	neurologist	physician specializing in the treatment of the nervous system
	neuropsychiatry	branch of medicine dealing with the mind and the nervous system
	neurodermatitis	inflammation of the skin caused by a nervous disorder
	neurosurgery	surgery on some part of the nervous system, including the brain and spinal cord

• *ophthalm-,* "eye"

Base	Word	Meaning
ophthalm-	**ophthalm**ia	inflammation of the eye and membranes lining the eyelids
	ophthalmologist	physician specializing in the eye and its diseases
	ophthalmoscope	an instrument for examining the inside of the eye

• *oste-,* "bone"

Base	Word	Meaning
oste-	**oste**opath	a practitioner who treats diseases by manipulation; based on the theory that disease is caused by a faulty alignment of the bones
	osteotomy	surgical cutting of a bone
	osteoma	a tumor composed of bone tissue

- *ot-*, "ear"

Base	Word	Meaning
ot-	**ot**oscope	instrument for examining the interior of the ear
	otorrhea	discharge from the ear
	otomycosis	a fungal infection of the external ear

- *phleb-*, "vein"

Base	Word	Meaning
phleb-	**phleb**itis	inflammation of a vein
	phlebectomy	surgical removal of a vein
	phlebostenosis	constriction or contraction of a vein
	phlebosclerosis	hardening of the walls of a vein

- *psych-*, "mind"

Base	Word	Meaning
psych-	**psych**ology	scientific study of the human mind and its functions, especially those affecting behavior in a given context
	psychopathology	scientific study of mental disorders

- *sthen-*, "strength"

Base	Word	Meaning
sthen-	**sthen**ia	a condition of strength, vigor
	a**sthen**opia	weakness of the eyes
	myo**sthen**ia	muscular strength
	neura**sthen**ia	a condition of nervous debility

- *tachy-*, "swift"; *tach-*, "speed"

Base	Word	Meaning
tachy-	**tachy**cardia	abnormally rapid beating of the heart
	tachylogia	extreme rapidity of speech
tach-	**tach**ometer	instrument for measuring speed

- *tox-*, "poison"

Base	Word	Meaning
tox-	in**tox**icate	(originally) to poison
	toxin	poisonous substance produced by micro-organisms or by plants and animals
	toxicology	the scientific study of poisons
	zoo**tox**in	toxin derived from an animal

Word for Word

- *xanth-*, "yellow"

Base	Word	Meaning
xanth-	**xanth**emia	a condition in which the blood contains a yellow pigment
	xanthoderma	yellowness of the skin
	xanthin	yellow pigment found in flowers

KEY WORDS DERIVED FROM LATIN

Word	Meaning	Sample Use of Word
antenatal (from *ante*, "before" + *natus* (past participle of *nasci*, "to be born")	before birth	**antenatal** classes where mothers prepare for the birth of their babies
anterior (from *ante*, "before")	near the front	**anterior** lobes of the brain
atrium (from *atrium*, the central courtyard of a Roman house)	one of the two upper chambers of the heart	**atrium** of the heart

Word	Meaning	Sample Use of Word
biped (from *bi-*, "two")+ extended form of *pes, pedis*, "foot"); adjective **bipedal**	two-footed animal (for example, man)	**bipedal** locomotion
cerebral (from *cerebrum*, "brain")	relating to the brain	**cerebral** palsy
dorsal (from *dorsum*, "back")	of, on or near the back	**dorsal** fin (zoology)
femur (from *femur, femoris*, "thigh"); adjective **femoral**	thigh	**femoral** artery
inject (from *in-*, "in," "into" + *iacere*, "to throw"); noun **injection**	to administer medicine by means of a syringe	intramuscular **injection**
jugular (from *jugulum*, "collarbone," "throat," *jugum* "yoke")	relating to the collarbone or throat	**jugular** vein
lachrymal (from *lacrima*, "tear")	relating to tears	**lachrymal** duct
lateral (from *latus*, "side")	at, towards or from the side	**lateral** movement
maxilla (from *maxilla*, "jaw," "jawbone"); adjective **maxillary**	upper jawbone	**maxillary** surgery
muscle (from *musculus*, "muscle")	fibrous tissue with the ability to contract	**muscle** strain
nasal (from *nasus*, "nose")	relating to the nose	**nasal** passages
ocular (from *oculus*, "eye")	of or connected with the eyes	**ocular** movement
pectoral (from extended form of *pectus, pectoris*, "chest," "breast")	of or relating to the chest	**pectoral** muscle
pulmonary (from *pulmo*, "lung")	relating to the lungs	**pulmonary** embolism
renal (from *renes*, "kidney"; compare Greek *nephr-*)	of or concerning the kidneys	**renal** dialysis
subcutaneous (from *sub*, under + *cutis*, "skin")	under the skin	**subcutaneous** injection
uterus (from *uterus*, "womb"); adjective **uterine**	womb	**uterine** contractions

BIBLIOGRAPHY AND FURTHER READING

Allbutt, T. C., *Greek Medicine in Rome* (New York 1970).

Ayers, D. M., *Bioscientific Terminology: Words from Latin and Greek Stems* (Tucson 1972).

Clendening, L., *Source Book of Medical History* (New York 1960).

Dunmore, C. W. and Fleischer, R. M., *Medical Terminology: Exercises in Etymology* (Philadelphia 1985).

Edelstein, L., *Ancient Medicine* (Baltimore 1967).

Grmek, M. D., *Diseases in the Ancient World* (Baltimore 1989).

Jackson, R., *Doctors and Diseases in the Roman Empire*, 2nd Ed. (London 1988).

Lloyd, G. E. R., *Hippocratic Writings* (Harmondsworth 1983).

Longrigg, J., *Greek Rational Medicine: Philosophy and Medicine from Alcmaeon to the Alexandrians* (London 1993).

Majno, G., *The Healing Hand: Man and Wound in the Ancient World* (Cambridge, Mass. 1975).

McCulloch, J. A., *A Medical Greek and Latin Workbook*, 2nd Ed. (Springfield 1984).

Phillips, E. D., *Aspects of Greek Medicine* (Philadelphia 1987).

————, *Greek Medicine* (London 1973).

————, *Philosophy and Medicine from Alcmaeon to the Alexandrians* (London 1973).

Scarborough, J., *Roman Medicine* (Ithaca 1969).

————, *Medical Terminologies: Classical Origins* (Norman 1992).

Sigerist, H. E., *A History of Medicine* 1–2 (New York 1951).

Tebben, J. R., *A Course in Medical and Technical Terminology*, 2nd Ed. (Minneapolis 1996).

WEB SITES: NAMES AND URLS

"Ancient Greek Medicine"
        http://www.nlm.nih.gov/hmd/greek
"Ancient Greek Medicine"
        http://www.historyforkids.org/learn/greeks/science/medicine
"Antiqua Medicina: From Homer to Vesalius"
        http://www.hsl.virginia.edu/historical/artifacts/antiqua
"Foundations of Hippocratic Medicine"
        http://www.indiana.edu/~ancmed/foundations.htm
"Medicine in Ancient Greece"
        http://www.indiana.edu/~ancmed/greekmenu.HTM
"Medword"
        http://www.medword.net
"The Presocratic Influence upon Hippocratic Medicine"
        http://www.perseus.tufts.edu/GreekScience/Students/Chad/pre-soc.html
"The Surgery of Ancient Rome"
        http://www.hsl.virginia.edu/historical/artifacts/roman_surgical

EXERCISES

1. (a) List two basic differences between Greco-Roman medical practice and modern Western medical practice. Be sure to identify the ancient and modern practices in each difference you cite.
   (b) List two similarities between Greco-Roman medical practice and modern Western medical practice. Be sure to identify the ancient and modern practices in each similarity you cite.
   (c) How is the practice of traditional medicine similar to the Greco-Roman practice? List two similarities.

2. (a) Describe what you think it would have been like to have been a doctor in ancient Greece.
   (b) Describe what Roman medical practice was like. Be sure to include in your answer brief comments on some of the following topics: the social standing of doctors, their medical training, illnesses, treatments, women, and contraception.

3. (a) Why is a specialized vocabulary for science and medicine useful?
   (b) How did Greek and Roman doctors receive their training?
   (c) What methods of contraception and abortion were available in the Roman world?
   (d) What topics did Greek and Roman medical writers discuss in their manuals?
   (e) What form did Roman medical training take?
   (f) How did Greek doctors obtain experience of dealing with injuries?
   (g) What illnesses and ailments afflicted Romans? (Name at least two.)
   (h) What accounts for the low social standing of doctors in antiquity?
   (i) Explain the origin of the word **diagnosis**.
   (j) Why were Greek doctors weak in the field of diagnosis?
   (k) What role did women play in the practice of Roman medicine?
   (l) Explain the origin of the word **anatomy**.
   (m) Explain the derivation and meaning of the word **optometrist**.
   (n) Explain the derivation and meaning of the word **hysteria**.
   (o) Explain the derivation of the word **pediatrician**.

4. Write out the base (first part of the word) of each of the following words, then give the meaning of the base and a brief literal meaning of the English word.

Example: **osteopathy**
Base: *oste-*
Meaning of base: *bone*
Meaning of English word: *bone disease*

a. **xanthin**
b. **hysterectomy**
c. **enteritis**
d. **mycology**
e. **neurologist**
f. **melanosis**
g. **hydropathy**
h. **ophthalmology**
i. **optician**
j. **psychopathy**
k. **tachycardia**
l. **otomycosis**
m. **phlebitis**
n. **chloroma**
o. **toxicology**
p. **nephritis**
q. **mastectomy**
r. **myology**
s. **cephalitis**
t. **dendrologist**
u. **arthrectomy**
v. **mycetoma**

5. Write out the combining form (base at the end of the word) of each of the following words, then give the meaning of the combining form and a brief literal meaning of the English word.

Example: **leukemia**
Combining form: *-aemia*
Meaning of combining form: *condition of the blood*
Literal meaning of English word: *condition of white blood*

a. **hydrotherapy**
b. **psychopath**
c. **ophthalmologist**
d. **xanthemia**
e. **cardiopathy**
f. **osteotomy**
g. **tachometer**
h. **otorrhea**
i. **neuropathy**
j. **phlebectomy**
k. **psychotherapy**
l. **myotomy**
m. **osteologist**
n. **nephrology**
o. **enterectomy**
p. **neurasthenia**

6. Write out the suffix (the form at the end of the word) of each of the following words, then give the meaning of the suffix and a brief literal meaning of the English word and the current meaning of the word (dictionary definition).

Example: **toxin**
Suffix: *-in*
Meaning of suffix: *chemical substance*
Meaning of English word: *poisonous substance*

a. **chlorine**
b. **melanoma**
c. **arthritis**
d. **psychosis**
e. **osteoma**
f. **mastitis**

g. **cirrhosis**
h. **neurosis**
i. **melanin**
j. **carditis**
k. **myositis**
l. **mycosis**

CHAPTER 6

POLITICS AND LAW

J. L. Hilton and S. M. Masters

THE GREEK POLIS

The English words **politic, politico, politics, political, politician, politicize,** and **polity** all share the same base form *polit-*, which is derived from the Greek word *politēs* ("citizen"). The related Greek word *polis* ("city"), from which **police** and **policy** originate, first meant "citadel," an area distinct from the rest of the city known as *astu* ("town"). A citadel is a fortified hill-top (later called the "high city" or **acropolis**: *acro-,* "high" + *polis,* "city"). The ancient citadel of Athens is still called the Acropolis today.

The Acropolis of Athens as it is today

The Greeks, however, also used the word *polis* to mean "the body of citizens." This meaning of the term *polis* is best illustrated by Homer's description of two cities, one at peace and the other at war (*Iliad* 18.490–540). In this passage Homer describes various civic functions such as a marriage, a legal dispute and the siege of a city. The cities are described in terms of their social structures: the family, the legal system, and the army. In later times the Greeks did not speak of Athens so much as "the Athenians." During the Persian attack on Athens, for example, the inhabitants of the city abandoned the citadel and took to the sea on their ships. The citadel was burned, but the citizens returned after the departure of the Persians and Athens continued to exist. The Greek city was therefore not necessarily dependent on its fortified citadel. The connection between these two meanings ("citadel" and "body of citizens"), however, is easy to see: in times of danger the people in the area around a fortified hill-top would congregate there and co-operate in the defense of their position.

The Greek philosopher, Aristotle, explains the development of cities in terms of natural evolution. According to him, man is a "political animal" (Aristotle, *Politics* 1253a) and society came into being for a natural purpose: human beings need to form communities in order to survive. A key passage in his work reads as follows.

> The *polis* is the complete integration of several villages that have reached the limit of self-sufficiency. The *polis* comes into existence for the sake of life and continues to exist for the sake of a good life. And, therefore, every *polis* is created by nature, just as the first communities were, for the *polis* is the final stage of growth (*telos*) of these communities, and the final stage of growth of anything (such as a man, a horse, or a house) determines its nature . . . Hence it is clear that the state is a creation of nature and that a man is by nature a political animal (*politikon zōon*). And he who by nature and not by accident is without a state, is either unimportant or superhuman.
>
> (Aristotle, *Politics* 1252b–1253a)

Aristotle's argument is that human beings by nature tend to live in cities. The basic unit of society is the family, which fulfils basic needs of food, shelter, love and so on. Families naturally band together into villages and these in turn unite into a "single complete community," the *polis* or state, as a matter of necessity.

Like all Greeks of his time, Aristotle does not allow for a higher level of communal life than the *polis*. Therefore a modern state like the United States, which is composed of numerous cities, would have been inconceivable to him and his contemporaries. The Greek word *polis* is therefore often translated as "city-state." In the Classical period (fifth century BCE) the area we know as Greece today consisted of several hundred independent *poleis* ("city-states"), such as Athens, Sparta, Thebes, and Argos. Their inhabitants all spoke various dialects of Greek and were largely cut off from one another by mountains. Wars between these Greek city-states were common. It was only when the city-states were threatened by a larger, more unified power, Persia, that they managed to bring about a system of uneasy alliances that fell apart once the crisis had passed. On the other hand, the independence of the Greek city-states meant that they enjoyed a high degree of political freedom and **autonomy** ("self-rule").

Aristotle also does not allow for the element of individual choice in his account of the origin of human society. This reflects the general Greek view that society is not based on a "social contract" and consequently the question of human rights does not arise. In the ancient world citizenship was largely based on a person's participation in the armed forces, and women and children were not considered full citizens. A citizen was therefore "a free male lt who lives in a city," a *politēs* (plural *politai*). Slaves and foreigners (or metics, *metoikoi*) also not included among the citizens, although the latter were subject to tax. It is ing that Aristotle himself was only a resident alien in Athens and would not have been d citizenship or its privileges.

lition to providing for the survival of their citizens, however, Aristotle argues that e formed "with a view to some good purpose" (*Politics* 1252a). Underlying this is theory that "in their actions all men do in fact aim at what they think good" and that humans differ from animals because of their capacity for speech and their ability to discuss what is right and wrong. The laws *(nomoi)* by which a state was governed were therefore also a matter of contention. Over time, the various Greek city-states recognized a wide variety of laws and traditions that regulated political life. These are what we would call constitutions *(politeiai)*. At no stage were these constitutions enacted as a legal code as some modern constitutions are.

LATIN WORDS FOR "CITY"

In Latin two separate words were used for the physical city and the body of citizens. The Latin word for the physical city was *urbs*, "stronghold," which produced **urban, urbane, urbanity, urbanize,** and **urbanization** in English. The story of how Romulus built a wall around the newly founded city of Rome and how he killed his brother Remus for mocking it illustrates the importance of fortifications for the development of communal life in Italy, which was populated by a large number of competing **tribes.** The establishment of a fortified place of refuge brought landowners together with the dispossessed and made negotiations between these two groups and the distribution of power between them increasingly necessary. The civil disturbances that characterized the early history of Rome is a good example of this.

Word for Word

The English word "city" is derived, however, from the Latin *civitas* (the middle syllable being dropped), which is in turn based on the word *civis* ("citizen"). The derivation shows a separation between the people who constitute the city and the place in which they meet. The Latin word *civitas* referred to the state as constituted by its citizens. The English words **civic, civics, civil, civilian, civility, civilization, civilize, citadel, citizen,** and **city** are all derived from the Latin *civis* ("citizen"). *Civitas* is therefore more abstract than *urbs* and was later used by St. Augustine to refer to the Christian church and its relationship with Rome in his best-known work *City of God*.

Word Study

- **Sovereign** is derived from the Latin *superanus* ("superior") + *reign* (from *regnum*, "kingdom"); the Latin verb *regere* ("to rule") has produced the English noun **regent.**
- Other words with the same base as **acropolis** are **acrobat** ("a performer of spectacular gymnastic feats," literally "highwalker"), **acromegaly** ("abnormal growth of hands, feet, and face [the extremities]"), **acronym** ("a word formed from the initial letters of other words"), and **acrophobia** ("fear of heights").
- The Latin word for a constitution was *constitutio* ("arrangement"), from which comes **constitute, constitution,** and **constitutional** in English.

MONARCHY AND RELATED FORMS

The first section of this chapter explained how the citizens of Greek and Roman cities agreed on laws and traditions, known as constitutions, by which the state would be run. One of the earliest forms of constitution in Greece and Rome was the monarchy, or government by a single ruler, as opposed, for example, to an oligarchy, the rule of a few. The word **monarchy** comes from the Greek *mon-* ("one") + *archē* ("beginning," "rule"), while **oligarchy** comes from *olig-* ("few") + *archē* ("beginning," "rule"). The English word **monarchy** is a general, constitutional term referring to a state traditionally ruled by one person, that is, government through a sovereign with the title of king, queen, or emperor.

The Greek term **monarchy** refers to a variety of different types of ruler such as kings, tyrants, and other despots. The early Greek city-states were ruled by kings (*basileis*; singular *basileus*). The Greek term has not been taken into English to refer to royalty; the Latin *rex* ("king") and *regina* ("queen"), which are still used as names in English, are used instead. These words are built on the very productive base *reg-* ("direct," "rule").

In early times the king was probably advised by a council of elders (Greek *boulē*, Latin *senatus*) drawn from the aristocracy. English also has another term for aristocrats, **nobles** (derived from Latin *noscere*, "to know"; old Latin form *gnoscere*, from the base *gno-* of Greek *gignoskein*, "to begin to know"). There also seemed to be some kind of assembly of the people (*ekklesia*) in the early monarchies. It is unlikely, however, that the assembly had any power during the monarchy. Homer gives the best illustration of the relationship between the early Greek kings and their followers (*Iliad* 2.84–392). In this passage Agamemnon (whom Homer calls "the shepherd of the people") tests the will of his troops to capture Troy; the attempt backfires and the situation is only saved by the forceful actions and words of Odysseus.

In the Archaic and Classical periods the monarchy was not strong in Greece. After Greece had been conquered by the Macedonians and after the Macedonian general, Alexander the Great, had defeated the Persian empire, however, a new and much stronger form of monarchy arose that used many of the characteristics of the Persian type. This became known as the Hellenistic monarchy. Many of the features of the Hellenistic monarchy influenced the Roman imperial system of government and the later European monarchies that we are familiar with today, for example, the use of a crown (Latin *corona*) or diadem (Greek *diadema*); the development of courts of advisers; the conferment of rank and title such as "Prince" (Latin *princeps*, "leader"), "Duke" (Latin *dux*, "leader"), "Count" (Latin *comes* "companion"), and "Viscount" (Latin *vicis* + *comes*, "in place of a companion"); and the idea of the divine right of kings (by which the legitimacy of the Roman emperors in particular was often established).

The early Greek kings often claimed to rule by virtue of the fact that they were descended from kings or were elected to the position. From time to time, however, these traditional monarchies were overthrown by revolutionary leaders known as tyrants. These leaders may have been able to seize power because they had become wealthy through trade, because of a change in military tactics in which individual soldiers were replaced by a formation of troops known as hoplites, or because of other socio-economic changes. Tyranny (from the Greek word *tyrannos*) is usually revolutionary and unconstitutional. In English the word **tyrant** means "an oppressive, unjust, or cruel ruler, a person exercising power or authority arbitrarily or cruelly," **tyranny** is "rule by a tyrant, the cruel, and arbitrary use of authority"; **tyrannize** means "rule despotically, exercise tyranny"; and **tyrannical** is defined as "acting like, characteristic of a tyrant." Greek tyrants, however, were not necessarily all tyrannical in the English sense of the word. Some of the tyrants were quite moderate and even popular. The rule of Peisistratus in Athens is a good example of a relatively benevolent tyranny. A tyrant's rule was arbitrary, however, and often resented by his fellow aristocrats. For example, Peisistratus' son Hipparchus was assassinated by Harmodios and Aristogeiton, who were then executed and became martyrs for the cause of equality before the law (*isonomia*).

DEMOCRACY

The English words **democracy, democratic,** and **democrat** originate in the combination of the Greek words *demos* ("the people") and *kratos* ("power, dominion"), hence *demokratia* ("popular government, power in the hands of the people"). The English derivatives and meanings are **democracy** ("state practicing government by the people, direct or representative"), **democrat** ("advocate of democracy"), and **democratic** ("practicing democracy"). *Kratos* has produced a number of similar compound forms such as **democracy, autocracy,** and **plutocracy** and the related noun forms **democrat, autocrat, technocrat,** and **plutocrat.**

Democracy in Athens arose when Hippias, the last tyrant, was expelled from Athens in 510 BCE and an Athenian aristocrat, Cleisthenes, introduced a new system of government in a bid to obtain popular support for himself. The main features of the Athenian democracy were: (1) the redistribution of the citizens of Athens into artificial rather than ethnic tribes; (2) the election of councilors by lot; (3) the short term of office for political leaders; (4) the sovereignty of the *ekklesia* ("popular assembly"); and (5) the payment of political officers. Cleisthenes is also said to have introduced the practice into Athenian politics whereby the assembly could ostracize unpopular citizens from Athens for a period of ten years.

Word for Word

Despite the fact that democracy is now widely considered to be the most desirable constitution, it was very unusual in Greek and Roman times. Most writers believed that government by the wealthy, educated class was preferable to a radical democracy in which decisions were taken by majority vote and carried out by amateurs. Some critics of democracy believed that the popular assemblies could be easily influenced by persuasive speakers. Indeed most ambitious politicians diligently studied the art of speaking in public *(rhetorica technē)*, precisely because success as a speaker guaranteed political leadership. An example of such rhetoric is given by Thucydides in his *History of the Peloponnesian War,* in which he reports the speech of the Athenian statesman, Pericles, in praise of the democratic government of Athens.

> Let me say that our system of government does not copy the institutions of our neighbors. It is more the case of our being a model to others, than of our imitating anyone else. Our constitution is called a democracy because power is in the hands not of a minority but of the whole people. When it is a question of settling private disputes, everyone is equal before the law; when it is a question of putting one person before another in positions of public responsibility, what counts is not membership of a particular class, but the actual ability that the man possesses. No one, so far as he has it in him to be of service to the state is kept in political obscurity because of poverty... We are free and tolerant in our private lives; but in public affairs we keep to the law ... Our city is open to the world and we have no periodical deportations to prevent people observing or finding out secrets that might be of military advantage to the enemy... Here, each individual is interested not only in his own affairs but in the affairs of the state as well: even those who are mostly occupied with their own business are extremely well-informed on general politics—this is a peculiarity of ours: we do not say that a man who takes no interest in politics is a man who minds his own business; we say that he has no business here at all.
>
> (Thucydides, *History of the Peloponnesian War* 2.37)

Word Study

- **Draco,** the seventh century BCE Athenian lawgiver, has given his name to the English adjective **draconian** due to the stringency of his laws.
- The term **despot** comes from the Greek *despotēs* ("lord," "master").
- **Senate** is built on the base *sen-* ("old"); compare English **senile, senior** and Spanish **señor, señora, señorita.**
- *Ekklesia* survives in English in the word **ecclesiastic** ("to do with the church").
- In English the word **martyr** means one who suffers on behalf of a cause. The Greek word *martyr* simply means "a witness," "someone who testifies." The change in meaning is due to the use of the term **martyr** to describe the early Christians who "bore witness" for Christ and were put to death for their faith. This meaning became attached to the word and now in English martyrs are those who suffer on behalf of a cause.
- The base *iso-* ("equal") is still widely used in scientific terminology, for example, in **isonomia, isometric, isochronous, isomorphic, isosceles, isotherm, isotonic, isotope, isotropic,** and **isobar.**
- The following words also contain the base *demo-* ("people"): **demography** ("the scientific study of populations") and **demagogue** ("leader of the people," "political agitator"). **Demagogue** is the combination of the Greek noun *demos* ("people") and the verb *ago* ("I lead"); hence the Greek word *demagogos* ("popular leader").
- The Latin word *orator* referred to a public speaker. The Latin *ars oratoria* ("the art of speaking") gives us the English **oratory.** An **oration** is "a formal address or discourse, especially of ceremonial kind" and it is derived from *oratio* ("a speech").

THE ROMAN REPUBLIC

The Romans referred to their system of government as a "Republic" (from *res publica*, "the affairs, or property, of the people"). The modern term means "a form of government in which the people or their elected representatives possess the supreme power" and is virtually synonymous with "representative democracy." For the Romans, however, the important element in the *res publica* was not democracy but freedom (*libertas*). *Libertas* in Rome meant the freedom of the wealthy, political classes to compete for political office without the domination of a monarch. It was to secure this political freedom that the kings had been driven out of Rome (an event traditionally dated to 510 BCE).

The Roman Republic was a mixed constitution consisting of executive magistrates, an advisory Senate drawn from the wealthy citizens, and popular assemblies. Such a constitution aimed at achieving a balance of the competing elements in the state, which was organized in the following way.

Magistracies

At the time of the establishment of the Roman Republic, the king was replaced by several magistrates whose power was limited by the principles of collegiality (there were normally more than one of them), accountability (they had to give an account of their actions at the end of their term), and by time (they were elected annually and could not normally continue in office for consecutive terms). During the early years of the Republic, access to these magistracies was bitterly contested by the "founding fathers" of the state, known as **patricians,** and immigrants from the surrounding tribes, known as **plebeians.** The plebeians gathered in a separate assembly from the rest of the population (known as the *concilium plebis*) and elected tribunes to protect their rights.

The other magistracies were at first elected from the patrician class, but gradually plebeians won the right to stand for these offices too. The senior magistracies (**consuls, praetors,** and **censors**) were elected by the assembly of citizens in centuries (*comitia centuriata*), while the junior offices (**quaestors, aediles,** and **tribunes**) were elected by the assembly of citizens by tribes (*comitia tributa*). The magistracies of the Republic and their functions are listed below.

Magistracy	Functions	Related English Derivative
consul	executive power over the army	**consulate**
praetor	administer the law	**Pretoria**
quaestor	administer the finances of the Republic	**question**
aedile	administer the city, roads, temples	**edifice**
censor	take census, review citizen body, award contracts	**censorship**
plebeian **tribune**	veto legislation, convene Senate, help citizens	**tribunal**

The executive power (*imperium*) of the magistrates was symbolized by the *fasces*, a bundle of sticks containing an axe. The consuls were awarded twelve *fasces*; dictators, who were appointed in times of political emergency, were given twenty-four. The dictator was given supreme authority in Rome for a limited period (six months) whereafter he relinquished his powers. The Latin word *dictator* originates from the verb *dico* ("to speak"). The English term describes a person who has unrestricted authority and has usually usurped power, that is, an unconstitutional position. To describe someone as a **dictator** or as **dictatorial** implies that they are harsh, domineering, and overbearing. In the Roman context the word did not always (or necessarily) have these negative associations: the word simply referred to the person elected into the office of dictator.

The Roman Class Structure

*a*t some point in the early history of the Republic, the population of Rome was classified according to a wealth requirement. When the Roman citizens met in these groups the assembly was known as the "assembly by centuries" (*comitia centuriata*). Otherwise the citizens assembled in tribes (*comitia tributa*). The classes were as follows.

Class, Property Qualification and Equipment	Seniors	Juniors	Total
Class 1 (100,000 asses: helmet, shield, greaves, breast-plate, sword, spear)	40 centuries	40	80
Equites / Equestrian class or "knights" (Grant of 10,000 asses and 2,000 asses for feed)			18
Subtotal			98
Engineers			2
Class 2 (75,000 asses: helmet, long shield, greaves, sword, spear)	10	10	20
Class 3 (50,000 asses: helmet, long shield, sword, spear)	10	10	20
Class 4 (25,000 asses: sword, spear)	10	10	20
Trumpeters			2
Class 5 (11,000 asses: slings and stones)	15	15	30
Class 6 (Proletarian class)			1
Total			193

THE ROMAN CLASS STRUCTURE

(Compare Dionysius of Halicarnassus, *Roman Antiquities* 7.49.2–8; Livy 1.42–43; Cicero, *On the Republic* 2.22.39)

Voting for the most important positions (consul, praetor, and quaestor) was done in the assembly by centuries. As the above chart shows, the voting favored the rich since the combined votes of the Class 1 and the equestrian class provided a simple majority of the votes. An individual's vote had no weight in this system of voting; there were, for example, fewer individuals in the wealthy centuries than in those of the proletariat.

The Roman Senate

During the Roman Republic, the Senate was very powerful. It was made up of ex-magistrates and it discussed and decided all issues of foreign and domestic policy. While it did not have legislative authority (it could not enact laws), it was responsible for discussing and drafting the laws to be proposed to the assembly; it was the Roman deliberative body of state.

The Roman Assemblies

The assemblies of the people were the elective and legislative councils: they elected politicians to office and they voted on the passing of laws that had been proposed by the Senate. When a law was passed by the assembly it became a statute.

THE ROMAN EMPIRE

The Roman Republic, at first in order to survive but later as an instrument of imperialism, developed an army *(exercitus)* that was, for many centuries, superior to any other within the Mediterranean basin. First, Rome established control over Italy by means of **colonies** *(coloniae),* treaties *(foedera;* compare **federation**), free tributary states *(municipia;* compare **municipality**), and the client-patron relationship *(clientela)* with other tribes. After many wars against rival powers in the Mediterranean (Carthage, the Hellenistic kingdoms, and the developing nations such as Gaul, Britain, and Germany), Rome came to control Europe south of the Rhine-Danube river from Britain to Iraq. As a result of the socio-economic changes that the expansion of Roman territory brought about, however, the Republican system of government collapsed in a series of civil wars that resulted in the emergence of one military leader, Augustus, who became the first emperor of Rome.

Augustus, however, did not do away with Republican magistrates or the Senate. Instead he opted for a **dyarchy,** a system of government in which power was shared between the Senate and the emperor. He himself no longer occupied Republican offices, but was content with a grant of consular *imperium* and the powers of the plebeian tribunes. He retained control over the army in the imperial provinces, but handed over some provinces to be administered by senators. On his death he was careful to hand over control of the state to his adopted son, Tiberius. Therefore the forms of the Republic persisted alongside of the establishment of an imperial dynasty (Greek *dynasteia,* "power," "sovereignty").

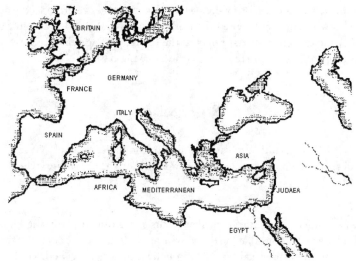

Map of the Mediterranean area ruled by Rome in the first century BCE

Word Study

- From *publica* come the English words **public, publican,** and **publish.**
- The word **magistrate** comes from the Latin base *magistr-* ("master").
- The term **patrician** refers to a member of a group of families that, according to tradition, Romulus had appointed as his advisers. The term is related to *patres* ("fathers"), a word used to refer to senators.
- The term **plebeian** refers to the immigrants who joined the Roman state in her early history. The word is related to the Latin *ple-* ("fill"; compare **complete**). It is unclear whether the plebeians were racially, economically, or socially distinct from the patricians. One of the early laws of Rome, the Twelve Tables, prohibited plebeians from marrying into a patrician family. Plebeians were also prevented from being elected to the patrician magistracies such as the consulship. Over time, however, the plebeians gradually won the right to intermarry with patricians and to hold the consulship and other offices of the state.
- Originally there were two praetors, the urban **praetor** (*praetor urbanus*), who dealt with cases involving Roman citizens, and the foreign **praetor** (*praetor peregrinus*), who heard cases involving foreigners. Under Sulla (first century BCE) the number of praetors was increased to eight because of the increase in the number of standing courts.
- The Latin word *imperium* produces such English words as **imperative, imperial, imperialist, imperialism, imperious,** and **emperor** in English.
- The word **fascist** (believer in the principles of right wing nationalism in Italy) derives from the fact that Mussolini's Fascist party used the Roman *fasces* as its emblem.
- The word **dictator** is constructed on the base *dict-* ("speak"); compare, for example, **diction, dictionary, dictate, dictation,** and **dictatorial.**

- The **proletarian** class, or **proletariat,** in Roman times referred to the class of citizens who only contributed their offspring (*proles*) to the state. In Marxist theory the term **proletariat** refers to the industrial wage earning class, whose only property consists in their labor (the "working class").

ROMAN LAW

It is no exaggeration to say that next to the Bible, no book has left a deeper mark upon the history of mankind than the *Corpus Iuris Civilis*.
(A. P. d'Entrèves)

One of the most significant achievements of the Roman civilization was their law. The legal heritage that the Romans have left us has had a pervasive effect on modern legal systems and many legal systems throughout history have modeled themselves directly on Roman principles of law. Its influence can be attributed to its clarity, simplicity, and orderliness. In its ultimate form Roman law incorporated a coherent and efficient means of defining and regulating all relationships in society.

The Latin word for law is *lex* (the base of the extended form is *leg-*), which in its general sense refers to "a contract, a set form of words, a binding agreement" and can also specifically denote "a law that has been passed by an authoritative body"—in other words what we term a statute as opposed to a bill. During the Republican period, such laws were passed by the popular assemblies, while plebiscites (*plebiscita*, literally "decrees of the common people"), which were ultimately binding on the whole community, were passed by the plebeian assembly.

In the later Republic changes were made to make the law more applicable to the vastly expanded Roman context and the diversity of people it incorporated. In addition to the *ius civile,* or body of laws, another body of "laws" or authoritative statements was introduced in the form of the edicts issued by each *praetor* at the beginning of his office. These were manifestos, or statements of policy that outlined how the magistrates were going to apply the law in that year. The body of edicts formed a separate body of law, the *ius honorarium,* which was basically what we would term procedural law (as opposed to substantive law, which is the actual body of laws). The Romans also introduced another body of laws that regulated contact with foreigners called the *ius gentium* ("law of the nations") that demonstrated how the Romans recognized the need for change, flexibility, and development in their law to deal with different legal traditions.

The government that replaced the Republican system in Rome after the civil wars was termed the **Principate** from the fact that the first emperor, Augustus, referred to himself as the *princeps* ("leader"). During the principate, the law-making and election of magistracies was taken out of the hands of the assemblies and given to the Senate. In effect, however, the Senate was influenced and controlled by the emperor, whose edicts and rescripts (replies to questions by governors) had the force of law. During the later Principate, the emperor's powers became unashamedly unlimited. This period is termed the **Dominate** since the Emperor called himself *dominus* ("lord," "master"), a term often used to describe the master of slaves.

During the reign of the Emperor Justinian (527–565 CE), the great legal code, the *Corpus Iuris Civilis*, was compiled. The emperor wanted to gather together all actual bodies of laws, imperial edicts, and the writings of the Roman jurists and to set it out in an orderly, systematic, and thorough collection. The purpose was to preserve the law for posterity and also to assist in the education of law students. The *Corpus Iuris Civilis* consisted of four main sections: the *Digests* or *Pandects*, the *Institutes* (first principles in the law), the *Codex* (imperial statutes), and the *Novellae Constitutiones* (Justinian's new legislation). From the sixth to the eleventh centuries Roman law was largely eclipsed by the laws of the Germanic kingdoms of Western Europe. A revival of interest in the maxims, principles, and laws of the Romans occurred in the eleventh century.

The Influence of Roman Law upon American Law

No doubt in reaction against English rule, the civil law, which was a combination of Roman law with non-Roman elements, had a stronger influence upon American lawyers and legal scholars in post-Revolutionary America than the Common law, which was a body of doctrine based on cases tried in England and in English colonies. This influence was felt particularly in the areas of legal education, commercial law, maritime law, and in the entrenchment of human rights in the constitution of the United States.

Roman law made itself felt in American law schools directly through readings from Justinian's *Corpus Iuris Civilis* and indirectly through the work of European legal scholars such as Hugo Grotius (1583–1645), Samuel von Pufendorf (1632–1694), and Gottlieb Heineccius (1681–1741). Leading intellectuals such as John Adams, James Kent, and Thomas Jefferson made use of Roman law to lend weight to their arguments in particularly contentious cases. In 1812, for instance, Jefferson justified his decision to forbid building on alluvial land in New Orleans on the basis of citations from Justinian's *Digest* and *Institutes* in which alluvial land, such as a beach or river-bank, is considered *terra nullius* ("land belonging to no one").

Some American legal scholars in the nineteenth century considered Roman law to have been the foundation of maritime and commercial law in Europe. French civil law texts in these fields were translated into English by French immigrants to America and the *American Law Journal* published a number of translations and discussions of chapters from the *Digest* that related to legal obligations of mariners and inn-keepers. It was felt that Roman law provided general principles to guide judges in new and problematic cases in this area.

As a result of this interest, many works on Roman law were published in America. In 1812 Thomas Cooper's translation of Justinian's *Institutes* was published in Philadelphia, while in 1817 David Hoffman published in Baltimore his *Course of Legal Study*, in which he urged the study of Roman law as a foundation for a proper understanding of American law. American law schools prescribed the study of Roman law texts and the principles of Roman law were applied to actual litigation, particularly in the law of contract. The high point of interest in Roman law in America came in 1817 with the discovery in Verona of a manuscript of the *Institutes* of Gaius, which focused attention on the primary texts once again.

Another area of interest for American legal scholars was the Roman idea of the "law of nations" (*ius gentium*), which provided them with a body of universal law of general applicability in contrast with the more haphazard collection of legal precedents in the Common law.

Therefore civil law was used to approximate to a more systematic body of legislation that could be deduced from the rules of natural justice. The influence of the idea of natural law can be seen most clearly in the formulation of the American Declaration of Independence, with its strong emphasis on universal human rights. The concept of natural law originates with the Stoic concept of a law of "reason" (*logos*) inherent in the universe, which manifested itself in the form of fate or divine providence. According to Stoic philosophy it was the duty of every human being to live his or her life in accordance with natural reason.

The Influence of Roman Law upon South African Law

O ne of the countries whose legal system has been particularly influenced by Roman law is South Africa. The South African legal system is based on Dutch law, which was heavily "Romanized" between the twelfth and sixteenth centuries. The resultant combination, which was brought in 1652 to South Africa, is termed "Roman-Dutch" law. Both Roman and Dutch texts became authoritative sources of South African common law. In 1860 a judge presiding over a case in the Western Cape relied on the *Corpus Iuris Civilis* of Justinian in reaching his verdict. Roman-Dutch law still forms the basis of the modern South African legal system. The Roman influence upon South African law is pervasive in a number of areas such as maxims, legal principles, legal concepts, institutions, and actions.

Roman Maxims and Legal Principles

R oman maxims (from Latin *maxima* [*propositio*], "greatest [proposition]") are general truths or rules of conduct that are expressed in a sentence. They are not laws as such, but they are presumptions or guidelines that stand unless successfully rebutted. For example, the Latin maxim *qui facit per alium facit per se* ("one who does something through another does it by himself") means that if you get somebody else to commit a crime for you, even though you may not have carried out the physical action yourself, in the eyes of the law you may as well have. So if you hire someone to kill a person, you will receive the same penalty as the hit-man, although you did not pull the trigger.

Roman Legal Concepts

T he Roman legal concepts of *vis maior* ("superior force") and *casus fortuitus* ("unavoidable accident") occur in the law of contract. In a contract a person undertakes to perform a certain action and, if he does not do so, he is liable for breach of the contract. If, however, he is prevented from performing the contract through a *vis maior* ("superior force") or *casus fortuitus* ("unavoidable accident"), then he is discharged from liability due to "supervening impossibility of performance." If someone undertakes to deliver a product by a certain time, for example, and the delivery van is prevented from getting to the destination because a hurricane arrives and no vehicles can travel on the roads, the person cannot be held in breach since he is unable to fulfil his obligation through a natural phenomenon over which he has no control.

Roman Institutions

The Romans had various institutions, including the institution of a soldier's will, which existed until recently in South African law. Ordinarily, for a will to be valid there were certain requirements that had to be fulfilled, including the signing of the will by witnesses. If these requirements were not fulfilled, the will would be declared invalid. A soldier on active service, however, could make an informal will that did not fulfil all the requirements. The absence of these elements did not make the will invalid.

Roman Actions

These actions refer to legal processes or remedies of law. In Roman law a *delictum* is simply a "fault," "misdeed," or "crime," while a *crimen* is "guilt," "fault," or "misdeed." The distinction in Roman law is not entirely clear. In modern law, the law of delict describes the law that seeks personal reparation for certain behavior, compensation on a private level while criminal law seeks reparation or punishment on behalf of the public or the state. In the event of a car accident the state may prosecute a perpetrator for "reckless and negligent driving" since he is a threat to the community's safety. The other party, who has had his car destroyed, has incurred massive hospital bills, and has lost earnings because he had to be in hospital for three months, has a private remedy or action in the law of delict against the reckless driver. In the South African law of delict about ninety per cent of cases brought against individuals in private disputes are for *damnum iniuria datum* ("damage wrongfully caused"). Damages pursued or awarded may be pecuniary through the "action of Aquilian law" (*actio legis Aquiliae*) or non-pecuniary (for example, loss of physical integrity, self-respect, and reputation) through an *actio iniuriarum* ("an action for a personal injury").

LATIN DERIVATIVES IN LEGAL VOCABULARY

Since Latin derivatives feature heavily in legal vocabulary, having a basic knowledge of the most important Latin derivatives can be an aid to those interested in the study and practice of law. The following lists contain some common words used in various areas of law and lists their Latin bases and English meanings.

Public Law (Criminal)

English Word	Latin Components and English Meaning
abduct	(*ab*, "away " + *ducere*, "to lead"): to carry off or kidnap (especially a woman or child) illegally by force or deception (verb)
abscond	(*abscondere*, "to conceal," "lose sight of"): to leave quickly and secretively, especially in wrongdoing (verb)
alias	(Latin: "at other times"): called or known at other times as (adverb); an assumed name (noun)
alibi	(Latin: "elsewhere"): a plea that when an alleged act took place one was elsewhere (noun)
allegation	(*allegare*, "to adduce"): assertion, especially unproved (noun)
assault	(*ad*, "to," "towards," "on" + *saltus*, "leap"): violent physical or verbal attack (noun)
capital	(*caput*, "head"): involving punishment by death, as in a **capital** offence (adjective)
conspiracy	(*con*, "together" + *spirare*, "to breathe"): plot together in secret for unlawful or harmful business (noun)
crime	(*crimen*, "guilt," "fault," "misdeed": an act (usually a serious offence) punishable by law (noun); **criminal:** a person guilty of crime (noun); of or involving or concerning crime (adjective)
culpable	(*culpare*, "to blame"): deserving of censure or blame (adjective)
detain	(*de*, "down," "away" + *tenere*, "to hold"): keep in confinement or under restraint (verb); **detention** (noun)
deterrent	(*de* + *terrere*, "to frighten"): something that discourages or prevents through fear or dislike of the consequences (noun)
exoneration	(*ex-*, "out of," from" + *onus*, "load"): free or declare free from blame; clearing from accusation (noun)
extenuation	(*ex-*, "out of," from" + *tenuis*, "thin"): partial justification; that which causes a matter to seem less serious (noun)
extortion	(*ex-*, "out of," from" + *torquere, tort-*, "to twist"): obtain money by force, threat or intimidation (noun)
homicide	(*homo*, "man" + *caedere*, "to kill"): killing of one person by another (noun)
incarcerate	(*in*, "in," "into" + *carcer*, "prison"): imprison (verb)
penal	(*poena*, "punishment"): concerned with punishment (adjective)
penitentiary	(*paenitere*, "to repent"): reformatory prison (USA) (noun)
posthumous	(*posthumus*, "last"): after death (adjective)

Private Law (Persons)

English Word	Latin Components and English Meaning
abortion	(*ab*, "away," "from" + *oriri*, "to be born"): expulsion of fetus from womb before it is able to survive (noun)
adopt	(*adoptare*, "to choose," "accept"): to take a person into a relationship, especially as a child or heir (verb)
annul	(*ad*, "to" + *nullus*, "nothing"): to declare invalid; to reduce to nothing (verb)
consanguinity	(*con*, "with," "together" + *sanguis*, "blood"): blood relationship (noun)
custody	(*custos, custod-*, "guard"): guardianship, protective care (noun)
divorce	(*di* [reversal of state] + *vert-*, "turn"): legal dissolution of marriage (noun)
domicile	(*domus*, "home"): place of permanent residence (noun)
majority	(*maior*, "greater," comparative of *magnus*, "great"): full legal age (noun)
minority	(*minor*, "less," comparative of *parvus*, "little"): state of being under full legal age (noun)

Property and Wills

English Word	Latin Components and English Meaning
administer	(*ad*, "to," "near," "at the home of" + *minister*, "servant"): manage affairs, person's estate (verb)
beneficiary	(*beneficium*, 'kindness," "favor"): person designated to receive funds, property or other benefits from an insurance policy, will, or other settlement (noun)
codicil	(diminutive of *codex*, "book," "tablet"): addition to will explaining, modifying, or revoking parts of it (noun)
heir	(*heres, hered-*, "heir"): person entitled to property or rank as legal successor of its formal owner (noun); **hereditary:** descending by inheritance (adjective)
legatee	(*lego*, "bequeath"): recipient of **legacy** (gift left in a will) (noun)
residuary	(*residuus*, "remaining," "outstanding"): of the residue of an estate (noun)
testament	(*testamentum*, "will"): a will, especially a last will and testament (noun)
testate	(*testis*, "witness"): having left a valid will at death (adjective); **intestate:** not having left a will before death (adjective)
testify	(*testis*): to bear witness, give evidence (verb)
usufruct	(*usus*, "use," "application" + *fructus*, "enjoyment," "proceeds," "profit," "fruits"): the use of others' property (noun)

Commercial Law (Contracts)

English Word	Latin Components and English Meaning
annuity	(*annus*, "year"): an amount, especially of money, payable annually (noun)
contract	(*contrahere*, "to draw together," "unite," "collect"): written or spoken agreement, especially one enforceable by law; document recording the agreement (noun)
conveyance	(*con-*, "with," "together" + *vehere*, "carry"): an instrument or deed carrying or transferring property to another (noun)
covenant	(*convenire*, "to agree"): an agreement between persons or parties; an undertaking or promise of legal validity (noun)
creditor	(*credere*, "to trust"): person to whom money is owed (noun)
latent	(*latere*, "to be hidden"): concealed, dormant; not existing or developed or manifest yet (adjective)
liable	(*ligere*, "to bind"): legally bound (adjective)
patent	(*patere*, "to lie open"): official document conferring right or title, etc., especially a sole right to make use of or to sell some invention (noun); obvious, plain (adjective), as in **patent** defects

Other Legal Words

English Word	Latin Components and English Meaning
adjudicate	(*adjudicare*, "to award as a judge"): act as judge in a court or a tribunal (verb); **adjudication:** a judicial decision or sentence (noun)
appellant	(*appellare*, "to address"): one who appeals a court decision (noun)
defame	(*de-*, "down" + *fama*, "talk," "report," "reputation"): attack good reputation, speak ill of (verb)
defendant	(*defendere*, "to repel," "protect," "defend"): person accused or sued in a lawsuit (noun)
injunction	(*iniungere*, "to join," "attach"): a court order prohibiting a certain action (noun)
jurisdiction	(*iuris*, "law" + *dicere*, "to say," "speak"): the right and authority to apply the law: extent of authority and control (noun)
prosecutor	(*prosequi, prosecut-*, "to pursue"): one who institutes legal proceedings against a person, especially in a criminal court (noun)

LATIN LEGAL PHRASES

Latin phrases are often used in the practice of law in countries such as the United States and South Africa. The list below includes some of the Latin phrases used in the legal profession.

Latin Phrase	English Meaning
ab initio	from the beginning
actio in rem	action for a thing
ad litem	for the purpose of a lawsuit
animus testandi	the intention of making a will
audi alteram partem	hear the other side
bona fide	in good faith
caveat emptor	let the buyer beware
caveat scriptor	let the signer beware
compos mentis	sound of mind
culpa lata	gross negligence
curator bonis	a guardian for goods or estate
de facto	according to fact
de iure	according to law
de minimis non curat lex	the law takes no account of trifles
doli capax	capable of crime
doli incapax	incapable of crime
dolus	criminal intention
ex facie	at face value
ex parte	from one party
habeas corpus	you must have the person (physically present in court before a judge)
in loco parentis	in the place of a parent
in re	in the matter of
inter alia	among other things
ipso facto	by the fact itself
ipso iure	by the law itself
iusta causa	just cause
locus standi	a right to appear in court
mala fide	in bad faith
mens rea	guilty mind; criminal intention
modus operandi	manner of working
non compos mentis	not sound of mind

Latin Phrase	English Meaning
obiter dictum	incidental remark; non-binding opinion
per annum	per year
per capita	per head
per se	by itself
persona non grata	an unacceptable person
prima facie	at first sight
pro forma	as a matter of form
pro rata	according to one's share
qui facit per alium facit per se	one who does something through another does it by himself
quid pro quo	one thing for another
sine qua non	without which not; a necessary condition
sub judice	under the judge

BIBLIOGRAPHY AND FURTHER READING

Abbott, F. F., *A History and Description of Roman Political Institutions* (New York 1963).

Berger, A., *Encyclopedic Dictionary of Roman Law* (Philadelphia 1953).

Borkowski, J. A., *Textbook on Roman Law*, 3rd Ed. (Oxford 2005).

Earl, D., *The Moral and Political Tradition of Rome* (Ithaca 1967).

Kunkel, W., *An Introduction to Roman Legal and Constitutional History*, 2nd Ed. (Oxford 1973).

Nicholas, B., *An Introduction to Roman Law* (Oxford 1962).

Passerin d'Entrèves, A., *Natural Law* (New Brunswick 1994).

Phillipson, C., *The International Law and Custom of Ancient Greece and Rome* 1 (New York 1979).

Staveley, E. S., *Greek and Roman Voting and Elections* (Ithaca 1972).

Stein, P. G., *The Character and Influence of Roman Civil Law* (London 1988).

Taylor, L. R., *Party Politics in the Age of Caesar* (Berkeley 1949).

Thomas, J. A. C., *Textbook of Roman Law* (Amsterdam 1976).

Winton, R. I. and Garnsey, R. I. W. P., "Political Theory," in M. I. Finley (ed.), *The Legacy of Greece: A New Appraisal* (Oxford 1984) 37–64.

WEB SITES: NAMES AND URLS

"Ancient Law"
   http://avalon.law.yale.edu/subject_menus/maineaco.asp
"Athenian Politics"
   http://ancienthistory.about.com/od/greekpolitics/Athenian_Politics.htm

"Greece — Greek Law — Ancient Greek Government"
    http://ancienthistory.about.com/od/greeklaw/Greece_Greek_Law_Ancient_
    Greek_Government.htm
"Edward Gibbon: The Idea of Roman Jurisprudence"
    http://www.fordham.edu/halsall/ancient/gibbon-chap44.html
"Law and Politics"
    http://ancienthistory.about.com/od/law/Law_and_Politics.htm
"Notes on Roman Politics"
    http://www.vroma.org/~bmcmanus/politics.html
"Roman Law"
    http://www.newadvent.org/cathen/09079a.htm
"Roman Law Resources"
    http://www.iuscivile.com
"Rome — Roman Law — Government"
    http://ancienthistory.about.com/od/romelaw/Rome_Roman_Law_Government.htm

EXERCISES

1. (a) Briefly explain what you think Aristotle meant when he described man as a
        "political animal." In your explanation you should discuss the Greek word from
        which the English word **political** is derived.
    (b) In your own words briefly explain the terms **monarchy, oligarchy,** and
        democracy and discuss whether any of these terms are sufficient to describe the
        constitution of the Roman Republic.
    (c) Give a short definition of **tyranny** in ancient Greece and suggest one explanation
        for how tyrannies were established in Greece.

2. (a) Give the meaning of the Latin word *urbs*. Then supply one English derivative from
        this word and explain its meaning.
    (b) Give the Greek and Latin words from which **noble** is derived and explain how
        their meanings relate to the English word.
    (c) Give the two bases of the English word **monarchy** and give one example of
        monarchy in ancient Greece (you may suggest either a type of monarchy or give
        the name of an ancient Greek monarch).
    (d) Give one English word that originates from the Greek work *basileus* and explain
        the derivation. Use an English dictionary if necessary.

3. For each of the following words give the base and its meaning and explain how the meaning of the English word is related to the meaning of the base.

a.	**politic**	f.	**ecclesiastic**
b.	**regulate**	g.	**rhetoric**
c.	**anarchy**	h.	**martyr**
d.	**diction**	i.	**tribune**
e.	**proletariat**	j.	**Senate**

4. Use each of the following Latin legal terms in a sentence to illustrate its meaning.

a.	*mala fide*	f.	*alibi*
b.	*de facto*	g.	*habeas corpus*
c.	*caveat emptor*	h.	*compos mentis*
d.	*ex parte*	i.	*sub judice*
e.	*in loco parentis*	j.	*de jure*

5. Consider the following passage from the *Republic* of Plato in relation to the questions that follow it.

> *Socrates:* What sort of a society will it be and how will its affairs be run? The answer, obviously, will show us the character of the democratic man.
>
> *Adeimantus:* Obviously.
>
> *Socrates:* Would you agree, first, that people will be free? There is liberty and freedom of speech in plenty, and every individual is free to do as he likes.
>
> *Adeimantus:* That's what they say.
>
> *Socrates:* Granted that freedom, won't everyone arrange his life as pleases him best?
>
> *Adeimantus:* Obviously.
>
> *Socrates:* And so, there will be in this society the greatest variety of individual character?
>
> *Adeimantus:* There's bound to be.
>
> *Socrates:* I dare say that a democracy is the most attractive of all societies. The diversity of its characters, like the different colors in a patterned dress, make it look very attractive. Indeed, perhaps most people would, for this reason, judge it to be the best form of society, like women and children when they see gaily colored things.
>
> *Adeimantus:* Very likely.
>
> *Socrates:* And, you know, it's just the place to go constitution hunting.
>
> *Adeimantus:* How so?

Socrates: It contains every possible type, because of the wide freedom it allows, and anyone engaged in founding a state, as we are doing, should perhaps be made to pay a visit to a democracy and choose what he likes from the variety of models it displays, before he proceeds to make his own foundation.

Adeimantus: It's a shop in which he'd find plenty of models on show.

Socrates: Then in a democracy, there's no compulsion either to exercise authority if you are capable of it, or to submit to authority if you don't want to; you needn't fight if there's a war, or you can wage a private war in peacetime if you don't like peace; and if there's any law that debars you from political or judicial office, you will nonetheless take either if they come your way. It's a wonderfully pleasant way of carrying on in the short run, isn't it?

Adeimantus: In the short run, perhaps.

Socrates: And isn't there something rather charming about the good temper of those who have been sentenced in court? You must have noticed that in a democracy men sentenced to death or exile stay on, nonetheless, and go about among their fellows, with no more notice taken of their comings and goings than if they were invisible spirits.

Adeimantus: I've often seen that.

Socrates: Then they're very considerate in applying the high principles we laid down when founding our state; so far from interpreting them strictly, they really look down on them. We said that no one who had not exceptional gifts could grow into a good man unless he were brought up from childhood in a good environment and trained in good habits. Democracy with a grandiose gesture sweeps all this away and doesn't mind what the habits and background of its politicians are; provided they profess themselves the people's friends, they are duly honored.

Adeimantus: All very splendid.

Socrates: These, then, and similar characteristics are those of democracy. It's an agreeable anarchic form of society, with plenty of variety, which treats all men as equal, whether they are equal or not.

Adeimantus: The description is easy to recognize.

(Plato, *Republic* 557a–558c [adapted])

(a) What are the characteristics of democracy according to this discussion in Plato's *Republic*?

(b) Do you think that Socrates believed democracy was a good form of government or not? Can you explain why he would have felt this way?

6.   Read the following passage carefully from the *Politics* of Aristotle.

> The idea of the democratic constitution is freedom. One part of freedom is "ruling and being ruled in turn," since popular justice regards people as equal in terms of numbers rather than merit, and on this view the masses must be sovereign and whatever the majority decides that is final and that is justice. This is one feature of freedom, which all democrats regard as definitive for their constitution. Another is the "live as you like" principle. This is the second defining feature of democracy and from it has come the principle of "not being ruled," not by anyone at all if possible, or at least only in turn, and this principle is as much a part of democracy as freedom based on equality.
>
> Since these are its fundamental principles and the nature of its government, democracy has the following features:
>
> all citizens are eligible for all offices;
>
> all rule over each and each, in turn, over all;
>
> offices are filled by lot, either all or at any rate those not calling for experience or knowledge;
>
> no tenure of office is dependent on the possession of a property qualification or only on a very low one;
>
> the same man may not hold the same office twice or only very rarely or a few offices, except for the military ones;
>
> term of office for all offices or as many as possible is short;
>
> jury-courts are all chosen from all the citizens who judge all or most matters, or on the most important and significant ones, such as those concerned with the constitution, the investigation of corruption, or private fraud;
>
> the assembly is the sovereign authority in all or most matters, while officials having no sovereign power over anything, or as few matters as possible;
>
> all officials (the assembly, jurors, and magistrates) are paid; if not, the magistrates, law courts, and important assemblies, or the magistracies that have to board together;
>
> since oligarchy arises from birth, wealth, and education, democracy seems to imply the opposite: low birth, poverty, and ignorance; no office is unlimited in time and if any office survives the change in government, it is restricted and officials are appointed by lot rather than by election.
>
> (Aristotle, *Politics* 6.2 [adapted])

(a)   Define the most important features of a modern democracy.

(b)   To what extent are Aristotle's features of democracy true of modern democracies?

CHAPTER 7

COMMERCE AND ECONOMICS
J. L. Hilton

ANCIENT ECONOMIC THEORIES

Greek Theories

conomics is concerned with the scarcity of resources available to a community and how these resources are allocated. In ancient Greece scarcities were frequent. Greece is a highly mountainous country with a relatively low rainfall. In ancient times the soil in Attica was so poor and difficult to plow (Menander, *The Angry Old Man* 604–606) that the historian Thucydides thought that the political stability of Athens was the result of the absence of competition over land (1.2.5): "The same people always lived in Attica as a result of the fact that it was for the most part politically stable because of the poverty of the soil." According to Hesiod, who describes the harsh farming conditions in his poem *Works and Days*, the difficulties of life are the result of the anger of the gods (42): "The gods keep the means of life hidden from men." He tells the myth of how the gods created a beautiful woman, Pandora, whom they sent to the earth with a jar containing all the bad things in life (sickness, old age, vice). When the jar was opened these evils were released into the world for the first time. In another myth he explains how life has deteriorated since the beginning of the world in a series of ages, each worse than the previous one, until his own day.

> People today are like iron;
> Neither by day nor by night will men cease
> To be worn down by toil and sorrow.
> (Hesiod, *Works and Days* 176–178)

Hesiod's answer to the scarcity brought about by such conditions is to be frugal (368–370), to work in order to avoid starvation ("If desire in your heart longs for wealth . . . then work, work, work!", 381–382; "I tell you to find a way to pay your debts and to keep hunger at bay," 403–404), and to outdo other workers in competition.

> She (Strife) stirs up even the helpless to work;
> For a man craves work when he sees someone else's
> Wealth, a man who is eager to plough and sow
> And put his house in order. Neighbor competes with neighbor
> As they strive for riches. This strife is good for men.
> Potter is jealous of potter and builder of builder;
> Beggar envies beggar and one poet vies with another.
> (Hesiod, *Works and Days* 20–26)

In giving this advice Hesiod was thinking of the work of a peasant farmer and his family. This reflects the fact that the ancient Greek and even the Roman economies were relatively underdeveloped. The basis of the economy was the *oikos* ("house"); the individual "house," for the most part, generated the income for its members. Aristotle, for example, defined the state as a collection of households (*Politics* 1253b), each household consisting of a master (*despotēs,* which is the Greek word from which the English words **despot, despotic,** and **despotism** are derived) and his slaves, husband and wife, and father and children. Therefore the Greek family was governed by three hierarchical relationships: despotic, marital, and paternal (all focused on the mature male citizen). A book on household management, the *Economicus* by Xenophon, survives that provides a good idea of the level of economic activity in the Greek *oikos.*

The Greek philosophers were aware, however, that in a well-regulated state there should a division of labor, since production would be most efficient if workers specialized in particular jobs. Therefore Plato argued that, instead of each family building its own house, growing its own food, and making its own clothing, one family should specialize in building, another in farming, and a third in weaving cloth (*Republic* 370; compare Xenophon, *Cyropaedia* 8.2.5). According to him, people are innately suited to different occupations and therefore should specialize in what they are best able to do. Furthermore, Plato knew that money functioned as a medium of exchange and that trade with other nations was a necessary part of an economy. Such commercial activity resulted in the generation of wealth, but it created extreme imbalances between rich and poor in the community. For this reason, commerce and even private property were condemned. Plato states, for example, that the guardian class in his ideal republic should live a communal life without private property.

> First, no one should possess private property unless absolutely necessary. Secondly, no one should have a building or a warehouse that people are prevented from entering if they should want to do so. As far as the supplies that disciplined and courageous men trained for war need, they should be rated to receive just enough pay for their services from the other citizens so that they have neither more nor less than they need for a year. They should dine together regularly and live communally like soldiers in a camp.
>
> (Plato, *Republic* 416e)

Plato also proposed that guardians should even have their wives in common. Both suggestions were later criticized by Aristotle, who, while acknowledging that common ownership promoted unity in the state, pointed out:

> What is common to most people is cared for least. For people think most of their own things and least about what is shared or only as much as concerns them individually. Apart from anything else people think little of such things, as if someone else were taking care of them.
>
> (Aristotle, *Politics* 1261b)

Aristotle, however, was opposed to the creation of monopolies (*Politics* 1259a) and the acquisition of money for its own sake.

Roman Theory

*T*he Romans were not greatly interested in theory and were generally pragmatic in outlook. Nevertheless they did make a contribution to economics in respect of the definitions of price, money, sale, and loans in Roman law. They were also aware of the laws of supply and demand. After the emperor Augustus returned to Rome after capturing Egypt from Cleopatra, for example, the interest rate on loans dropped sharply while the prices of property rose (Suetonius, *Augustus* 41).

Inflation, however, was not clearly understood. Toward the end of the Roman Empire, in the fourth century CE, the money was devalued to such an extent that hyper-inflation set in. To combat the situation, the emperor Diocletian published an edict listing the maximum prices that could be charged for various items, but this simply had the effect of creating a flourishing black market. Because of inflation, the economy ceased to operate as a money economy and reverted to the barter system.

Another area in which the Romans made a significant contribution to economics was in agriculture. Surviving textbooks on the management of farms give detailed advice on how to run large estates.

Word Study

- **Agriculture** comes from the Latin word *ager* ("field," "land") and *cultura* ("cultivation," "tillage," "care"). Related words are **agronomy** and **agrarian.**
- **Commerce** is derived from the Latin prefix *com-* ("together") and *merx* ("goods," "merchandise"). Related words are **merchant, mercantile, merchandise, meretricious, mercury,** and **mercy.**
- **Communism** comes from the Latin word *communis* ("common"). Hence communism is (in simple terms) a society in which property is held in common.
- **Competition** is derived from the Latin prefix *com-* ("together") and *petere* ("to seek," "to look for") with the noun suffix *-tion* at the end.
- **Economy** comes from the Greek term *oikonomia*, which is derived from *oikos* ("house") and *nomos* ("law"), and means "household management." The base derived from *oikos* was later spelled *oeco-* and then *eco-*. Other words related to this base include not only **ecology, ecosphere,** and **ecosystem,** but also **ecumenical** and **parochial.**
- **Inflation** is derived from the Latin prefix *in-* ("into") and verb *flare* ("to blow"; base *fla-*) with the noun suffix *-tion* at the end. Inflation refers to the blowing up of or increase in prices.
- **Manage** comes from Latin *manus* ("hand") and has the meaning "take in hand," "take charge of." Compare **mandate,** "instruction" (something placed in one's hand) and **demand,** "ask for," "require."

- **Monopoly** is derived from the Greek *monos* ("alone") and *polein* ("to sell") and is used to refer to a situation in which one person has cornered the market in a particular commodity and is alone able to sell goods.

AGRICULTURE IN THE ANCIENT WORLD

Greek Agriculture

Greek farmers concentrated mainly on the cultivation of barley, wine, and olives, but grain had to be imported from the Black Sea (see below on "Greek Trade and Transport"). Olives were pressed to make olive oil, which was exported. This situation was true of Greece in general since Herodotus states (7.102) that the land had always been poor. What fertile soil there was had been eroded by floods over the years (Plato, *Critias* 111b): "As in the case of the small islands . . . now the rich and soft parts of the land have been eroded and only the thin skeleton of the land remains, like the bones of a diseased body." The poverty of the land in Attica should not be exaggerated, however, since Aristophanes (frag-

An early Greek lever press

ments 109, 110, 387, 569) and Sophocles (*Oedipus at Colonus* 668–719) give a more positive picture and, according to Aristotle, the climate was ideal, neither too cold nor too hot, and therefore the Greeks had both energy and intelligence unlike the Europeans and Asiatics, who had one or the other of these qualities (*Politics* 1327b; compare also Hippocrates, *On Airs, Waters, and Places* 12.23: "Climates differ and cause differences of character"; Xenophon, *Revenues* 1.3, 6).

Roman Agriculture

During the early Republic, farms in Italy were generally small but with the influx of wealth into the economy these small farms were bought up by wealthy landowners and converted to "estates" (*latifundia*) worked by gangs of slaves. Extensive use, of course, was made of animal labor as well. For example, mills for grinding grain (in agriculture) and ore (in mining), for example, were designed to be driven by oxen or donkeys. This process can be seen in the work of Cato, who admired the efficiency of Carthaginian agriculture, which was based on large estates worked by slave labor with a high degree of specialization and run on a profit-making basis. Cato wrote a practical textbook *On Agriculture* based on the work of a Carthaginian, Mago, which has survived until today.

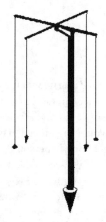

Roman surveying instrument (groma)

In some cases land that belonged to the state (*ager publicus*) was taken by force (Appian, *Civil Wars* 1.26; Sallust, *Jugurthine War* 41.8). The Licinian-Sextian law, which allowed a maximum of 500 *iugera*, or "acres" (a *iugerum* is about two-thirds of an English acre), of land to any one citizen, was ignored. The consul of 131 BCE, Publius Licinius Crassus, was said to have had at least 100,000 *iugera*. Public land from time to time was divided up, however, and allotted to the citizens of Rome. In order to do this the land was carefully surveyed (by *agrimensores*) and measured into strips. This process was known as **centuriation** (*centuriatio*) since it was composed of *centuriae* consisting of "100" (*centum*) "plots" (*heredia*). Each *centuria* was separated from the others by "boundary lines" (*limites*).

The Grain Supply

The supply of grain to Rome was carefully regulated by the Senate although it was essentially a private market. At the end of the second century BCE the Roman assembly passed a "grain law" (*lex frumentaria*) under which a limited amount of grain was supplied to Roman citizens at a fixed price. Most of the grain was imported from Egypt and Africa. Egyptian grain was transported in massive cargo ships from Alexandria to the port of Ostia, the nearest harbor to the city of Rome, from where it was brought to the city by the Tiber River or by road. Water was brought to the city by aqueducts such as the *Aqua Appia* ("Appian Aqueduct," completed in 312 BCE) and the *Aqua Anio Vetus* ("Old Anian Aqueduct," completed in 272 BCE).

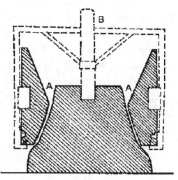

Grain or ore mill
(A = grinding stones; B = wooden frame)

Food Welfare

The price of grain was gradually reduced in Rome until eventually it was distributed free in the middle of the first century BCE, although the number of people who qualified to receive it was restricted. Julius Caesar, for example, who was dictator in Rome from 49 until 44 BCE, only allowed 150,000 citizens of Rome to receive the grain free.

During the first and second centuries CE a feeding scheme for children of the poor (*alimenta*) was established in Italy. This scheme was financed by interest from investments of money raised by mortgages of land. Often money was given by the emperors on security of land put forward by landowners. The purpose of the scheme was to increase the birth rate with a view to the eventual conscription of young men into the army.

FINANCIAL SYSTEMS

Greek Money and Coinage

Money is any medium of exchange that is widely accepted in payment for goods and services and in settlement of debts. The functions of money as a medium of exchange and a measure of value greatly facilitate the exchange of goods and services and the specialization of production. Without the use of money trade would be reduced to barter, the direct exchange of one commodity for another. In a barter economy a person that has something to trade must find another who wants it and has something acceptable to offer in exchange. In a money economy the owner of a commodity may sell it for money, which is acceptable in payment for goods, and therefore avoids the time and effort that would be required to find someone who could make an acceptable trade. Money is therefore indispensable for an effective economy.

Cattle were used as money in early times; other kinds of money were tools such as axes, tripods, cauldrons, rings, anchors, or metal bars. The word for the Greek unit of money, the talent, originally meant "balance" (in the sense of an instrument for weighing). Another unit, the obol (compare **obelisk,** from *obeliskos*), came from the word for "spit," or "nail," which was used as money, with six nails making a handful (*drachmē*). Money in the form of coinage was invented at about 630 BCE by a king in Asia who hit upon the idea of shaping precious metal into bean-shaped lumps of fixed weight and purity and stamping them with official symbols guaranteeing their value. By 550 BCE the practice of striking coins was established in all the important trading cities throughout the known world. The study of such coinages is known as **numismatics** (from *nomisma*, "custom," "coin"). The study of coins, such as the one following from Cyrene, can shed much light on social, political, and economic conditions in antiquity since images, words and symbols were struck on Greek and Roman coins. For centuries all but the very lowest denominations of coins had intrinsic value; that is, they

*Drachma from Cyrene (North Africa) showing the head of Zeus Ammon
(obverse) and a silphium plant (reverse). Silphium (now extinct) was the
source of the wealth of Cyrene and was used as food, medicine and perfume.
(Courtauld Collection 114)*

contained gold or silver equal to their face value. The weight and purity of the metal of these coins had to be tested every time it changed hands. Later, however, precious-metal coins were replaced with coins made from inexpensive metals and that had face value only. Because the Athenian coins had intrinsic value they could be used to trade anywhere in the Mediterranean (compare Xenophon, *Revenues* 3.2) and at some time in the fifth century BCE (the date is uncertain), the Athenians passed a decree enforcing the use of their coins, weights, and measures as a standard and requiring other coinages to be exchanged for them. This decree increased the control Athens had over trade in the Aegean. The most important denominations were the drachma, mina, and talent.

Greek Finance

$\mathcal{A}$thens had a coinage and banking system that arose from the necessity of changing one currency into another (money changing). Private banks were probably first established in Mesopotamia in the seventh century BCE, but "bankers," *trapezitai*, entered the public domain in Greece, where bankers set up their "tables," *trapezai* (compare **trapeze,** "a set of crossbars used as a swing by acrobats," and **trapezium,** a quadrilateral with one set of sides parallel) around temples. Another important service that bankers provided was usury, or money-lending, a practice that initially aroused strong moral condemnation (as it has done when introduced to other cultures) but that was later tolerated.

Various insurance schemes were devised; for example, bankers sometimes lent money at high rates of interest (up to 120 per cent) on the security of the cargo of a ship. When the cargo came into harbor safely the loan had to be repaid, but if the ship and its cargo sank the loan was written off. Such loans were know as a bottomry loans and were important for the development of sea trade, which was a risky business in the classical period (the first known loan was issued in 421 BCE). This kind of loan contains an element of insurance in it. The loans were sometimes subject to frauds (compare Demosthenes, *Against Sdenothemis* 32.5).

Banking was further developed in Ptolemaic Egypt, where a network of banks was established in the provinces and towns of the country with a central bank in Alexandria. These were private banks which employed large numbers of people to pay out money on behalf of the state and to collect taxes and revenues. Endorsements and bills of exchange were known to have been used here. This model of banking was eventually extended by the Roman administration all over the Mediterranean.

Roman Money

$\mathcal{T}$he economy of the Roman empire was clearly a money economy as opposed to a barter economy. As in Greece, the Romans at first used cattle as a standard of monetary value. The Latin word for "money," *pecunia*, is derived from *pecus*, the Roman word for "cattle"; English "fee" and Indian "rupee" are also derived from words meaning "cattle." Up to the time of the first Roman laws, the Twelve Tables, all fines were paid in units of cattle and sheep.

Coins (from the Latin *cuneus*, "wedge," which was used in striking coins) were originally made of copper and were introduced into Italy from Sicily, where they were known as *litrae* (*litra*, from which **liter** is derived, is related to *libra*, "measuring scales"). Rough ingots of bronze, *aes rude* (literally, "rough bronze"), were also used but later replaced with ingots engraved with an image, *aes signatum* (literally, "marked bronze"). *Aes* ("bronze") is the basis of the Latin word *aestimare* ("to estimate"), which later became the English word **esteem.** Bronze coins known as *asses* were used during the early Republic but lost a lot of their value during the Carthaginian Wars when the silver *denarius* (*denarius* gave rise to the **dinar** now used in the Middle East), the *sestertius* ("sesterce"), the gold *aureus*, and later the *solidus* started to be struck.

Word for Word

Money was stored in the temple of Juno Moneta; a building next to this temple was also the place where coins were minted, but later, other mints were established in the provinces of the empire, particularly Lugdunum (modern Lyon). The writing on these coins often advertised the policy of the Senate, politicians, and emperors. The example below shows that coins can also give important information about the provinces of the Roman empire.

The Roman Treasury and the Imperial Fisc

The **tribute** (*tributum*) from the subject nations of the Roman empire was paid into the treasury (*aerarium*, literally, "a place for bronze"), which was located in the temple of Saturn in Rome. Legal documents concerning tribute were also housed here. The treasury was originally administered by quaestors with the assistance of **scribes** (*scribae*), but later, the quaestors were replaced by **prefects** (*praefecti*). Later, money from the provinces was kept in the imperial fisc in each province rather than being transferred to Rome. The fisc of the emperors was managed by **procurators** (*procuratores*) and fiscal **advocates** (*advocati*).

Tetradrachm showing Cleopatra VII of Egypt (obverse) and Antony (reverse). Writing around the edge of the coin reads "Queen Cleopatra, new goddess" and "Antony, ruler and triumvir," respectively. At this time Antony and Cleopatra were allied against Octavian (later Augustus). (Courtauld Collection 53)

Word Study

- **Commodity** comes from Latin *commodum* ("convenience," "useful thing").
- **Finance** is derived from the Latin *finis* ("end"). Try to explain the reason for this derivation.
- **Fiscal,** "to do with public revenue," is derived from the Latin word *fiscus.*

Word for Word

- **Money** is derived from *moneta*, an adjective referring to the goddess Juno, since money was stored in her temple. The word **mint,** a place where money is coined, is related to *moneta.*
- **Specialize** is derived from Latin *species* ("appearance"). What other terms in English have the same base?
- The English word **talent,** "innate ability," is derived from Greek, *talanton* ("balance," "weight," "sum of money"). How do you think this meaning arose?
- **Usury** comes from the Latin *usura* (the base of this word means "use"). Compare also **credit** (Latin *credere,* "to believe") and **debt** (Latin *debere,* "to owe"). The Latin word *mutuari* ("to borrow") has produced **mutual** in English.

ROMAN BUSINESS

Company Organization

Public works like the aqueducts and roads of Rome were undertaken by *publicani* ("contractors"). They always acted in association, perhaps to minimize the risk. In many ways these associations of contractors resemble modern companies. For the temple of Sarapis at Puteoli, the small total of 1,500 sesterces was bid by five contractors (105 BCE). The chief of the contractors was the bidder *(manceps)* and acted as *praes,* a security for the bid. Land was generally demanded as collateral. The other four contractors were *socii* ("partners") in the company. In bigger deals probably more than one *praes* would be required. The partners had to be registered and constituted the company. Normally Roman law did not recognize a group of individuals acting as a company, but this status was conferred on some publican corporations, which enabled them to own property and transact business like modern companies. The conferring of legal corpus on a company was probably done by a law passed through the assembly. Mention is also made of *adfines*, who had likewise to be registered. They were probably less privileged partners in the company.

Public Contracts

Public contracts in Rome were awarded by the censor. The contractors were used for a wide variety of contracts (particularly provisions for the army, for religious ceremonies and for public buildings) and Polybius emphasizes that no one was unaffected by them. As in all company affairs, the ruin of the company affects many people. Two examples of contracts follow.

> When the day came, three companies of nineteen men were present to undertake the contracts. These men demanded two things: first, that they should be exempt from military service while they were engaged in public business; secondly, that the state should take on the risk from storms and enemy action to the freight they loaded on their ships. Both demands were accepted and they undertook the contract; the state was administered by private funding.
>
> (Livy 23.49.1–2)

> When the censors suspended the auctioning of contracts for the maintenance of sacred buildings and the supply of horses for ceremonies and similar matters because of the shortage of funds in the treasury, those who usually bid for these contracts assembled in large numbers and urged the censors to carry on with public business as if there were money in the treasury; they said that no one would ask for money from the treasury unless the war was ended.
>
> (Livy 24.18.10)

The publicans had a very bad reputation in the Republic (Livy 45.18.4; Cicero, *Letters to His Brother Quintus* 1.1.32), but they kept the armies supplied throughout the critical times of the Republic's history. Occasionally the contractors were unable to repay the amount they had bid. In 169 BCE the censors of this year, Tiberius Sempronius Gracchus and Gaius Claudius Pulcher, did not allow any of the contractors of 174 BCE to bid (Livy 43.16.2). The tribune Publius Rutilius tried to get the edict of the censors cancelled. The people and the Senate, however, stood by the censors in their move.

Clubs

There were a number of clubs (*collegia,* **college**) in Roman society that met in temples and later clubhouses (*scholae,* **schools**). These were originally religious in character (for example, the Bacchanalian cult), but later became political (the emperor Augustus legislated that every club had to be approved of by the emperor or the Senate).

Clubs were sometimes established to pay for burials. Members met once a month to pay their contributions into a fund and to enjoy a communal dinner on special occasions such as birthdays. The clubs elected leaders (*patroni*, **patrons**) and their money was administered by accountants (*quaestores*, **quaestors**). Often these clubs were composed of members of the same craft, but there is no indication that they tried to improve their working conditions, as modern unions do.

GREEK TRADE AND TRANSPORT

Athenian Sea Power

In classical times Athenian politicians developed the harbor at Piraeus, a natural triple harbor which was only eight kilometers from Athens, and rebuilt the long walls between Athens and Piraeus after they had been pulled down during the Persian Wars. They also insisted on maintaining the strength of the Athenian fleet, which played a vital role in protecting the economy and maintaining democracy in Athens. In wartime landowners could be persuaded to tolerate the destruction of their crops only because they could transfer their property to the islands and ensure that it was protected by the fleet.

Greek Trade

One consequence of the relative poverty of Attic agriculture was that Athens turned to the sea as a source of food and wealth (Greek *ploutos*, from which the English words **plutocrat** and **plutocracy** are derived) through trade. The coastline of Greece is uniquely long for an area of its size, and numerous islands dot the Aegean Sea.

The central position of Athens in the Aegean helped the city to control trade which was certainly vital for her prosperity (compare Xenophon, *Revenues* 6–8) and Athens naturally attracted large numbers of immigrants (*metics*). Trade itself was only possible in the first place because Athens controlled the sea and certain imports such as timber and grain were essential and had to be protected, but others such as ivory from Africa, carpets and cushions from Carthage, and ropes and papyrus from Egypt were luxury goods. Merchants traded in grain not only between the Black Sea area and Athens, but they also took the grain to wherever it was in most demand. Piraeus was an important center not only for the Athenian navy but also for industry (Latin *industria*, "diligence") and commerce.

Athens did not hesitate to restrict the markets of other Greek city states such as Megara by banning her merchants from the "market places" (*agorai*) controlled by Athens. Although the precise terms of the decree are not certain, the effect of it was similar to trade sanctions. Athens also managed the shipping that passed through the straits of the Hellespont and regulated the trade in grain. Athenian merchants had a preferential trade agreement with the rulers of the Black Sea area.

ROMAN TRADE AND TRANSPORT

Trade

Entrepreneurial trade by "merchants" (*mercatores, negotiatores*) was limited in the Roman empire, although there are instances of venture capitalism, such as that of Trimalchio (Petronius, *Satyricon* 76) who shipped wine and other commodities from Asia to Italy. Most trade consisted of the movement of raw materials and foodstuffs and this was often undertaken by the imperial government. Trade both inside and outside the Roman empire at the height of the *pax Romana* (a long period of peace and prosperity within the borders of the empire known as the "Roman peace") was extensive. The balance of trade did not necessarily favor Rome; the emperor Tiberius is said to have been concerned at the drainage of gold to India in payment for cloth and precious stones (Tacitus, *Annals* 2.33, 3.53; Pliny, *Natural History* 6.101; 12.84).

Road Transport

The Romans built an extensive network of roads from an early date. The *Via Appia* ("Appian Way") from Rome to Capua (later to Brundisium) was constructed in 312 BCE; the *Via Flaminia* ("Flaminian Way") from Rome to Ariminum in 268 BCE, extended to Bononia as the *Via Aemilia* ("Aemilian Way") in 187 BCE. By the end of the Republic, most of Italy was connected by roads. During the Empire this road system was extended throughout the provinces. The roads were financed by the public treasury, local contributions, and imperial assistance and served an economic and social as well as a strategic role.

Sea Transport

The Romans built large freighters to carry bulk cargoes. One such freighter, which was used by the emperor Caligula to bring an obelisk from Egypt to Rome (Pliny, *Natural History* 16.201; Lucian, *The Ship* 5), could handle about 1,300 tons of freight; by way of comparison, the largest supertanker today carries 550,000 metric tons of oil.

*A drawing based on a mosaic
showing a Roman cargo ship with a freight of amphorae*

The major trading commodities, their provenance and names are listed below.

Commodity	Latin Name	Provenance
glass	*vitrum*	Egypt, Italy
gold	*aureum*	Spain, Dacia, Egypt
grain	*frumentum*	Egypt, Sicily, Africa
ivory	*ebur*	Africa
lead	*plumbum*	Spain, Britain, Sardinia
marble	*marmor*	Greece, Italy, Carthage
myrrh	*myrrha*	Somalia
olive oil	*oleum*	Spain, Carthage, Syria
paper	*papyrus*	Egypt
pearls	*margaritae*	India, Britain
pitch	*bitumen*	Judea
pottery	*fictilia* (Greek *ceramica*)	Greece, Italy, Spain
purple dye	*purpura*	Syria
silk	*serica*	China
silver	*argentum*	Spain, Gaul, Greece
tin	*plumbum, candidum*	Spain, Britain
wine	*vinum*	Gaul, Italy, Spain, Greece

After the *pax Romana* was established throughout the empire and pirates were driven from the seas during the late Republic, travel among the various regions of the Mediterranean increased. This freedom of movement on the seas greatly facilitated trade, since transport by sea was much cheaper than by land. In addition, Greek merchants had discovered the monsoon winds that prevailed between India and the Red Sea. As a result, trade was possible between the Mediterranean and Africa, India, and even China (from which the Romans imported silk). Details of this trade are given in a work entitled *Circumnavigation of the Red Sea*, which still survives. One passage from this work discusses Arab trade with East Africa, specifically modern Zanzibar.

> Two days' sailing beyond there lies the very last market-town (*emporium*) of the continent of Azania which is called Rhapta, which has its name from the sewed boats already mentioned and in which there is ivory in great quantity and tortoise-shell. Along this coast live men of piratical habits, very great in stature, and under separate chiefs for each place. The Mapharitic chief governs it under some ancient right that subjects it to the sovereignty of the state that is become first in Arabia. And the people of Muza now hold it under his authority and send many large ships there, using Arab captains and agents who not only are familiar with the natives and intermarry with them but also know the whole coast and understand the language.
>
> (*Circumnavigation of the Red Sea* 16)

Another passage lists goods traded at Ozene, a city in India.

> There are imported into this market-town wine, Italian preferred, also Laodicean and Arabian; copper, tin, and lead; coral and topaz; thin clothing and inferior sorts of all kinds; bright-colored girdles a cubit wide; storax, sweet clover, flint glass, realgar, antimony, gold and silver coins on which there is a profit when exchanged for the money of the country; and ointment, but not very costly and not much. And for the King there are brought into those places very costly vessels of silver, singing boys, beautiful maidens for the harem, fine wines, thin clothing of the finest weaves, and the choicest ointments. There are exported from these places spikenard, costus, bdellium, ivory, agate and carnelian, lycium, cotton cloth of all kinds, silk cloth, mallow cloth, yarn, long pepper, and such other things as are brought here from the various market-towns.
>
> (*Circumnavigation of the Red Sea* 16)

Word Study

- Latin *conventio* (Latin; "coming together," "agreement") has produced **conventional** and **convention.**
- Latin *manceps* ("a bidder," "a purchaser"), which is derived from from *manus* ("hand") and *capere* ("to take"), means literally "to take in hand." Compare **emancipate**, "to take out of someone's power," "to liberate."
- **Entrepreneur** ("businessman," "risk-taker") comes from Latin *prehendere* ("to seize," via French *entreprise*, "bold undertaking"). Compare **comprehend** and **apprehend.**
- Latin *industria* ("activity") produces **industry, industrial,** and **industrious.**
- **Island** is derived from Latin *insula*, which also produces **insulate, insulin,** and **isle**.
- Latin *navis* ("ship") results in **navigate** and **navy**. This word is related to Greek *naus*, which produces **nausea, nauseous,** and **nautical.**

Word for Word

- Latin *negotium* ("lack of leisure [*otium*]") produces **negotiate**. *Otium* gives **otiose** ("redundant," "unnecessary").
- Latin *pax* ("peace") produces **pacify** and **pact** in English.
- Latin *publicanus* ("relating to the public revenues," "a contractor") comes from *populus* ("people"), which gives **publish, publican, populace,** and **popular.**
- Latin *sancire* ("to make sacred," "to establish," "to fix unalterably") produces **sanction.** Compare **sacrosanct, sanctuary,** and **sanctify, sanctimonious.**
- Latin *socius* ("ally," "partner") produces **social, society, associate,** and **sociology.**

THE ROLE OF SLAVERY IN THE GREEK AND ROMAN ECONOMIES

a contemporary film such as *Amistad* reminds us that slavery was openly practiced in the fairly recent past and, of course, slavery still persists in the form of sexual bondage and child labor. In Greece slavery was present from the earliest times and continued until the time of the Roman Empire. The economies of Greece and Rome are therefore often described in terms of the slave mode of production. Enslavement often resulted from defeat in war or from piracy, poverty, or punishment. Often people were born into slavery; the Romans called such slaves *vernae*.

Although some Greeks believed that slavery was natural, others viewed it as an unjust convention, as the following passage by Aristotle shows.

> We must consider whether a person is a slave by nature or not, and whether it is right and just for someone to be a slave or not, or whether all slavery is contrary to nature. . . It is clear that some people are free and others slaves for whom enslavement is advantageous and right. . . But many lawyers criticize this law as they would someone who proposes something illegal, saying that it is monstrous that people who are oppressed by force should be ruled and enslaved by those who are able to use violence as a result of their superior power.
>
> (Aristotle, *Politics* 1254 [adapted])

One consequence of slavery was that Greeks and Romans often considered work to be something that a free man should not have to do. Yet in Athens, slaves (Greek *douloi*) and free men often worked together and strangers often found it hard to tell them apart. Slaves in Greece were relatively inexpensive and most Athenians owned one or two, sometimes more. They were therefore employed in industry. According to Lysias, a shield factory employed 120 slaves; a sword factory employed thirty-three slaves; a couch factory had twenty slaves; and a shoemaking business thirteen slaves.

The greatest use of slaves, though, was in mining. The silver mines at Athens were run by wealthy men, who hired 1,000 slaves to the manager of the mines at a price of one obol per slave per day (Xenophon, *Revenues* 4.15). The Athenian historian Xenophon suggests setting up a subscription scheme to finance the further exploitation of the silver in the mines (*metalla*; *Revenues* 3.6–11). Conditions in the mines were often very primitive, and mortality must have been high.

Slavery was also practiced in the Roman world. The continuous cycle of wars that Rome fought against Carthage, Macedonia, and other Mediterranean powers resulted in the influx of vast numbers of slaves (Latin *servi*) from newly conquered provinces and provided ample labor for building projects despite the slave wars that broke out from time to time; the most famous was the revolt of Spartacus in 72 BCE. There was a certain amount of social mobility for slaves at Rome, however, since Roman law recognized the slave's right to own property (*peculium*) and allowed various ways in which a slave could be **manumitted**. (On this word see "Word Study" below.)

Manumitted slaves were known as "freedmen" *(liberti)*. Freedmen frequently acted as business managers for their previous owners, and many became rich in the process. This relationship was a special case of what was known as the patron-client relationship. Many **clients** (even freedmen) were buried with their patrons, and it is clear that the relationship was close.

It is apparent that Roman slave owners were dependent on the labor of their slaves and that self-interest must have compelled them to look after the health of their workers. On balance, however, the system of slavery probably had a negative effect on the economy of the Roman empire since there was little incentive to develop technology when slave labor was readily available.

Word Study

- Latin *cliens* has produced English **client** and **clientele.**
- Latin *libertus* ("freedman") is derived from *liber* ("free"), which also produced Latin *libertas* ("freedom"), from which Middle French *liberté* and in turn English **liberty** are derived.
- Latin *manumittere* ("to release from power"); literally, "to send" *(mittere)* + "from the hand" *(manu)* gives **manumit**. Other words from *manus* are **manufacture, manuscript, manual,** and **maneuver** (compare **manure,** from Middle French *manouvrer,* "to do work by hand," "to cultivate," from Latin *manu operare,* literally, "to work with the hand").
- Latin *servus* ("slave") has produced **servant, service,** and **servile.**

THE ROLE OF TECHNOLOGY
IN THE GREEK AND ROMAN ECONOMIES

lthough Greeks and Romans did not exploit their technology (Greek *technē*, "art," "craft," "skill") for commercial advantage, they did apply it to military inventions such as catapults (Latin *catapultus*, from Greek *catapeltēs*, "through the hide," that is, capable of piercing leather shields). There were a great number of these ranging from the small *gastraphetēs* ("stomach bowman"; compare **gastric**) to the larger *ballista* ("thrower"). These machines were the forerunners of modern artillery and were capable of propelling missiles over considerable distances with great force, although they were not particularly accurate. A catapult built by Hieron II of Syracuse was capable of firing a bolt 5.5 meters long up to 185 metres. Other ballistic machines could throw stones of about eighteen kilograms over a similar distance.

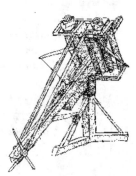

A Roman catapault (ballista)

Some of the most impressive structures throughout the Roman empire were the aqueducts. These aqueducts were major feats of mechanical (Greek *mekhanē*, "contrivance"; Latin *machina*) and hydraulic engineering and involved tunnels and vaulted bridges that sometimes spanned extensive ravines and considerable distances. The water was used principally for baths, which played an important role in daily life in the entire Roman empire.

Another area in which technology was developed in the Roman world was in agriculture. During the early Republic, farms in Italy were generally small, but with the influx of wealth into the economy these small farms were bought up by wealthy landowners and converted to estates *(latifundia)* worked by gangs of slaves. Because of the relative scarcity of land, the Romans invented techniques of land surveying, which is referred to above in the section on "Roman Agriculture." Mills powered by animals (oxen or donkeys) or by water were invented to boost productivity.

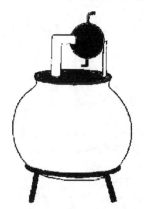

Steam turbine of Heron of Alexandria

The development of technology in the Roman world probably was impeded by the system of slavery that sustained the economy. Greek scientists had discovered the principle of steam propulsion and they knew about metal cylinders, pistons, and valves, as in the case of the manual force pump of Ctesibius, for instance, but no steam engine was invented because the work that a machine could perform could be done less expensively by slaves.

Word Study

- Greek *ballein* ("to throw") has given **ballistic, anabolic, emblem,** and **problem.**
- **Hydraulics** is the study of the properties of water in pipes and is derived from Greek *hydr-* ("water") and *aulos* ("pipe"); the base *hydro-* is commonly used in scientific terms such as **hydrogen** and **hydrochloride.**
- Latin *ingenium* has produced **engine.** Related words are **ingenious, genius, gene,** and **photogenic.**

Word for Word

- Greek *mekhanē* ("contrivance"; Latin *machina*), has produced **machine, mechanical,** and **mechanize.**
- Greek *metallon* ("mine") has produced **metal, metallic, metallurgy,** and **metalloid.**
- Greek *technē* ("art," "craft," "skill"), has resulted in **technology, technique, technocracy,** and **technobabble.**
- The Latin word *verna* ("home-bred slave") has produced the English word **vernacular** ("commonly spoken language").

BIBLIOGRAPHY AND FURTHER READING

Cohen, E., *Athenian Economy and Society: A Banking Perspective* (Princeton 1992).

Duncan-Jones, R., *The Economy of the Roman Empire: Quantitative Studies,* 2nd Ed. (Cambridge 1982).

Finley, M. I. (ed.), *Economy and Society in Ancient Greece* (London 1983).

Garnsey, P. and Saller, R., *The Roman Empire: Economy, Society and Culture* (Berkeley 1987).

Jones, A. H. M. (ed. P. A. Brunt), *The Roman Economy: Studies in Ancient Economic and Administrative History* (Totowa 1974).

Klemm, F. (tr. D. W. Singer), *A History of Western Technology* (Ames 1991) 17–52.

Kranzberg, M. and Pursell, C. W. (eds.), *Technology in Western Civilization* (New York 1967) 47–66.

Laistner, M. L. W., *Greek Economics: Introduction and Translation* (New York 1974).

Landreth, H. and Colander, D. C., *History of Economic Thought,* 4th Ed. (Boston 2001) 24–35.

Neuburger, A. (tr. H. L. Brose), *The Technical Arts and Sciences of the Ancients* (New York 1969).

Schumpeter, J. A. (ed. E. B. Schumpeter), *History of Economic Analysis*, 2nd Ed. (New York 1994) 51–72.

Singer, C. J., Holmyard, E. J., Hall, A. R., and William, T. I. (eds.), *A History of Technology 2: The Mediterranean Civilizations and the Middle Ages c. 700 B.C. to c. A.D. 1500* (Oxford 1956).

White, K. D., *Greek and Roman Technology* (Ithaca 1984).

WEB SITES: NAMES AND URLS

"Ancient Greek Methods of Boating and Sailing"
http://www.mlahanas.de/Greeks/ships/ships.htm
"Aqueducts and Roads of Ancient Rome"
http://ancienthistory.about.com/od/aqueductsroads/Aqueducts_and_Roads_of_Ancient_Rome.htm
"Economics, Coins, and Taxes"
http://ancienthistory.about.com/od/economics/Economics_Coins_and_Taxes.htm
"Greece — Rome — Engineering — Mechanics"
http://ancienthistory.about.com/od/greekmechanics/Greece_Rome_Engineering_Mechanics.htm
"Greek Cities"
http://www.historylink101.com/lessons/farm-city/greece-city.htm
"Greek Farming"
http://www.historylink101.com/lessons/farm-city/greece1.htm

EXERCISES

1. (a) Name three features of the economy of Athens that you think were most important for its growth. Explain why you think these features were important.

   (b) Name two actions undertaken by the Roman state that promoted economic activity in the Mediterranean. Explain why you think these actions were important for the development of the Roman economy.

   (c) Briefly explain how public contracts were awarded in Rome.

   (d) Name two ways in which the Romans attempted to deal with the problem of poverty in Rome and Italy.

   (e) Name two functions performed by banks in Greek and Roman times.

2. (a) From what you have read, name one factor that inhibited Greek and Roman technology and one factor that promoted it.
   (b) Briefly explain why you think the manual force pump illustrated below in question 5 was important for the ancient Roman economy.
   (c) Give a brief description of Roman farming.
   (d) Explain what was, in your opinion, the most important difference between Greek (especially Athenian) and Roman agriculture.

3. (a) From what you have read, give two reasons why Athens became a strong trading power.
   (b) Based on your reading, give two reasons why trade links were established between the Roman empire, India, and east Africa.
   (c) Give one reason why trade between the Mediterranean and India became significant at the time of the Roman Empire.

4. (a) Give the bases and the meaning of the bases of the word **agriculture.**
   (b) Give the base of the words **spectacle** and **specious** and its meaning, then explain how the meanings of the English words are derived from this base.
   (c) Give the base of the words **commerce** and **mercy** and its meaning, then explain how the meanings of the English words are derived from this base.
   (d) For each of the following words give the base and its meaning, then explain how the meaning of the English word is related to the meaning of the base. Use an English dictionary if necessary.

1.	**mercury**	9.	**genius**
2.	**metallic**	10.	**finance**
3.	**otiose**	11.	**aquarium**
4.	**profit**	12.	**emblem**
5.	**servile**	13.	**specimen**
6.	**negotiate**	14.	**engine**
7.	**populace**	15.	**finesse**
8.	**nausea**	16.	**utility**

5. Consider the following diagram and the list of Latin words carefully, then answer the account and the questions that follow it.

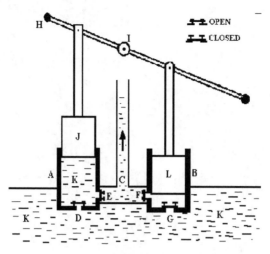

A manual force pump

Latin Words

(A, B) *cylindrus* ("a hollow roller"; Greek *kylindros*)
(D, E, F, G) *valva* ("a folding door")
(H) *levare* ("to lift," "to raise")
(I) *fulcire* ("to support")
(J) *pinsere* ("to beat"; *pistum*)

(a) Complete the following account of how this manual force pump worked by inserting the letters corresponding to the parts mentioned in the description in the spaces provided between brackets. Some terms have been left out. Supply the correct English terms using the Latin words as clues. The terms and letters may be used more than once.

Two brass _____ (A) and (B) are connected by an inverted T-shaped pipe (C). Inserted into the bottom and inner sides of these are four _____ (D), ( ), ( ), and ( ). When the handle of the _____ (H), which is attached to a _____ (I) is pushed down, the _____ (J) forces water (K) inside the _____ (A) down, closes _____ (D), opens _____ ( ), closes _____ ( ), and forces the water up the pipe (C). At the same time the _____ (L) in the other _____ ( ) is raised. This opens _____ ( ) and draws water into the _____ (B) ready for the next downstroke.

(b) What are the possible applications of this force pump?
(c) What other inventions could cylinders, pistons, and valves have been used in?

CHAPTER 8

PHILOSOPHY AND PSYCHOLOGY

A. Gosling and W. J. Dominik

INQUIRY

The idea of **inquiry** is essential to Greek philosophy. The earliest Greek philosophers pursued inquiries not only about the nature and origin of the universe but also about the nature of man, so that eventually they extended their inquiries to the field of ethics. Inquiry is also fundamental to the discipline of psychology. There was no such subject as psychology, however, in ancient Greece or Rome. Although the word psychology is coined from two Greek bases, the subject itself was only developed as a separate discipline in the nineteenth century. The Greeks and Romans were interested in human psychology, the study of the behavior and reactions of individuals in particular circumstances and under particular stresses. Their mythology, tragedies, and poetry raise many psychological questions, while ancient historians laid great stress on the role played by individuals in the causes and course of historical events and consequently included analysis of character as an important part of historiography.

Word Study

- What are the bases of **philosophy** and **psychology?** Use an English dictionary, if necessary.

Word	First Base	Second Base
philosophy		
psychology		

- Think of some English words with these Greek bases: *phil-, log-, soph-*.
- Use an English dictionary to establish the meaning of the following words: **psychic, psychosis, psychedelic, psychogenetic** (compare Greek *genesis*), and **psychokinesis.**
- Study the following Greek words. Combine their bases with the base *psych-* to form English words, then work out the meaning of the words so formed.

Greek Word	Meaning	English Word	Meaning
analysis			
iatros			
pathos			
soma			
therapeuein			

LOGOS

Word Study

*T*he word *logos* (discourse) has a wide range of meanings in ancient Greek. It can mean:

- the actual word by which the inward idea is expressed
- the idea itself; hence "thought," "reason"
- "word," "language," "talk," "proverb"
- "story" (What other Greek words mean "story"?)
- "proportion," "relation" (compare Latin *ratio* below)
- "reason," that is, "cause"
- "reason," that is, "rationality"

Word for Word

KNOWLEDGE

GNOTHI SAUTON
("Know Yourself")

Word Study

- There are three words for "to know" in Greek: *eidenai* (*oida*, "I know"), *gignōskein*, and *epistasthai*. *Eidenai* is used of knowing by reflection, *gignōskein* of knowing by observation. *Gignōskein* is the base of the Latin verb *noscere* (originally *gnoscere*) and the English verb **know**. *Epistasthai* is related to the noun *epistēmē* ("knowledge"), from which the English noun **epistemology** is derived.
- What is an **agnostic**? How is an **agnostic** different from an **atheist**?
- Greek and Latin words concerned with knowledge appear in the following table. Give one English derivative for each of the Greek and Latin words where indicated.

Word	Meaning	Derivative
aisthesthai (Greek verb)	to perceive	
aisthetikos (Greek adjective)	perceptive	
apo- (Greek prefix) +	off, from, away from	**apodeictic** (necessarily true, beyond contradiction)
deigma (Greek noun)	sample, pattern, plan	
apodeiknusthai (Greek verb)	to show, point out, prove	
cogitare, cogitatum (Latin verb)	to think	
cognoscere, cognitum (Latin verb)	to find out, get to know, learn	
genus, generis (Latin noun)	kind, sort	
ingenium (Latin noun)	inborn ability, characteristic	
intellegere, intellectum (Latin verb)	to realize, understand	
mens, mentis (Latin noun)	mind	
sapiens, sapientis (Latin adjective)	wise	
scire, scitum (Latin verb)	to know	

Word for Word

WE TAKE MANY WORDS FOR GRANTED! FOR INSTANCE, ALTHOUGH THE TERM SCIENCE (FROM THE LATIN *SCIRE*.. TO KNOW) HAS BEEN AROUND FOR MANY CENTURIES, THE TERM SCIENTIST IS RELATIVELY NEW! IT WAS COINED BY WILLIAM WHEWELL, OF CAMBRIDGE, UK, IN 1840!

@ATCHISON

- What is the main base of the words **conscience** and **consciousness**?
- What is *homo sapiens*?
- Why is an **anesthetic** referred to by this name?

GREEK PHILOSOPHY

Aspects of Greek Philosophy

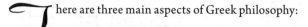here are three main aspects of Greek philosophy:

- speculative and scientific inquiry—the nature and origin of the universe; the study of scientific and natural phenomena.
- practical application—the study of man, his nature, his place in the world, his relations with others; ethics; political philosophy.
- critical philosophy—the study of *being* and *knowing;* epistemology (theory of knowledge); how we perceive or know things; logic.

Word Study

- Give English derivatives from the following Greek and Latin words and word combinations.

Word	Meaning	Derivative
esse (Latin infinitive)	to be	
ethikos (Greek adjective)	ethical, moral	
ethos (Greek noun)	way, custom, moral nature	
kosmos (Greek noun)	order, world, universe	
meta (Greek preposition)	after	
+ *phusis/physis* (Greek noun)	nature	
mos, moris (Latin noun)	manner	
mores (plural)	manners, morals	
phainomai (Greek verb)	I appear	
phainomenon (Greek present participle of *phainomai*)	appearance	
unus (Latin djective) +	one	
vertere, versum (Latin verb)	to turn	

Metaphysics, the derivative to be supplied in the table above, literally means "after physics" in reference to Aristotle, who published his *Physics* and later *Metaphysics*. This title has come to mean the subject of metaphysics, which is concerned with attempts:

- to characterize existence or reality as a whole, instead of, as in the various natural sciences, particular parts or aspects thereof;
- to explore the realm of the **suprasensible,** beyond the world of experience;
- to establish indubitable first principles as a foundation for other knowledge;
- to examine critically what more limited studies simply take for granted.

(A. Flew 1979: 212–213 [abridged])

Word for Word

The Pre-Socratic Philosophers

The earliest Greek philosophers before the time of the famous philosopher Socrates are often referred to as "natural philosophers" because they were interested in the natural world and how it functioned. These philosophers asked questions about the natural world and attempted to develop a system that described its fundamental laws, its origins, and man's role in it. Their approach was essentially rational, since they looked beyond supernatural explanations of the world and attempted to find universal principles that would explain the natural world without recourse to religion or mythology.

The Ionian Philosophers

The Ionian philosophers of the sixth century BCE were the first Greek thinkers to try to explain the origin and nature of the **cosmos** (Greek *kosmos*). These philosophers believed the universe had a single basic substance. They are called Ionian because they lived in Ionia, a region in the eastern part of the Mediterranean on the western coast and islands of what is now Turkey. The first three philosophers below belonged to the Milesian school, so named after Miletus, the chief city of Ionia.

Thales

*T*hales argued that the origin of all matter was water or moisture which could be solid (in the form of ice), liquid, or gas (steam). He is famous for having predicted an eclipse of the sun in 585 BCE.

Anaximander

*A*naximander saw the world as a conflict of opposites such as heat and cold, wet and dry. This conflict is cyclical and constant; for instance, heat in the form of the sun dries up water, but water puts out heat in the form of fire. Therefore these basic elements which destroy each other could not be the primary elements of the cosmos; there must, he argued, be an undefined mass without any limits from which the basic elements are derived; this he termed *apeiron* ("boundless," "limitless").

Anaximenes

*A*naximenes believed that the primary substance was *aer* ("air," "mist"). He maintained that if mist could condense into water, it could then condense further to form solids; he felt that this was how the earth must have been formed. The most extreme form of condensed *aer* is fire; the purest form of *aer* is the life-force. As the earth was considered to be a living being in early Greek religious thought, so Anaximenes believed that there was a small part of "the god," that is, "the universe," in every person.

Heracleitus

*H*eracleitus, who flourished around 500 BCE in Ephesus, taught that the universe consisted of a conflict of opposites controlled by an unchanging principle, which he called *logos*, and that this conflict was creative. He rejected the idea of the Ionian school that the world originated in a single substance.

Heracleitus was the first Greek writer to explore the nature of knowledge and of the soul, maintaining that one must seek knowledge, including self-knowledge, in order to understand the world. One should search within oneself for the *logos* which meant the "word" as spoken, the truth as contained in the word, and the external reality. For Heracleitus the external reality was a concept that the world is in a constant state of flux, strife, and destruction; for him, in fact, it was an ever-living fire.

The Pythagoreans

Pythagoras

*P*ythagoras emigrated from the island of Samos to south Italy *circa* 530 BCE, taking Greek philosophy to the West. His followers, known as the Pythagoreans, regarded philosophy as a way of life and lived in a brotherly community of philosophers. They believed in the "transmigration" of souls (the passing of a soul after physical death from one body to another); for this reason they did not eat meat.

The Pythagoreans also believed that the universe was a living creature and that each individual contained a fragment of the divine whole that was trapped inside the physical body. Their aim was to free themselves from the corruption of the body, to become pure spirit, and to be united with the universal spirit. Studying the rules by which the cosmos worked would bring them closer to it; therefore they made important contributions to the study of mathematics and music.

Pythagoras was interested in ratios and proportions. He taught that mathematical ratios give order (Greek *kosmos*) to the limitless range of sound. Musical sound can be mathematically represented; for example, there is a fixed ratio between the length of a string on a guitar and the sound it produces when plucked.

The Monists

Parmenides

P armenides, who was born in about 515 BCE, was the first Greek philosopher to introduce abstract thought. He taught that what exists must be "one, eternal, indivisible, motionless, and changeless" and that there is no validity to sense perception and no reality to what is perceived by the senses.

The Pluralists (Fifth Century BCE)

Empedocles

E mpedocles taught that all four elements (air, earth, water, fire) were real and that combinations of these, in various proportions, led to all phenomena. The opposing principles of Love and Strife created the various combinations of elements; to him Love and Strife were not abstract qualities but were concrete in the same way as the material elements were.

Anaxagoras

A naxagoras was the first to distinguish clearly between matter and mind; he maintained that the mind ruled the universe and brought order (Greek *kosmos*) out of confusion (*chaos*).

The Atomists (Late Fifth Century BCE)

Democritus

D emocritus put forward an atomic theory in which he claimed that the world was made up of atoms or small particles. These were solid, hard, and indestructible (but could differ in shape and size) and were in a constant state of motion. Their chance combinations in varying densities produced various forms of matter.

To Empedocles, birth and death were an illusion; he believed that there was not real beginning or end but rather simply a constant rearrangement of atoms in new combinations. Democritus, however, unlike Empedocles, did not suggest what it was that caused the atoms to move; he stressed the importance of sense perception and the reality of substances.

Word for Word

Word Study

- Give English derivatives from the following Latin and Greek words.

Word	Meaning	Derivative
materia (Latin noun)	timber, building material	
res (Latin noun)	thing, matter, circumstance	
realis (Late Latin adjective)	real	
abstrahere, abstractum (Latin verb)	to draw (*trahere*) away (*abs-*)	
concrescere, concretum (Latin verb)	to grow (*crescere*) together (*con-*)	
atomos (Greek noun) (*a + tomos*)	"particle" (not divided)	

Socrates

Socrates (469–399 BCE) was one of the major figures of the intellectual revolution in fifth century Athens. He never wrote down his philosophy. This was done by some of his pupils, most notably Plato who increasingly introduced his own ideas into his Socratic dialogues which were conversations of a formal or imaginary nature between Socrates and other people that involved an exchange of views in the hope of ultimately reaching agreement. Socrates taught through discussions with people in public using the dialectic method which involved asking questions and using the rules and modes of reasoning.

Socrates

> The life without inquiry is not worth living for a human being.
>
> Socrates (Plato, *Apology* 38a)

Socrates claimed that the Delphic oracle had said that he was the wisest man in the world and that this had shocked him into trying to disprove the oracle. He determined, however, that people were *not* wise because they thought that they knew things when they did not. It was only in the sense that he was aware of his own ignorance that he found he was wiser than other people.

> As I talked with this man, it seemed to me that he appeared to be wise to many other people, and most especially to himself, but not to be so. And then I tried to demonstrate to him that he considered himself to be wise, but was not... And so as I went away, I thought to myself that I was wiser than that man. Very probably neither of us knows anything beautiful or good, but this man thinks he knows something when he doesn't; on the other hand, I, when I don't know, don't think that I know... The wisest among you, humans, is whoever understands that he is in reality quite worthless in regard to wisdom.
>
> Socrates (Plato, *Apology* 21c–d, 23b)

Socrates was friendly with many of the aristocratic youth of Athens and this brought him into disfavor with the democrats. His constant questioning, moreover, led to him being perceived as a nuisance.

> History is one long chain of reflections. Hegel . . . indicated certain rules that apply for this chain of reflections. Anyone studying history in depth will observe that a thought is usually proposed on the basis of other, previously proposed thoughts. But as soon as one thought is proposed, it will be contradicted by another. A tension arises between these two opposite ways of thinking. But the tension is resolved by the proposal of a third thought which accommodates the best of both points of view. Hegel calls this a *dialectic* process.
>
> (J. Gaarder 1994: 280)

Since Socrates believed in a single "divine being" and was accused of not worshipping the gods of the state, he was regarded by some Athenians as politically subversive. Eventually, he was brought to trial on charges of religious unorthodoxy and of corrupting the young, whereupon he was found guilty and condemned to death.

The Sophists

*T*he fifth century was a time of great intellectual questioning. The Sophists were teachers who traveled from city to city, teaching the practical skills needed for public life, such as rhetoric and how to present a weak argument so as to make it seem better. They claimed to teach *aretē*.

Most Sophists were skeptical about the possibility of absolute knowledge or truth. They argued that sense perception is not absolute but relative (for instance, if you are eating a very sweet cake, your coffee can taste bitter even if it does have sugar in it). From this, they went on to argue that there is no absolute justice or right and wrong, but that these are relative; laws and moral codes are not divine in origin, but develop as societies evolve in order to make it easier for communities to get along together.

The rationalism and relativism of the Sophists led many people to regard them as immoral and subversive. Socrates also criticized them for taking money for their teaching, something he never did.

Plato

A pupil of Socrates, Plato (*circa* 429–347 BCE) wrote his philosophical ideas in the form of *Dialogues* in which Socrates discusses philosophical concepts through the dialectic method. Among Plato's dialogues are *Phaedrus*, *Meno*, and the *Republic*. The *Apology* is his version of Socrates' defense speech at his trial for blasphemy and corrupting the youth.

At Athens, Plato founded the Academy over which he presided for forty years. The Academy was a small area in the center of Athens where teachers and students could mingle while they discussed issues in the fields of philosophy and mathematics. Although the Academy was quite informal by modern standards, it is generally considered to have been the first establishment of higher education in the Western World.

Plato

Word for Word

THE FAMOUS GREEK PHILOSOPHER, PLATO (c 428–c347 BC) OFTEN TAUGHT IN A GROVE ONCE OWNED BY A FARMER NAMED ACADEMUS!

THE GROVE WAS CALLED ACADEMEIA!

THIS IS THE SOURCE OF TODAY'S WORDS... ACADEMY, ACADEMIC... ETC!

ATCHISON

Plato's Academy

One of Plato's aims in establishing the Academy was to provide a philosophical training ground for statesmen. His attempts to produce an ideal king through philosophical education failed, however; he was friendly with Dionysius I, the ruler of Syracuse in Sicily, and Dion, a Syracusan politician, but his pupil Dionysius II proved to be a tyrannical ruler and imprisoned Plato.

Plato's "theory of forms" developed out of attempts to make abstract and absolute definitions. For example, we may ask, "What is justice?" We can only arrive at the idea of justice by considering various practical examples or manifestations of justice, but these are not justice itself. There is a reality behind what we perceive, which is the true "idea" or "form."

Let us assume that you have dropped in from outer space and have never seen a baker before. You stumble into a tempting bakery—and there you catch sight of fifty identical gingerbread men on a shelf. I imagine you could wonder how they could be exactly alike. It might well be that one of them has an arm missing, another has lost a bit of its head, and a third has a funny bump on its stomach. But after careful thought, you would nevertheless conclude that all gingerbread men have something *in common*. Although none of them is perfect, you would suspect that they had a common origin. You would realize that all the cookies were formed in the same mold. And what is more, Sophie, you are now seized by the irresistible desire to see this mold. Because clearly, the mold itself must be utter perfection—and in a sense, more beautiful—in comparison with these crude copies.

If you solved this problem all by yourself, you arrived at the philosophical solution in exactly the same way that Plato did.

. . . He was astonished at the way all natural phenomena could be so alike and he concluded that it had to be because there are a limited number of *forms* "behind" everything we see around us. Plato called these forms *ideas*. Behind every horse, pig, or human being, there is the "idea horse," "idea pig," and "idea human being. . ."

Plato came to the conclusion that there must be a reality behind the "material world." He called this reality *the world of ideas*; it contained the eternal and immutable "patterns" behind the various phenomena we come across in nature. This remarkable view is known as Plato's *theory of ideas*.

(J. Gaarder 1994: 67)

Plato's Forms

In the dialogues of Plato doubts about whether we can really know anything are constantly expressed. The character Socrates claims that the only way in which he can claim to be wise is that he *knows that he does not know anything,* whereas others think they know things when they do not. Several earlier philosophers had expressed doubts about the reliability of sense perception and about the stability of the material world, for example, the Pluralists (or Atomists), or Heracleitus, whose saying *panta rhei* ("everything is in a state of flux") suggests the modern notion that one can never step into the same river twice.

Plato put forward a representational theory of reality in which he suggests that when we view an object, for example, a table, we are not seeing the real object but something that represents it in our mind. In the *Republic* he develops the "theory of forms" which are the true reality but which cannot be fully known by human perception. To illustrate what he means he employs the simile of a cave.

> Suppose that there are people who have spent all their lives in a cave with their backs to the entrance and unable to turn around. All that is within their field of vision is the inner wall of the cave. When the sunlight shines in from the cave mouth, it causes the shadows of people or things outside the cave to fall on this inner wall. These shadows are what the people in the cave see. They do not know that there are "real" people moving about outside the cave because they have never been outside into the "real" world; since all they can know is the shadows they see of people moving, they imagine that these shadows are the reality. But if a man were taken outside the cave, he would at first not be able to see because of the brightness; even when his eyes grew accustomed to the light, he would not believe what he saw because it would be different from what he had always seen and known. Yet what is outside would be the true reality, while what was seen on the inside of the cave would only be the idea of the reality.
>
> (Plato, *Republic* 514a–515d [adapted])

A rough modern analogy of this cave simile might be television, especially if we can imagine someone who has been reared in isolation and has only ever seen the outside world on the screen. While Plato, then, would regard what people saw on the inside of the cave as only the idea of the reality, he would consider the true reality outside the cave to be the "forms." We can attempt to define justice, for instance, by describing various instances of just behavior, but these are not the ultimate real justice. Absolute justice (the "prototype" of justice) is the "form" (Greek *eidolon*) of justice.

Many later Western philosophers have doubted the accuracy of sense perceptions as a gauge of reality. The seventeenth century French philosopher René Descartes, for instance, believed that we can only be sure of our own existence because we perceive through the activity of the mind.

> *Cogito, ergo sum.*
> "I think; therefore I am."
>
> Descartes (1596–1650)

Word Study

- What is the **Socratic method?**
- What is **Socratic irony?**
- What are the Greek bases of **dialogue** and **dialectics?** Use an English dictionary if necessary.
- What is **sophistry?**
- What is meant by **platonic** love?

Aristotle

Aristotle

Aristotle (384–322 BCE) was a pupil of Plato, whom he succeeded as head of the Academy. He spent some years as tutor to Alexander the Great. Eventually, Aristotle established his own school in Athens, the Lyceum, where he lectured, wrote, and discussed philosophical, scientific, and other topics with his associates and students. Driven by a desire for knowledge and understanding in virtually every possible field, Aristotle wrote biological and botanical studies, political studies on the constitutions of various states, and literary criticism on tragedy and comedy. His works consist of abstract speculations of a general type as well as detailed observations about the natural world. He combined his philosophical and scientific interests with an absolute faith in the power of the human mind, assisted by precise observations of natural phenomena and his system of deductive logic, to perceive the basic nature of objective reality.

Aristotle had a huge influence upon the subsequent practice of philosophy. From Late Antiquity through the Middle Ages it was routine practice for philosophers to expound upon their own views by referring to his works. In the history of human thought he is probably without parallel in terms of his vast influence and the breadth of his intellectual interests.

For Consideration

- How does the empirical approach of Aristotle contrast with Plato's ideas?

The Epicureans

The Pluralist philosopher Democritus had taught that people, like all matter, consist of different kinds of atoms. Those atoms that make up the soul are in more rapid motion than those that make up the body. The purpose of the philosophy of Epicurus (341–270 BCE) was to achieve freedom from fear and anxiety. Epicurus built on Democritus' "theory of atoms" and used it to prove that the soul does not survive death but, as with the body, its atoms disperse. One therefore need not fear death since there was no afterlife in which one could be punished. He taught that the gods did exist, but were not concerned with human affairs and therefore need not be feared. Epicurean philosophy advocated withdrawal from the world of affairs and politics in order to avoid disturbing influences that created anxiety. The Roman poet Lucretius used Epicurus' teaching as the basis for his philosophical didactic poem *De Rerum Natura (On the Nature of Things)*.

The Stoics

The Stoics derive their name from the Stoa, a public portico, where their founder Zeno taught. They did not accept the survival of the soul after death, but taught that the whole cosmos goes through cycles that end in destructive conflagration and renewal in which the cosmos and all life are infinitely recreated. According to the Stoics, every person was part of the whole cosmic being and everything happened in accordance with fate. In common with several other Greek philosophical schools, the Stoics believed that each human soul is a spark of the divine fire that makes up the cosmos and that it strives for unity with that universal soul.

Like the Epicureans, the Stoics believed that the goal of people was happiness, which could be achieved by expelling everything that disturbed the mind such as desire, delight, fear, and grief. They taught that the passions are subject to control by reason. Unlike the Epicureans, however, the Stoics thought that it was important for the individual to become involved in public life in order to improve oneself and for the common good. Their ultimate goal was virtue which they defined as harmony with nature. In order to achieve this one needed first to acquire self-knowledge; this in turn would lead to altruism since man is a social creature and needs other men.

In the eyes of the Stoics all good acts, such as honoring parents, friends, and country, constituted progress towards virtue. The Stoics valued especially the virtues of good sense, self-control, justice, and courage since they believed they were forms of knowledge. The teachings of the Stoics appealed strongly to the Romans because of their involvement in public life and sense of moral duty.

The Cynics

Diogenes founded the school called the Cynics. He preached the supreme importance of individual freedom and self-sufficiency and rejected the conventions of society such as wealth, social status, and reputation. He despised pleasure and was ostentatiously ascetic, living in a large pottery barrel instead of a house. The name **Cynic** is derived from the Greek word for "dog" (*kuon, kun-*) and was originally a nickname referring to Diogenes' shamelessness and extreme poverty.

Word Study

- Form the English derivatives from the Greek and Latin words given in the first column of the following table.

Word	Meaning	Derivative
absolvere, absolutum (*ab-*, "away," "from" + *solvere, solutum*; Latin verb)	to loosen from, make loose	
docere, doctum (Latin verb)	to teach	
dogma, dogmatos (Greek noun)	opinion, decree	
dokein (Greek verb)	to be of the opinion	
ducere, ductum (Latin verb)	to lead	
nihil (Latin noun)	nothing	
non sequitur (Latin verb)	it does not follow	
ratio, rationis (Latin noun)	proportion	
sumere, sumptum (Latin verb)	to take, take up	
thesis (Greek noun)	proposition	
tithenai (Greek verb); first person *tithemi*; base *the-*	to place	

ARETĒ

For the Greek epic poet Homer who wrote about a warrior society, *aretē* most often meant "courage." By itself, however, the Greek word *aretē* was incomplete, since it was linked with what one does, for example, with one's job or political activity; therefore one could refer to the *aretē* of a general, a statesman, a shoemaker, a horse trainer, or a slave. *Aretē* meant skill or efficiency at a particular job.

When the Sophists claimed to be able to teach *aretē*, they were not necessarily saying that they would teach moral virtue, although some of them were concerned with ethics; rather, they were saying that they could teach "efficiency" in areas such as intellectual activity, public speaking, debating, law, and politics.

For Socrates, Plato, and Aristotle, a major philosophical question was the search to define *aretē anthropinē* ("human virtue"; compare Greek *anthropos*, "human being"). They maintained that each type of person, for example, a soldier, a shoemaker, or a politician, had *aretē* that was related to his vocation. This concept of *aretē* was specific, but it was also possible to generalize about being a human being and therefore about the *aretē* of a human being. If the philosopher could decide what the vocation of a human being was, then he could decide what made him a "good" or "efficient" human who possessed *aretē anthropinē*.

These philosophers argued that *aretē* in connection with a particular sphere of activity, for example, horse training, implied a thorough knowledge of that job. So when they tried to generalize about *aretē* they stressed its connection with knowledge; hence arose the Socratic paradox "virtue is knowledge."

Word Study

- What do you think is the connection between the Latin nouns *vir* and *virtus*? If necessary, find the simple English derivative of *virtus* in an English dictionary and note the meaning of the Latin from which the English word is derived.

PSYCHĒ

There is no single, simple translation for the Greek word *psychē*. Among its meanings are "breath," "soul," or "spirit." The word *psychē* has been taken into English and covers a range of meanings. When defining **psyche,** most English dictionaries make reference to the "soul," "spirit," and "mind" and sometimes expand upon these synonyms to explain it as the principle of conscious and unconscious mental and emotional life.

For Consideration

- Why is there no simple meaning for the English word **psyche?**
- What does **psyche** mean to you?
- Does the word "soul" denote the same thing in every culture and system of beliefs?
- Does the word "soul" mean something specifically different to a Hindu, a Jew, a Muslim, a Chinese, or an African?

Homer and the Early Greeks on **Psychē**

In Homer the *psychē* is the part of a person that lives on after death in Hades, the underworld or realm of the dead. The *psychē* is thought of as feeble, shadowy, and insubstantial. When Hector killed Patroclus,

> His *psychē* fled from his body and went off to Hades,
> Bewailing its fate as it left behind manhood and youth.
>
> (Homer, *Iliad* 16.856–857)

In *Odyssey* 11 the hero Odysseus must go down to the underworld to consult the soul of the seer Teiresias. When Odysseus performs a blood sacrifice, the spirits of the dead are drawn to the blood. Odysseus can see the spirits, but they show no awareness of him at all. Only after drinking the blood are they able to communicate with him.

> So he [Teiresias] spoke, and in answer I said to him,
> "Teiresias, these things the gods themselves have made my fate.
> But come, tell me this and speak of it truthfully:
> Here I see the *psychē* of my dead mother;
> But she sits in silence near the blood and does not
> Dare to look straight at her son or speak to him.
> Tell me, lord, how may she know that I am he?"
> So I spoke, and at once in answer he said to me,
> "It is a simple thing that I shall say and put in your mind.
> Whichever of the spirits of the dead you allow
> To go right up to the blood will speak the truth to you;
> But whichever you refuse will go back again."
> When he had spoken and given these prophecies,
> the *psychē* of lordly Teiresias went off to the house of Hades;
> But I remained there determinedly until my mother
> Came to the dark blood and drank it. At once she knew me
> And mournfully spoke to me in winged words:
> "My child, how have you come beneath the gloomy darkness
> While still alive? It is difficult for the living to see these things.
> For on the way are great rivers and terrible streams,
> The first of which is Ocean, which it is not possible to cross
> On foot but only if one has a well-made ship.
> Do you come here from Troy only now after wandering
> For a long time with your ship and your companions? Have you not yet
> Come to Ithaca and not yet seen your wife in your palace?"
> So she spoke, and in answer I said to her,
> "My mother, need led me down to Hades
> To seek advice from the *psychē* of Theban Teiresias."
>
> (Homer, *Odyssey* 11.138–165)

For Consideration

- Later in Greek lyric poetry, much of which is love poetry, *psychē* began to mean the seat of the emotions. What part of the body is the equivalent seat of the emotions in other cultural forms you may have heard about, for instance, in English love poetry?

Plato on Psychē

By the fifth century BCE the word was used in the sense of something conscious and vital. Plato uses three terms for various aspects of the non-physical element of human beings:

- *psychē*
- *nous* ("mind," "intellect")
- *thumos* ("spirit," "passion")

The soul consists of three parts:

- rational, logical, concerned with thinking
- irrational, illogical, concerned with appetites and desires
- passionate, concerned with the emotions

Plato sees the rule of reason as being in opposition to the rule of the appetites and the passions. For him, the soul is not only separate from the body but is also immortal; whereas the body is subject to material laws, the soul is not. The passage that follows is a dialogue between Socrates and Glaucon, the brother of Plato, which is recorded in Plato's *Republic*. Socrates and Glaucon are considering the nature of the individual mind or soul (*psychē*). Socrates speaks first.

> *Socrates:* Could we say that there are sometimes some people who are thirsty but are unwilling to drink?
>
> *Glaucon:* Certainly there are many such people, and this happens often.
>
> *Socrates:* And what can we say about them? Surely there is in their *psychē* something that commands them to drink, and also something that prevents them which is different and overcomes the element that commands them?
>
> *Glaucon:* That's how it seems to me.
>
> *Socrates:* Well, then, doesn't the element that prevents such things arise from one's reason whenever it does arise, while that which leads and drags one on appears as a result of passive and unhealthy conditions?
>
> *Glaucon:* It seems so.
>
> *Socrates:* Then it will not be unreasonable for us to say that these are two elements that are different from each other. We can call the part of the *psychē* with which it reasons the rational element, and the part with which it feels love and hunger and thirst, and is stirred by the other desires, the irrational and desiring element, which is associated with certain satisfactions and pleasures.
>
> *Glaucon:* No, we'd be quite right in thinking this way.

Socrates: So these elements may be distinguished as two forms within the *psychē,* but what about the passionate part *(thumos),* the one with which we become angry? Is it a third element or would it be of the same nature as either of these two elements?

Glaucon: Perhaps it is the same as the second part, the desiring element.

Socrates: But I rely on the following story I once heard. As Leontios, son of Aglaion, was on his way up from the Peiraieus under the outer side of the north wall, he noticed some corpses lying at the place of the public executioner. He desired to look at them, yet at the very same time he was disgusted at himself and turned away. For some time he struggled and covered his face, but eventually, overcome by his desire, he opened his eyes wide, rushed up to the corpses, and said, "There you are, you wretched things—look all you want at this wonderful sight!"

Glaucon: I too have heard this.

Socrates: Well, this story shows that rage sometimes makes war on the desires as one thing against something different.

Glaucon: It does show that.

Socrates: And in other cases, too, don't we often see that, when desires force themselves on someone in opposition to reason, that person becomes angry with himself and rages against the force within him, and that, like two warring factions, the person's passionate anger *(thumos)* becomes an ally of reason? But its taking the side of the desires against reason, when reason indicates that it should not, is something I don't think you would say you have ever seen happening in yourself or in anyone else.

Glaucon: No, by Zeus.

Socrates: And whenever someone believes he has done wrong, is it not the case that, the more noble his character, the less capable he is of anger at being hungry and cold and suffering any other things like that at the hands of someone he believes is inflicting these things fairly? As I say, his passionate anger *(thumos)* is unwilling to be roused against that person.

Glaucon: That is true.

Socrates: But whenever someone believes he has been wronged, doesn't that same anger seethe and grow fierce and take sides with what seems right and, enduring through hunger and cold and all such sufferings, emerge victorious? It will not abandon what is noble until it succeeds or perishes, or is called back and calmed by reason, as a dog is by a herdsman.

Glaucon: It is exactly the way you describe it, and in our [ideal] city-state we established the "assistants" to act like dogs in obedience to the "rulers," who are like the shepherds of the city-state.

Socrates: You understand very well what I want to say, but have you considered this additional point?

Glaucon: What point?

Socrates: That the opposite seems true of the passionate part *(thumos)* from what we thought just now. Then we were thinking it might be some aspect of the desiring element, but now we are saying something very different—that in the struggle within the *psychē* it is far more likely to place its forces on the side of the rational element.

Glaucon: Absolutely.

Socrates: But then is it something different from this element also, or is it some form of the rational element, so that there are not three but two forms in the *psychē*, the rational and the desiring? Or is it that, just as in our [ideal] city-state there were three constituent categories—the money-makers, the assistants, and the council—so also in the *psychē* there is a third part, the element of passion which assists the rational element by nature if it is not ruined by bad upbringing?

Glaucon: It must be a third element.

Socrates: Yes, *if* it can be shown to be something different from the rational element, just as it seemed to be different from the desiring element.

Glaucon: But that's not difficult to show. You can see this even in children: as soon as they are born they are full of passion *(thumos)*, but some, it seems to me, never acquire reason, while most acquire it quite late.

Socrates: Yes, by Zeus, you have said it very well. And in animals too one can see that what you say is the case...

(Plato, *Republic* 439c–441b [adapted])

Aristotle on Psychē

Aristotle is not so much interested in what the *psychē* is as in what it does, that is, how it relates to the world around it. For him the *psychē* is responsible for thought and sense perception. In *On the Soul* he maintains the following view of the soul.

The *psychē* is the cause and originating force of the living body... [I]t is the origin of movement... [T]he *psychē* is also the thing for which [the body exists]. The mind acts for some reason and nature behaves in just the same way. This reason is its eventual purpose... [A]ll physical bodies are instruments of the *psychē* and ... they exist for the psyche.

(Aristotle, *On the Soul* 415b)

Aristotle is an empiricist and believes that man perceives his environment through his senses. He lists the abilities of the soul as seeing, hearing, smelling, tasting, and feeling and maintains that these five senses are synthesized by a sixth, "common," sense which is the ability to be aware of things such as number, form, shape, and duration of time. Whereas for Plato, knowledge was to be achieved by intellectual activity and by attempting to understand the "forms" (see above), for Aristotle, knowledge was to be gained empirically, that is, by experience.

The divisions of knowledge acquisition listed by Aristotle are still recognized by psychologists today:

- *Association* occurs when we remember things because they are similar to things with which we are already familiar.
- *Contrast* takes place when we remember things because they are the opposites of things we already know.
- *Contiguity* refers to things that occur together which are not ordinarily associated and afterward one reminds us of the other; for instance, if we meet someone at a party while a particular piece of music is being played, hearing the music afterward may cause us to think of that person.

Psyche in Mythology

In late Greek mythology Psyche was the personification of the soul. She was depicted as a young woman with wings shaped like those of a butterfly. Psyche was loved by the Greek god Eros who was called Cupid by the Romans. The story of Cupid and Psyche has often been a favorite theme in western literature, art, and music.

Psyche and Eros pulling a chariot containing Aphrodite and Hermes

Word Study

- Latin has two cognate words for *psychē*; these are *animus* ("mind," "spirit") and *anima* ("breath," "soul," "spirit").
- What do you think is the main difference between *animus,* which is a masculine noun, and *anima,* which is a feminine noun?
- Look at the section of an English dictionary that contains words built on the Latin base *anim-* from *animus* and *anima.* Look up particularly the words **animadvert, animal, animus, animism, animate,** and **animosity.** Which of these words are derived from *animus* and which are derived from *anima*?
- How do you think Latin *animus* ("mind," "spirit") is different from Latin *mens, mentis* ("mind")?
- What English words are derived from the Greek noun *peira* ("trial," "test")? (Combine with prefixes such as *em-* and *ex-*.)

MYTHS

Several myths have given rise to psychological terms. The ones described below concern Oedipus, Electra, and Narcissus. The Oedipus myth is told in greater detail in Chapter 4 ("Mythology").

Oedipus

The king and queen of Thebes, Laius and Jocasta, were warned by the Delphic oracle that their son would grow up to kill his father and marry his mother. When the baby was born, they gave it to a servant to expose it on Mount Cithaeron. Since he could not bear to do this, he gave it to the servant of the king and queen of Corinth, Polybus and Merope, who raised this baby, Oedipus, as their son. Oedipus did not know that they were not his natural parents until he was a young adult when someone taunted him with being a foundling. Polybus and Merope assured him he was their son, but he decided to consult the Delphic oracle and learn the truth. There he was told that he was destined to kill his father and to marry his mother.

Oedipus decided never to return to Corinth so that the oracle could not be fulfilled. But as he was leaving Delphi, he got into a fight with a man blocking his way at a crossroads and killed him. Unbeknown to him, this was his real father, Laius. Oedipus went on his way and came to Thebes, where a creature known as the sphinx was plaguing the city with a riddle. Oedipus solved the riddle and got rid of the sphinx, and in their gratitude, the Thebans offered him the hand of their widowed queen, Jocasta, in marriage; in this way he fulfilled the oracle by killing his father and marrying his mother.

Electra

Electra was the daughter of Agamemnon and Clytemnestra. Agamemnon not only sacrificed her sister Iphigenia in order to receive favorable winds for the Greek fleet to sail to Troy, but he also brought the Trojan princess Cassandra home to Greece as his concubine after the war ended. While Agamemnon was away fighting in the Trojan War, Clytemnestra had an affair with Agamemnon's cousin Aegisthus. After the return of Agamemnon, Clytemnestra and Aegisthus murdered him. Clytemnestra's son, Orestes, returned from exile and, encouraged and helped by his sister Electra, killed Clytemnestra and Aegisthus.

Narcissus

> Narcissus was a very handsome youth who happened to catch sight of his reflection in a pool of water. He fell in love with the beautiful image and became so obsessed by longing for it that he pined away or, in some versions, fell into the pool and drowned. He was turned into the flower that bears his name.

Word Study

- What is **narcissism?** How does the myth explain the meaning of the word?

FREUDIAN PSYCHOLOGY

Sigmund Freud (1856–1939) is one of the founders of the modern science of psychology. The terminology he used drew heavily on Greek and Latin words and concepts. Among his numerous and complex theories is the idea that trauma leads to repression in which the memory is relegated to the unconscious which in turn leads to **hysteria.** He believed that the resolution of this condition could be achieved by encouraging the patient to talk about the **trauma** through **hypnosis** or the interpretation of dreams which would eventually lead to **catharsis.**

Freud taught that the fundamental motives in our lives are bodily needs. He used the Latin word *libido* ("pleasure," "lust") to define a psychic energy that aggressively seeks pleasure. If we are to live comfortably in society, libido cannot be openly expressed or gratified and is therefore sublimated (from Latin *sublimis*, "high," "lofty"), that is, "purified" and redirected into a higher or nobler activity.

According to Freud, the stages of personality development of the infant and child include identification with the mother in a pleasure-seeking way through her provision of food and warmth. Because he believed that the sexual impulse is present even in infancy, Freud theorized that the young male child has sexual desire for the mother and wishes to rid himself of the father. This theory is Freud's famous **Oedipus complex,** whereas the **Electra complex** describes the female child's desire for her father and rejection of her mother. The stories of Oedipus and his family can be viewed in psychological terms as mythic representations of the horror of and societal taboo against incestuous relationships.

As the child grows up the **Oedipus complex** is resolved as he begins to identify with his father by imitating and adopting his character and moral system, which leads to the formation of what Freud calls the *superego*. The *superego* is the morality principle, whereas the *id* is the pleasure principle (unconscious, repressed wishes); the mediator between these is the *ego,* the reality principle.

The pronoun *ego* in both Latin and Greek means "I." English derivatives such as **egocentric** and **egoist** express the idea of an individual viewing the world in relation to oneself to the exclusion of almost everything else. *Id* is a Latin neuter pronoun meaning "it," while *super* is a Latin preposition meaning "above," as in *superego,* which controls or regulates the impulses of the unconscious *(id).*

Word Study

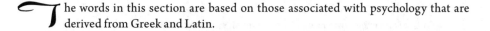 he words in this section are based on those associated with psychology that are derived from Greek and Latin.

- Try to think of English words derived from the Greek and Latin words in the first column, then use an English dictionary to check their meanings.

Word	Meaning of Latin/Greek Noun/Verb Base	Derivative	English Meaning
habere, habitum (Latin verb)	to have, hold		
inhibere (*in-*, "in," "into" + *habere, habitum*) (Latin verb)	to hold in, check, restrain		
hypnos (Greek noun)	sleep		
hystera (Greek noun)	womb		
katharsis (Greek noun)	cleansing, purification		
premere, pressum (Latin verb)	to press		
con- ("with," "together") + *premere, pressum*			
de- ("down") + *premere, pressum*			
ex- ("out of," "from") + *premere, pressum*			
in- ("in," "into") + *premere, pressum*			

Word	Meaning of Latin/Greek Noun/Verb Base	Derivative	English Meaning
ob- ("in the way of," "against") + premere, pressum			
re- ("back") + premere, pressum			
sub- ("under") + premere, pressum			
trauma, traumatos (Greek noun)	wound		
vertere, versum (Latin verb)	to turn		
extra- ("outside") + vertere, versum			
intro- ("inside") + vertere, versum			

- The base -gress- is derived from a Latin verb base meaning "to step" or "to go." (The cognate noun is gradus, "step.") Using the prefixes in the table below, form some English words that use this base -gress-. Which of them are used in psychological terminology?

Latin Prefix	Meaning	Derivative
ad (ag-)	towards	
con (from cum)	with	
di-	in different directions	
in	into	
pro	forward	
re	back	
trans	across	

- *Aitia* and *aition* (Greek nouns) mean "cause." Combined with the base *log-*, this gives the word _____, which is used in different ways in both mythography and psychology.
- The Latin pronoun *alius* ("other"; adjective *alienus*) gives rise to the term _____, defined by some psychologists as a sense that life has no meaning and the world is impersonal, mechanistic, and unsympathetic.
- The Greek noun *orexis* means "longing," "appetite" (from the verb *oregein*, "to reach out"). With the negating prefix *a-*, this gives us *anorexia*, meaning _____. The pathological condition **anorexia nervosa** is an eating disorder involving chronic fasting.
- Another Greek base connected with eating comes from the verb *phagein*, which means "to eat." With the prefix *a-* we can build the word _____, which means an inability to feed, and with the prefix *hyper-* we can form _____, which means a morbid voracity or a pathological overeating. The latter word is also known as **bulimia,** from the Greek *bous* ("ox") + *limos* ("hunger").
- **Phobia** is derived from *phobos*, the Greek word for "fear." Some words with *-phobia* do not describe actual pathological conditions but rather are semi-humorous.
- Give the meanings of the following words ending in *-phobia* and *-phobe*. Use an English dictionary if necessary.

Word for Word

English	Meaning
aichmophobia	
anthropophobia	
aviophobe	
cyclophobia	
galeophobia	
hobophobia	
pogonophobe	

- Combine the Greek words and Latin word below with *-phobia* to form English words, then give the meaning of the words you have formed. Use an English dictionary if necessary.

Greek Word	Meaning of Greek	English Word	Meaning of English
agora	assembly, market		
ailouros	cat		
akros (*acro-*)	topmost, top		
anemos	wind		
arachnē	spider		
brontē	thunderer		
claudere, claustrum (Latin verb)	to shut, close		
entoma (*en-*, "inside" + *tomos*, "slice")	insects		
hudor (base *hudr-*)	water		
nekros (*necro-*)	corpse, dead		
pharmakon (*pharmac-*)	drug, posion		
thalassa	sea		
xenos	stranger		

- Some of the words with *-phobia* have opposites based on the Greek *philos,* which means "friend", "lover," and "friendly." What, for example, is a **xenophile?** An **equinophile?** What is **necrophilia?** Use an English dictionary if necessary.

Word for Word

- The Greek word for "madness" is *mania*. This word is also used in English to denote intensely excited activity, including a speeding up of thought processes, incoherence, and aggression. What other English words begin with the base *man-* and end with *-mania*?

Base	Derivatives
man-	
-mania	

- What is **manic depression?** (Use a dictionary, if necessary.)
- The Latin verb *ludere, lusum* ("to play") combines with the prefix *de-* to give _____ and with the prefix *in-* to give _____.
- The Latin verb *pendere, pensum* ("to hang") is the base of a word such as _____.
- _____ is derived from the Greek prefix *dys-* ("ill," "bad," "abnormal") + *lexis* ("word"; compare *legein*, "to speak," "to read," and *logos*).
- _____, a severe mental disorder leading to disintegration of the personality and a loss of contact with reality (not, as is popularly supposed, "a split personality"), comes from the Greek bases *schizo-* ("split") + *phren-* ("mind," "will"). The Greek *phren, phrenos* means "the midriff," which the Greeks thought was the seat of the passions.
- What does **schizoid** mean?
- The Greek verb *mnaomai* ("I remember") and the cognate adjectives *mnemon* ("mindful") and *mnemonikos* ("belonging to memory") give the word _____.
- _____ is derived from the Latin verb *compellere, compulsum* ("to drive," "to force").
- What English words can be formed from the Latin adverb *frustra* ("in vain")?
- Can you think of a mental pathology derived from Latin *senex* ("old") and *senior* ("older")? (Combine with Latin *de-* + *ment-*.)
- _____ is derived from the Latin adjective *imbecillus* ("weak"), which itself is derived from *baculum*, which means a "staff" or "stick" (for supporting oneself).
- _____ is derived from the Greek word *moros* ("foolish").
- _____ is derived from the Greek *idios* ("own," "private"); the cognate noun *idiotēs* denoted someone who did not become involved in the life of the *polis* ("city-state").

Word for Word

- What are the bases of *idiosyncrasy?* Look up this word in an English dictionary to find any base you do not recognize.
- Use an English dictionary to find the bases and meanings of **latent, masochism,** and **subliminal.**

BIBLIOGRAPHY AND FURTHER READING

Armstrong, A. H., *An Introduction to Ancient Philosophy* (Totowa 1981).

Bréhier, E. (tr. J. Thomas), *The History of Philosophy 2: The Hellenistic and the Roman Age* (Chicago 1965).

Campbell, R. J., *Psychiatric Dictionary*, 9th Ed. (New York 2009).

Cornford, F. M., *Before and After Socrates* (Cambridge 1960).

Harre, R. and Lamb, R. (eds.), *The Encyclopedic Dictionary of Psychology* (Cambridge, Mass. 1983).

English, H. B. and English, A. C., *A Comprehensive Dictionary of Psychological and Psychoanalytical Terms: A Guide to Usage* (New York 1964).

Flew, A. (ed.), *A Dictionary of Philosophy*, 2nd Ed. (London 1984).

Gaarder, J. (tr. P. Møller), *Sophie's World: A Novel About the History of Philosophy* (London 1994).

Green, T. M., *The Greek and Latin Roots of English*, 4th Ed. (Lanham 2008).

Guthrie, W. K. C., *The Greek Philosophers from Thales to Aristotle* (London 1989).

Kayy, W. H., *Dictionary of Psychiatry and Psychology* (Paterson 1953).

Long, A. A., *Hellenistic Philosophy: Stoics, Epicureans, Sceptics*, 2nd Ed. (Berkeley 1986).

Warren, H. C. (ed.), *Dictionary of Psychology* (Boston 1934).

Weiner, P. P. (ed.), *Dictionary of the History of Ideas: Studies of Selected Pivotal Ideas* 4 (New York 1973).

Werner, A. (ed.), *A Psychiatric Glossary*, 5th Ed. (Boston 1980).

WEB SITES: NAMES AND URLS

"Classics in the History of Psychology"
     http://psychclassics.yorku.ca
"Aristotle"
     http://www.iep.utm.edu/aristotl
"Aristotle"
     http://plato.stanford.edu/entries/aristotle
"Epicureanism"
     http://plato.stanford.edu/entries/epicurus
"Greek Philosophy"
     http://www.utm.edu/research/iep/g/greekphi.htm
"Greek Philosophy"
     http://www.historyforkids.org/learn/greeks/philosophy/index.htm
"Greek Philosophy Archive"
     http://people.clemson.edu/~knox2/archive/Greek.html
"Hellenistic Philosophy"
     http://philosophypages.com/hy/2w.htm
"Historians and Philosophers: Classical Period (Until 500 A.D.)"
     http://www.scholiast.org/history/hp-clas.html
"Philosophy"
     http://ancienthistory.about.com/od/philosophy/Philosophy.htm
"Plato"
     http://plato.stanford.edu/entries/plato
"Pre-Socratic Philosophy"
     http://platostanford.edu/entries/presocratics
"Socrates"
     http://platostanford.edu/entries/socrates
"Stoicism"
     http://plato.stanford.edu/entries/stoicism

EXERCISES

1. Match each statement in *List B* with the names or terms in *List A* by listing the appropriate lower-case letter in *List B*.

List A	*List B*
Pythagoreans	_____
Socrates	_____
Plato	_____
Epicurean thought	_____

List B
(a) The soul does not survive after death because the atoms of which it consists disperse. Consequently there is no need to fear death.
(b) We can give examples of just acts, but these do not in themselves define justice. Behind the examples is the "form" (*eidolon*), which is the true idea of justice.
(c) "Very probably neither of us knows anything beautiful or good, but this man thinks he knows something when he doesn't; on the other hand I, when I don't know, don't think that I know."
(d) They did not eat meat because of their belief in the transmigration of souls.

2. From the list below choose one name to associate with each of the following:
Anaximander, Epicureans, Stoics, Thales, Aristotle, Plato, Narcissus, Pythagoras, Heracleitus, Sophists

a. The simile of the cave is an attempt to explain the inadequacy of sense perception.
Associated with _____.

b. There is no absolute right or wrong and no absolute justice: these things are all relative.
Associated with _____.

c. The *psychē* is responsible for sense perception and for physical movement.
Associated with _____.

d. To understand the world, one must seek to know the *logos* within oneself.
Associated with _____.

e. His followers avoided killing animals for food because they believed that all living creatures had souls that transmigrated to other creatures at death.
Associated with _____.

f. The cosmos (Greek *kosmos*) is made up of divine fire and each human soul is a spark of that divine fire.
Associated with _____.

g. The world exists through a conflict of opposites: heat and cold, wet and dry.
Associated with _____.

h. This mythological youth has given his name to a psychological pathology of obsessive self-love.
Associated with _____.

3. Consider each of the following statements. From your knowledge of the Greek and Latin
    origins of the words in bold, explain whether these words have been used correctly. Give
    reasons for your answers.
    (a) The way Socrates taught philosophy by means of question and answer is termed
         dialectic because he spoke in the dialect of Greek peasants instead of educated
         Greeks.
    (b) Aristotle's view of the psyche is more **empirical** than Plato's, for he is concerned
         with the soul's ability to know things through the experience of the senses,
         whereas Plato's theories are based on abstract reasoning.
    (c) Some perverts take a **narcissistic** pleasure in covering the walls and ceilings of
         their bedrooms with pictures of nude women in erotic poses.
    (d) People who have strong religious or philosophical beliefs are often able to bear
         misfortune **stoically**.
    (e) If we inquire into the **etiology** of a pathological condition, we will need to know
         not only the patient's medical history but also something about her or his lifestyle.
    (f) The Greeks used the term *kosmos* (English **cosmos**) to mean "universe" because
         they thought the universe was very beautiful.
    (g) The dinner was of **epicurean** proportions, with buffet tables groaning with
         lavishly prepared and artistically garnished delicacies.
    (h) If you blame your parents for being overstrict and repressive, you have an
         Oedipus complex.
    (i) A student explained: "What Socrates says is this. You have a crowd of people at
         a banquet, some strong, some weak. One of them is a doctor who is very wise
         because of his medical skills, but he is not as strong as the strongest people in the
         crowd. But because he is the wisest person there, he will be able to take the most
         food." Another student replied, "But that's a *non sequitur.*"

4. Read the following passage carefully and answer the questions that follow it.

> *Meno:* Can you tell me, Socrates, whether virtue *(aretē)* is something
> that can be taught? Or is it acquired by practice rather than by teaching?
> Or does it come to people not through learning or practice but by nature
> or some other means?
> *Socrates:* I must admit that I know nothing about virtue *(aretē)* at all,
> and if I do not know what a thing is, how can I know what it is like?
> Do you think that someone who had absolutely no idea who Meno was
> could possibly know whether he was good-looking or wealthy or of no-
> ble birth, or the opposite? Does that seem possible?
> *Meno:* Not to me. But, Socrates, is it true that you don't know what
> virtue *(aretē)* is?
> *Socrates:* Not only that, my friend. I don't think that I have ever met
> anyone who did know. What do you yourself say that virtue *(aretē)* is?

Meno: That isn't hard to explain. First of all, if you want to know what virtue *(aretē)* is for a man, the answer is simple: a man's virtue *(aretē)* lies in being able to handle the affairs of the city-state. And if you want to know what a woman's virtue *(aretē)* is, that is also not difficult to describe: she should manage her household well, be careful with the property belonging to it, and be obedient to her husband. Other types of virtue *(aretē)* exist for children, both female and male, and for elderly men, whether free or slaves. There are also a great many other virtues *(aretai)*, so it is no trouble to say what virtue *(aretē)* is.

Socrates: It seems I am really in luck, Meno. I was looking for one virtue *(aretē)*, but I have found a whole swarm of virtues *(aretai)* residing with you.

[Socrates then enlarges on the metaphor of a swarm of bees and compels Meno to admit that bees may differ in respect of characteristics such as size and beauty, but there is some essential nature that still makes them all bees.]

Socrates: The same is true of the virtues *(aretai)*. Even if there are many different ones, they all have one common element that makes them virtues *(aretai)*. Do you think that it is only in the case of virtue *(aretē)* that there is one for a man, another for a woman, and others as well, or is the same true of health and size and strength? Do you believe that there is one sort of health for a man and another for a woman? Or is the same element present wherever there is health, whether in a man or in any other thing?

Meno: I think health is the same in a man as in a woman.

Socrates: And isn't it the same with size and strength? If a woman is strong, won't she be strong in the same way and with the same strength? What I mean by "the same" is this: that strength does not differ in its nature as strength, whether it is found in a man or in a woman. Well, then: didn't you say that a man's virtue *(aretē)* was in managing the city-state well and a woman's in managing her household well?

Meno: I did.

Socrates: Is it possible to manage something well—a city-state or a household or anything else—unless you manage it sensibly and justly?

Meno: Certainly not.

Socrates: Then in order to be good, both women and men must have the same qualities of justice and good sense?

Meno: Apparently.

Socrates: And what about a child and an elderly man? Surely they could never be good if they were undisciplined or unjust?

Meno: Surely not.

Socrates: Would they have to be sensible and just?

Meno: Yes, they would.

Socrates: Then all humans are good in the same way, since they all become good by having the same qualities?

Meno: So it seems.

Socrates: But presumably if virtue *(aretē)* were not the same for them all, they would not be good in the same way?

Meno: Presumably not.

Socrates: Then, since virtue *(aretē)* is the same in every case, try to tell me what it is.

Meno: What could it be but the ability to rule people—if, that is, you are looking for a single answer to cover all cases?

Socrates: That is exactly what I'm after. But is virtue *(aretē)* then the same for a child and for a slave—the ability to rule their masters? Do you think that someone in a position to rule would still be a slave?

Meno: Absolutely not.

Socrates: It isn't likely, my good friend. And consider this: your definition is "the ability to rule"; shouldn't we add to this "justly and not unjustly"?

Meno: I think so, Socrates, since justice is virtue *(aretē)*.

Socrates: Virtue *(aretē)*, Meno, or a virtue *(aretē)*?

Meno: What do you mean?

Socrates: The same as in any other case. Consider roundness, for example. I should say that it is a shape but not that it is shape itself. My reason would be that other shapes exist as well.

Meno: And you'd be right. I too say that other virtues *(aretai)* exist besides justice.

Socrates: What are they? Tell me. I should name other shapes if you asked me to. So name some other virtues *(aretai)*.

Meno: I think courage is a virtue *(aretē)* and good sense and wisdom and magnificence and a great many other things.

Socrates: Well, Meno, we are back in the same predicament. We have found many virtues *(aretai)* while looking for only one, even though our method was different from the one we followed just now. What we can't find is the one that is common to them all.

(Plato, *Meno* 70a–74a [abridged])

a.   According to the definitions in this passage, is virtue the same in women as in men?

b.   In your own words, explain how Socrates uses the example of the slave to destroy Meno's argument (or the argument he has led Meno to formulate).

c.   What is your impression of Socrates' character as presented in this passage? Justify your answer from the passage.

d.   The Greek word that we translate as "virtue" is *aretē*. Briefly explain how *aretē* differs from modern western ideas of "virtue" and why Socrates seems to have difficulty in defining *aretē anthropinē* ("human virtue").

5. Read the section on *"Psychē"* in this chapter, then discuss the different meaning of the word *psychē* in the context of each of the passages below.
    (a) The sacrifice of a boar:

> They led up a boar, well-fattened and five years old.
> Then they made it stand by the fire, and the swineherd did not
> Forget the immortals—for he had sound thoughts—
> But to begin with cast on the fire hairs from the head
> Of the white-toothed boar, and prayed to all the gods
> For the return of the inventive Odysseus to his home.
> Then, rising up, he struck the boar with a piece of oak
> Left while splitting wood, and the *psychē* left it.
>
> (Homer, *Odyssey* 14.419–426)

(b) On the transmigration of souls:

> The Egyptians are the first who stated the theory that the *psychē* of a human is immortal and that, when the body passes away, it always enters another living creature at birth. When it has passed around all the creatures of the land and those of the sea and those able to fly, it once again enters the body of a human at birth.
>
> (Herodotus, *History* 2.123.2)

(c) A philosophical definition of the soul:

> First of all, perhaps, it is necessary to determine to which genus [the *psychē*] belongs and what it is; I mean whether it is a specific thing that has substance, or a quality, or a quantity, or an element of one of the other categories that have been distinguished. One must also determine whether it is a thing that exists potentially or rather something with an actual existence, since this makes no small difference. Next one must consider whether it consists of various parts or not and whether every *psychē* is of the same sort or not; and if they are not all of the same sort, whether they differ in species or in genus.
>
> (Aristotle, *On the Soul* 402a–b)

(d) On unacceptable risks:

> This is spring sailing-time. It I do not
> Praise, for to my heart it is no joy.
> A stolen chance. You would find it hard to escape harm.
> Yet even this men do with ignorant minds
> Since, to wretched mortals, money is their *psychē*.
> But death among the waves is terrible.
>
> (Hesiod, *Works and Days* 682–687)

6. (a) Combine the bases of the Greek words *soma* ("body"), *pathos* ("suffering"), and
         analysis ("unloosening," "separating into component parts") with the base *psych-*
         to form English words, then work out the meaning of the words formed. Use an
         English dictionary to check your answers, if necessary.
    (b) Explain the meaning of the following words by giving the meaning of the Greek or
         Latin bases from which they are derived. Use an English dictionary if necessary.
         1. **intellectual**   4. **dependency**
         2. **ontology**   5. **animosity**
         3. **dyslexic**   6. **egotist**
    (c) What aspects of the Greek myth led Freud to choose the phrase **Oedipus
         complex?**
    (d) What is "psychological warfare"?
    (e) Explain the meaning of **xenophobia, dependency,** and **amnesia** by giving the
         meanings of their Greek or Latin bases.

CHAPTER 9

HISTORY
A. Gosling and W. J. Dominik

WHAT IS HISTORY?

The Greeks and Romans were the first to record historical events in written form. There is a wide range of historical subjects and methodologies among the Greek and Roman historians. Their writings are concerned with public and private issues such as war and peace, wealth and poverty, and human nature and morality. These historians were not just interested in recording what happened but in explaining the reasons why something happened.

Although the Greek and Roman historians examined issues of divine and human causation and the relationship between gods and humans, they made an attempt to distinguish history from myth. Therefore historians today owe both the idea of history and the practice of historical writing to the ancient historians. The detailed study of ancient historiography and how we derive historical information from ancient texts and other evidence remains central to the approach taken by modern historians.

For Consideration

- What do we know about our own family backgrounds? How do we know this?
- How long has your family been living in the same place?
- If they were immigrants, when did the members of your family come to your country?
- Who founded the community where you live?
- What important buildings, statues, and other monuments are there in your community? What do they record?

Word Study

- What does the word **history** suggest to you? Express your thoughts briefly.
- Look up the word **history** in a dictionary that provides etymologies of the English words. What is the Greek word from which **history** is ultimately derived via Latin? This word means "learned," "expert," "knowledgeable," as, for example, a judge who is well versed in the law. The word **history** has the connotation of "finding out by investigation," or "inquiry."

Word for Word

- Note at least three different meanings of the word **history** in the dictionary. Note related words given in your dictionary such as **historian, historiographer, historic,** and **historical.**
- What are the meanings of the following Latin words? (For each of these Latin words think of an English derivative, then look this word up in an English dictionary that gives the derivations.)

Latin Words	English Derivative	Meaning of Latin
quaerere, quaesitum (verb)		
in- + quaerere, quaesitum (verb)		
vestigium (noun)		

- Determine the meaning of the following Latin verbs. (For help refer to the use of the Latin word in English. If necessary, look up the loan words in an English dictionary that provides etymologies.)

Latin Words	Meaning of Latin Verb	Use of Latin Word
agere, actum (plural of perfect passive participle *actum* is *acta*)		An **agenda** (plural) is a list of "things that must be done." *Acta* ("things done") *senatus* were the daily records of senatorial business at Rome, which were published and could be consulted by historians. The Romans also recorded achievements as *res gestae*, which literally means "things performed."
curare, curatum		A **curator** is a guardian, keeper, manager, or an overseer.
dare, datum (plural of perfect passive participle *datum* is *data*)		**data** (plural) means "things given."

METHODOLOGY AND TOOLS OF HISTORY

For Consideration

- In what ways is history recorded and passed on?
- Are these ways the same in all cultures?
- How did the ancient Egyptians, Jews, and Babylonians record and pass on their history? How about Indians? How about Africans?

> History is the framing of questions by a particular human being in a particular space-time context; he asks questions, and he adduces evidence to support his answers, and in both of these acts he makes use of hypothesis before ever he "finds" a fact.
>
> (A. Toynbee 1972: 486)

- If a historian is an expert in the same way as a judge is expert in legal matters, what does this suggest about how a historian works?
- Should a historian always be objective? *Can* a historian always be objective?
- What is a *fact?*
- How useful and how reliable are the following primary sources to the modern historian of the ancient world?

> The *primary sources* available for the study of the ancient Greek and Roman worlds include texts written by ancient authors such as historians, playwrights, poets, novelists, philosophers, medical and scientific writers, astronomers, geographers, and orators; other written documents such as commercial and legal documents (for example, contracts and wills) and private letters; epigraphical evidence, that is, inscriptions of laws, edicts, decrees, palace records, temple records, state records, and epitaphs; and other archaeological evidence and material remains, including the physical remains of cities and settlements, buildings (for example, temples, amphitheaters, and tombs), monuments, pottery, sculpture, wall paintings, mosaics, armor, weapons, jewelry, and other personal property.

- What are some of the problems with these primary sources? What affects the reliability of source material?
- What *secondary sources* are available?
- If you wanted to write a history of the town where you live, what sources would you use?
- What does the following epitaph, which was found at Rome and dates from the second century BCE, reveal?

Stranger, I don't have much to say; stop and read.
This is the lovely tomb of a beautiful woman.
Her parents named her Claudia.
She adored her husband with all her heart.
She gave birth to two sons; one of these
She leaves on earth; the other she has buried.
She was charming in speech, yet elegant in her bearing.
She minded the house; she spun wool. I've spoken. Move on.

(*Corpus Inscriptionum Latinarum* 1.2.1211)

Word Study

- For each of the following Greek and Latin words, think of at least one English derivative.

Greek/Latin Words	Meaning	Derivative
autos (Greek pronoun)	self	
bios (Greek noun)	life	
cor, cordis (Latin noun)	heart	
graphein (Greek verb)	to write	
memor, memoris (Latin adjective)	mindful of	
monere, monitum (Latin verb)	to warn, advise, remind	
monumentum (Latin noun)	something that preserves the memory of a thing; a memorial	
narrare, narratum (Latin verb)	to tell, relate	
obicere, obiectum (Latin verb)	to throw against, oppose; expose	
scribere, scriptum (Latin verb)	to write	
semeion (Greek noun)	mark, sign	
tradere, traditum (Latin verb)	to hand over	

RECORDING TIME

*a*ncient calendars and timekeeping were usually based on natural cycles, like day and night, the movements of the sun, moon, and stars, the cycle of the seasons. Prehistoric stone circles of Europe such as Stonehenge and Avebury were probably astronomical observatories for accurately marking the seasons.

The Egyptians were the first to use a solar calendar of 365 days, in contrast to most other ancient civilizations, including the Babylonians, Greeks, and Chinese who used a lunar calendar based on a lunar month of twenty-nine or thirty days. The Hebrew calendar is dated from the beginning of Creation, calculated to be 3760 BCE; the Islamic calendar is dated from Mohammed's flight from Mecca to Medina (July 16, 622 CE in the Gregorian calendar).

Because the lunar year is too short, lunar calendars do not keep pace accurately with the seasons, unless corrected from time to time by the insertion of intercalary days or months (compare the intercalary day in February of each leap year in the Gregorian calendar).

The Roman year, which began in March (the month of Mars, god of war, when the campaigning season began), originally consisted of ten months; the names of the months September, October, November, and December are derived from the Latin numerals *septem* ("seven"), *octo* ("eight"), *novem* ("nine"), and *decem* ("ten"). Later two additional months were included and the beginning of the year was moved to January (named after Janus, the god of beginnings and endings).

The month of July is named after Julius Caesar (100–44 BCE) and August after his successor Augustus, who were both interested in the calendar. Julius Caesar engaged the services of an Alexandrian astronomer for his calendar reforms, which is why the Julian calendar (and subsequently, the Gregorian calendar) used an adaptation of the Egyptian solar calendar instead of the lunar calendar used in early Rome.

While the seven-day week is derived from the Babylonians, the division of the day and the night into twelve hours originates in Egypt, where the first shadow-clock (a primitive sundial, *circa* 1500 BCE) and water-clocks were devised. A water clock (Greek *klepsydra*) consisted of a stone bowl out of which water flowed at a consistent rate into another bowl. Rings on the interior marked the minutes.

A water clock (klepsydra)

For Consideration

- In modern western thinking time is something measurable and linear. Is this so in all cultures? (Mythologies, for example, tend not to be chronological.) Contrast the idea of chronological time with concepts like eternity and timelessness.

Word for Word

Chronos referred to measurable time, but the ancient Greeks also had another word for time, *kairos*, which was the "right time," the moment of opportunity and fulfillment.

- Can you think of an English word for *kairos*? A Spanish word or phrase?

Word Study

 ive at least one derivative for each of the Latin and Greek words and abbreviations below, where indicated.

Word/Abbreviation	Meaning	Derivative
AD (*anno domini;* compare CE)	in the year of our Lord	————
aevum (Latin noun)	age	
antiquus (Latin adjective)	ancient	
BC (compare BCE)	(before Christ)	————
chronos (Greek noun)	time	
finis (Latin noun)	end	
primus (Latin adjective)	first	
primitivus (Latin adjective)	first of its kind	
protos (Greek adjective)	first	
tempus, temporis (Latin noun)	time	

- What do these terms mean: **diachronic, synchronic, anachronism?**
- What is meant by a **cyclic** view of history (compare Greek *kuklos,* "ring," "circle")?

GREEK AND ROMAN HISTORIANS

Approach and Methodology

*T*he Greeks and Romans did not distinguish, as we do, between myth, legend and history. In a sense the epic poems of Homer, for example, were regarded by the Greeks as part of their history. The first writer of history in our modern sense, however, was Herodotus, who is often referred to as "the father of history." Before Herodotus, writers of history had concerned themselves mainly with genealogies, geographical accounts, and local history.

Most ancient historians are conscious of history as a means of instruction, with a strong moral content. They regard the events and people they write about as providing examples, both good and bad, for others to follow, particularly in the political and military spheres.

Today we probably think of historians as doing most of their work in libraries, archives, and museums of archaeology, but many of the ancient Greeks and some Romans believed strongly that a man could not write history if he did not have personal experience of the things he wrote about such as politics and war.

Besides being instructive, history was expected to be entertaining for the reader and ancient historians felt free to embellish their material with descriptive passages and with rhetorical speeches. These speeches are meant to represent what might have been said on an occasion rather than to serve as a record of the actual words spoken; they are an opportunity for the writer to display his rhetorical skills and style.

The Romans took over the tradition of historiography from the Greeks (in fact, the earliest Roman writers of history wrote in Greek, not Latin). The first Roman historian to write in Latin was the senator, soldier, and landowner Cato (234–148 BCE; *Origines*). His successors mostly wrote *Annals*: the structure of their histories recounted events year by year rather than thematically. For example, Livy begins each year with the names of the consuls and other new magistrates, then proceeds to an account of political events at Rome and her wars abroad, and then notes any other occurrences of significance during the year, including religious portents. Therefore he does not always recount a war or a political struggle as a continuous episode, but may tell parts of it in the accounts of each year.

Word Study

- Give at least one derivative of the following Greek and Latin words.

Greek/Latin Word	Meaning	Derivatives
annalis (Latin adjective)	annual, yearly	
annus (Latin noun)	year	
archē (Greek noun)	beginning, governing power	
archeion (Greek noun)	the place where the archons (magistrates) had their offices and kept their records	
chronos (Greek noun)	time	
histor (Greek noun/ adjective)	adjective: "knowing," "well-versed in"; noun: "learned person," "expert"	
historia (Greek and Latin noun)	account, story, history	

The Major Historians

Herodotus

Herodotus (Greek *Herodotos*; born *circa* 484 BCE) was born at Halicarnassus (modern Bodrum). This was one of many Greek cities in Asia Minor that had been under Persian rule but were liberated by the Greek victory of Xerxes in 480 BCE. He spent much of his life travelling and on his travels collected material for his *History*. The main topic of this work is the Persian Wars (490–470 BCE), when the attempts of the Persian kings Darius and later Xerxes to invade and conquer mainland Greece were defeated at the battles of Marathon (490 BCE) and Salamis (480 BCE). Herodotus, however, also traces the legendary past of both the Persian and Greek nations and gives much geographical and antiquarian information about the countries he visited, which included mainland Greece and the Greek islands, Asia Minor and Mesopotamia, Scythia and

Herodotus and Thucydides

Thrace, Syria and Palestine, southern Italy, and Egypt. For a few years he lived in Athens and was therefore part of the beginnings of the great intellectual movement there in the fifth century.

Herodotus set great store by personal inquiry and investigation in composing his *Histories*. Although he was sometimes credulous and uncritical in accepting what local informants told him, his standards of accuracy were generally high.

Thucydides

*T*hucydides (Greek *Thoukudidēs*; born *circa* 464 BCE) was an Athenian citizen. As a naval commander he had firsthand experience of war, but he was forced to live in exile for some years after a military failure.

The subject of his work is the Peloponnesian War between Athens and Sparta and their respective allies (431–404 BCE) which he lived through; therefore he had first hand knowledge of at least some of the events and could talk to people who had taken part in others. This work, however, is unfinished, as Book 8 breaks off in the middle of his account of the events of 411 BCE.

He is respected for his insight into cause and effect and his accuracy on chronology and points of detail, but he is not free from bias. Like other ancient historians, he embellished his work with speeches that purport to give the gist of what was said on particular occasions, but which are rhetorical set pieces used for effect.

Xenophon

*X*enophon (*circa* 430–*circa* 356 BCE) who was born at Athens, was a general and a writer; he was also a friend and pupil of Socrates. In 401 BCE he joined an army of mercenaries raised by Cyrus, a Persian prince who was trying to take the throne from his brother. Cyrus' army was defeated and the Greek commanders were murdered; Xenophon, although a junior officer, led the surviving Greek army back through hostile territory to Greek shores. (An account of this is given in his *Anabasis*). With his soldiers he then joined the Spartans as a mercenary. Either because of his Spartan sympathies or because of his friendship with Socrates, he lost his Athenian citizenship for a while. His works include political and military studies, works about the life and teachings of Socrates, and a history of Greece from 411–362 BCE entitled *Hellenika*; this picks up where Thucydides' *History* breaks off and covers the end of the Peloponnesian War and its aftermath.

Polybius

olybius (*circa* 200–118 BCE) was a wealthy Greek aristocrat and politician. For political reasons he was banished from Greece and went to live in Rome, where he made friends with some of the most influential people of the time, in particular the Roman aristocrat and general Scipio Aemilianus, a man who was also a patron of literature and philosophy. With Scipio, Polybius traveled to Africa and was present when Scipio defeated and sacked Carthage.

In his research he had access to first hand information from men who had served in the campaigns and to public records and private letters as well as to the work of earlier historians. Like many other historians, he believed that the study of history was important in the training of statesmen. Because he was a Greek, writing for a Greek audience, he included in his history an explanation of Roman methods of government, the Roman constitution, and the functioning of the Roman army.

Polybius

His *Histories* cover the rise of Rome's power, from 264–146 BCE, the period when Rome began to expand into the Mediterranean and to come into conflict with her neigbours, notably Carthage, against whom Rome fought three Punic wars, and Greece, including not only Macedonia and its leader Philip V but also Corinth, which was sacked in 146 BCE.

Flavius Josephus

lavius Josephus (born *circa* 37 CE) was a Jew who was educated in the Rabbinical tradition and was sent to Rome as an ambassador. On his return to Judea he became one of the leaders of the revolt against Roman government and was a commander of the Jewish forces in Galilee. Josephus, however, was captured by the Romans. He was given a pardon and became a member of the entourage of Vespasian, the Roman general in command of the Jewish campaign, and his son Titus (he took their family name, Flavius). He wrote in Greek and his works include a *History of the Jewish War* and *Jewish Antiquities* (a history of the Jews from Adam up to his own days).

The triumphal celebration following the fall of Jerusalem described by Josephus

Caesar

Gaius Julius Caesar (100–44 BCE) was not only a very successful general who was responsible for the conquest of Gaul but he was also a powerful Roman politician. His political ambition led eventually to civil war in which he defeated the senatorial forces led by Pompey. He was made perpetual dictator (therefore in effect ending the Republican constitution of Rome), but was assassinated in 44 BCE by a Republican party led by Brutus and Cassius.

Julius Caesar

The *Commentaries* of Caesar are records of his campaigns in Gaul. Subsequently he also wrote a record of the *Civil War*. Although he writes of himself in the third person, his works are essentially intended to glorify his achievements and make him acceptable to the Roman people.

Sallust

Gaius Sallustius Crispus (86–34 BCE) was a Roman senator and supporter of Caesar who was expelled from the Senate and later tried for and acquitted of extortion in the province of Africa. He then retired from public life and devoted himself to writing a monograph on the *Conspiracy of Catiline* (an attempted revolution that took place in 63 BCE) and an account of the *Jugurthine War* (111–105 BCE; Jugurtha was a Numidian leader who was at first an ally of Rome but later her enemy). Both works show a thematic concern with the moral and political decline of Rome (compare Livy). They also show bias against the senatorial aristocracy. His narrative style, however, is dramatic and effective, with skillful depiction of character.

Sallust also wrote a longer work, the *Histories,* which deals with the period from 78–67 BCE, but unfortunately, only a few fragments of this work survive.

Livy

Titus Livius (59 BCE–17 CE), unlike most ancient historians, was not involved in political or military life. He had lived through the civil wars that followed the assassination of Julius Caesar and the struggle between Caesar's heir Octavian (later the emperor Augustus) and Mark Antony. Although Augustus claimed to have "restored the Republic," he in fact created a monarchy veiled in republican constitutional forms. Livy's sense of horror at the civil wars and his pessimism about Rome's moral and political decline (compare Sallust) are evident in the preface to his history, *From the Foundation of the City* (*Ab Urbe Condita*), a history of Rome from her legendary beginnings in the eighth century BCE to his own times.

By the time Livy died, he had written 142 books. The emphasis of his work was on the late Republican period and the Civil Wars. These later books, however, have not survived, and of the thirty-five books still extant, those most widely read are the accounts of the early history of Rome, the war against Hannibal (the Second Punic War, 218–201 BCE), and the spread of

Rome's power in the Mediterranean world in the second century BCE. Livy is traditional and conservative, with a great sense of pride in Rome's past. Although he praised Pompey (which implies some degree of support for the Republican cause), he was also a friend and admirer of Augustus and tutor to the future emperor Claudius.

Livy seldom shows evidence of original research and where accounts in his sources differ, he will often summarize both accounts and note the differences without attempting to decide between them.

Tacitus

Cornelius Tacitus (*circa* 56–*circa* 120 CE) was a senator and celebrated lawyer. His earliest works are a *Dialogue on Orators; Agricola,* a biography of his distinguished father-in-law, the great soldier and governor of Britain; and *Germania,* a monograph on the history and customs of the peoples of Germany (Roman attempts to conquer Germany had begun under Augustus, and during Tacitus' lifetime the provinces of Upper and Lower Germany became part of the Roman empire).

Tacitus' major historical works are the *Histories,* which cover the civil wars after the death of Nero and the reign of the Flavian emperors (68–96 CE), and the *Annals,* which cover the period of the early Empire, from the death of Augustus to the death of Nero. (Neither of these works survives in its entirety). Tacitus' early adult life coincided with the reign of Domitian, who was tyrannical and autocratic and who severely restricted the powers of the Roman Senate and freedom of intellectual and political activity. The bitterness of these memories colors the way in which the pro-Republican senator Tacitus depicts the reigns of previous emperors. Nevertheless, he took great care over the accuracy of his facts. Besides consulting the works of earlier writers, he used the state archives (the *Acta Senatus,* the record of the proceedings of the Senate) as source material.

SOURCE PASSAGES

Below are five extracts from Herodotus, Thucydides, Polybius, Livy, and Tacitus. All of these source passages are from the prefaces with which these ancient historians began their works. These extracts afford an idea of the aims and methods of each writer.

For Consideration

As you read each of the historical passages below, consider the following questions:

- Does the historian choose contemporary events of which he has personal knowledge, or does he have access to others with personal knowledge? Events in the recent past? Events in the more distant past?
- Does he give reasons for his choice?
- What does he say about how he researched his material? Personal inquiry? Books? Public records? Personal interviews?

- Does he distinguish between myth and history?
- Does he emphasize the importance in his work of any of the following?
  didactic function (that is, teaching by example)?
  moral example?
  the character of individual leaders?
  literary style?
  objectivity?
  accuracy?
- Does he display any bias?

Herodotus, Histories *preface, 1.5.3*

> This is a record of the research of Herodotus of Halicarnassus. Its aim is to ensure that . . . great and marvelous achievements—some by Greeks and some by non-Greeks—do not go uncelebrated. . . .
>
> These, then, are the stories Persians and Phoenicians tell. I am not going to state that these events happened in one way or another. Instead I shall speak of the man I personally know was the first to commit wrongs against the Greeks.

Thucydides, The Peloponnesian War *1.21–22*

> Judging from the evidence that I have presented, one would not be mistaken if one believed that things in the distant past were very much as I have described them. Adopting this view is preferable to trusting what poets have said about this period, since they embellish their subjects to make them more impressive. It is also preferable to the stories prosewriters have strung together with the aim of making their work more attractive to an audience rather than more accurate. The things they write about are impossible of proof and the majority of them have, through the passage of time, become so incredible as to have achieved the status of myths and fables. Rather than believing these versions, one should take the view that my account represents a sufficiently accurate investigation of these matters, considering that they belong to the distant past. . . .
>
> Various individuals made speeches when they were preparing to go to war or were already at war. It has proven difficult to recall precisely what was said, both for me, in the case of the speeches I heard myself, and for those who reported to me from other places. Therefore I have presented in the speeches what I believed each person was most likely to have said, given the demands of each occasion, while at the same time remaining as close as possible to the overall meaning of what was actually said. But as to the facts of what happened in the war, I have made it my policy not to write my account on the basis of the first evidence that happened to appear or of what seemed most probable to me.

Instead I have investigated as carefully as possible every detail both of those events at which I was present in person and of those I have heard about from others. The research was difficult nonetheless, as those who were present on each occasion did not give identical accounts of the same events but were influenced by their favor for one side or the other or by their own memories.

The absence of a mythological or fabulous element will perhaps make my work seem less enjoyable to an audience, but I shall be satisfied if it is considered useful by those who wish to understand clearly the events that occurred in the past and those that—given the nature of human history—will one day occur again in the same or a similar way. My work has been composed not as a fine piece of writing for an immediate audience but rather as a thing of value for all time.

Polybius, Histories 3.31.2–4, 7–8, 11–13

If there were anyone who believed that he was capable on his own of facing any possible situation, I should perhaps say that a knowledge of the events of the past was good but not essential. But if there is no one, or at least no human, who would be so bold as to say this about his own personal affairs or those of his community—since, even if all is well at present, no intelligent person will feel certain about the future on the basis of present circumstances—then I say that a thorough knowledge of the past is not merely good but absolutely essential. . .

In the immediate present all people continually adapt themselves and suit what they say and do to the circumstances, so that it is difficult to determine each person's policy and the truth is often very obscure. But past actions, because they can be examined in the light of actual facts, offer a true reflection of each person's principles and beliefs, and make it clear from whom we may expect favor, generosity, and assistance and from whom the opposite. . . Therefore both writers and readers of history should not pay the same attention to a mere narrative of events as to the question of what preceded, what accompanied, and what followed each of these events. For, if one removes from history the consideration of why, how, and for whose sake a deed was done and whether the outcome was a reasonable one, what remains will be a fine display of writing but will have no educational value. It will give immediate enjoyment, but will be of no use for the future whatsoever.

Livy, From the Foundation of the City *preface 6–7, 9–10*

The accounts that are handed down of events before the city of Rome was founded or its foundation planned derive their attraction more from the narratives of poets than from unquestionable records of historical events. I do not intend either to support these accounts or to refute them. The distant past may be forgiven when it makes the early beginnings of cities more impressive by mingling human elements with divine ones. . .

In my opinion, each person should consider closely the following points: how people lived, what their values were, and through which individuals and what skills (both at home and at war) Rome's power was established and increased. Next, one should follow in one's mind the story of how, as discipline gradually began to decline, there was an initial weakening of traditional values. One should observe how from that point they declined more and more and then began to collapse entirely until these times arrived, in which we are able to endure neither our own faults nor the measures needed to cure them.

What is especially beneficial and profitable in the study of history is this—that you observe examples of every sort as if they were set down on a great monument. From these you may select for yourself and your country things to imitate and other things, bad in their origins and bad in their results, to avoid.

Tacitus, Annals *1.1*

The early fortunes of the Roman nation, both good and bad, have been recorded by distinguished writers, and the period of Augustus did not lack suitable talents to tell its story, until they were discouraged by the growth of flattery. Accounts of events under Tiberius, Gaius, Claudius, and Nero were falsified during their periods of dominance because of fear, and after they fell were influenced by the hatred that remained from recent times. This is why I have decided to relate only a few events under Augustus (and only from the very end of his reign), and then to describe the rule of Tiberius and everything else, without anger or partiality, the motives for which I simply do not have.

The following source passage which relates a famous story of early Rome (490 BCE) illustrates aspects of Livy's style in *From the Foundation of the City*.

The Story of Coriolanus and Veturia
(*Livy*, From the Foundation of the City 2.40.1–11)

The story that Livy recounts features Coriolanus, who was a very successful Roman general, and his mother Veturia. He was regarded as a hero by the Romans until his political ambitions became suspect and he was accused of treason. He fled from Rome to a hostile tribe, the Volsci, and led them in war against the Romans. When the Volscian successes threatened the safety of the city of Rome itself, ambassadors and priests were sent to plead with Coriolanus, but neither of these delegations met with any success.

Then the married women went in large numbers to Veturia, Coriolanus' mother, and Volumnia, his wife. I am unable to determine clearly whether this was motivated by public policy or by the women's own fear. What is certain is that they succeeded in persuading both Veturia, who was quite old, and Volumnia to take Marcius' two young sons and go to the enemy camp. Since the men could not defend the city by force of arms, the women would defend it by tears and pleas.

They came to the camp and Coriolanus was informed that a large force of women had arrived. As one might expect of a man who had not been moved by ambassadors representing the majesty of the state or by priests who had set the power of religion before his eyes and heart, he was all the more stubborn in the face of women's tears. Then, one of his friends recognized Veturia, whose sadness marked her out from the others as she stood between her daughter-in-law and her grandchildren. "Unless my eyes are deceiving me," he said, "your mother, your wife, and your children are here."

Coriolanus sprang from his seat almost as if he were mad and went to meet his mother, but as he came to embrace her she turned from pleas to anger and said, "Before I accept your embrace, let me know whether I have come to my enemy or to my son and whether I am in your camp as your prisoner or as your mother. Have my long life and miserable old age brought me to this—that I should see you first an exile and then an enemy? Were you capable of destroying the land that bore and nurtured you? Though you had come with a heart full of rage and threats, did your anger not lessen as you crossed the border? When Rome was in sight, did this thought not cross your mind: "Within those walls are my home and the gods of my family. There too are my mother, my wife, and my children"? If I had never given birth, Rome would not be under attack. If I had no son, I should have died a free woman in a free country. But now, I could not suffer anything more painful to me or more disgraceful to you and, though I am extremely sad, I shall not be so for long. Think instead of these others who, if you go on, can expect death at an early age or a long period of slavery."

> Then his wife and his children put their arms around him and the whole crowd of women began to weep and raise laments for themselves and their country. At last they broke the man. He embraced his family and told them to go. Then he moved his camp back from the city. It is said that, after his armies had been marched out of Roman territory, he died under the weight of resentment at what he had done, though accounts of his actual death differ. In the work of Fabius, by far the most ancient of our sources, I find it said that he lived to reach old age. Fabius certainly says that toward the end of his life he often used to repeat the saying that exile is far more miserable when one is old.

- How does Livy present the character of Veturia? What qualities and actions does Veturia show in this account that would make her an admirable example in Livy's eyes?
- Why do you think Veturia and the other women succeeded in persuading Coriolanus not to attack Rome when priests and diplomats had failed?
- What preconceptions about gender and attitudes to women are evident in this story?
- How does Livy present the character of Coriolanus? Do you think Coriolanus, as portrayed by Livy, is intended to be a good example or a warning (or both)?
- How does Livy present the story in such a way as to make his readers sympathize with any particular character or viewpoint?
- Judging by the way this story is told, what expectations do you think Romans of Livy's time and class had about how a leader should behave?
- In his preface Livy observes that "in history you have a record of the infinite variety of human experience plainly set out for all to see; and in that record you can find for yourself and your country both examples and warnings." What is one such example in this extract?
- Livy says in his preface that he will "find antiquity a rewarding study" because he will be able to forget the problems of his modern world. What is there in the story of Coriolanus and Veturia, as he narrates it, that might have a positive message for Roman society in Livy's day?
- The speech Livy attributes to Veturia is not a historical record of her own words on the occasion, but a composition by Livy himself. How does this fact affect our judgment of Livy as an historian? What do you think Livy's intention was in including speeches like this in his history?
- Considering what Livy says about the last years of Coriolanus and about Fabius, what do you think of his historical method and use of source material? Do you find his historical method in this extract satisfactory? How does it compare with modern historical methods?

For Consideration

- What do these ancient historians have in common with each other and in what ways are they similar to and different from modern historians?
- Does bias exist only in the writer or also in the listener or reader?
- Are some of the words listed in this chapter value laden? Do they have negative or positive associations?

KEY WORDS FOR HISTORY

Greek/Latin Words	Origin	Meaning	English Derivative
aevum	Latin noun	age	**primeval**
agere, actum	Latin verb	to do, conduct	**agenda** ("things that must be done")
annalis	Latin adjective	year	**annals, annalist**
annus	Latin noun	year	**annual**
antiquus	Latin adjective	old, ancient	**antiquarian**
archē	Greek noun	beginning governing power	**archaeology; archive** (singular); **archives** (plural). French *archif* (singular)
archeion	Greek noun	the place where archons (magistrates) had their offices and kept their records	
autos	Greek pronoun	self	**autobiography**
bios	Greek noun	life	**biography**
chronos	Greek noun	time	**chronicles; chronology; anachronism,** from Greek *ana-* ("up") + *chronos* ("time") + Greek *-ismos* ("condition," "characteristic")
cor, cordis	Latin noun	heart	**record**
curare, curatum	Latin verb	to care for	**curate**

ad- + curare, curatum	Latin verb	to take care of	**accuracy**
dare, datum	Latin verb	to give	**data** ("things given")
facere, factum	Latin verb	to make, do	**faction, factual**
finis	Latin noun	end	**finish**
graphein	Greek verb	to write	**historiography**
histor	Greek adjective	knowing, versed in	**historian, prehistory, history, protohistory**
	Greek noun	expert	
historia	Greek and Latin noun	account, story, history	
memor, memoris	Latin adjective	mindful of	**memory, remember, commemorate**
monumentum	Latin noun	monument	**monument,** from *monere* ("to advise," "to warn," "to remind")
narrare, narratum	Latin verb	to tell, relate	**narrate, narrative**
obicere, obiectum	Latin verb	to throw against, oppose; expose	**objective**
primus	Latin adjective	first	**primeval,** from Latin *primus* ("first") + *aevum* ("age")
primitivus	Latin adjective	first of its kind	**primitive.** French *primitif*
protos	Greek adjective	early	**protohistoric**
semeion	Greek noun	mark, sign	**semiotics**
temporalis	Latin adjective	transitory	**temporal**
tempus, temporis	Latin noun	time	
tradere, traditum	Latin verb	to hand over	**tradition**

BIBLIOGRAPHY AND FURTHER READING

Breisach, E., *Historiography: Ancient, Medieval and Modern*, 3rd Ed. (Chicago 2007).

Collingwood, R., *The Idea of History*, 2nd Ed. (Oxford 1994).

Croce, B. (tr. D. Ainslie), *History: Its Theory and Practice* (New York 1960).

Gilderhus, M. T., *History and Historians: A Historiographical Introduction*, 7th Ed. (Upper Saddle River 2009).

Grant, M., *The Ancient Historians* (New York 1970).

Green, P., *Classical Bearings: Interpreting Ancient History and Culture* (London 1989).

Morley, N., *Writing Ancient History* (Ithaca 1999).

———, *Ancient History: Key Themes and Approaches* (London 2000).

Southgate, B. C., *History: What and Why? Ancient, Modern and Postmodern Perspectives*, 2nd Ed. (London 2001).

Speake, G., *A Dictionary of Ancient History* (Oxford 1994).

Toynbee, A., *A Study of History* (London 1972).

WEB SITES: NAMES AND URLS

"Ancient History Timelines — Dynasties and Chronologies"
    http://ancienthistory.about.com/od/timelines/Ancient_History_Timeline_Dynasties_and_Chronologies.htm

"Ancient Rome"
    http://www.historylink101.com/ancient_rome.htm

"Ancient Rome Republic, Empire, and Fall of Rome"
    http://ancienthistory.about.com/od/romeancientrome/Ancient_Rome_Republic_Empire_Fall_of_Rome.htm

"Archaeology and Antiquity (Prehistory to 500 A.D.)"
    http://www.scholiast.org/history/hi-aran.html

"Biographies of Important Ancient People — Famous People"
    http://ancienthistory.about.com/od/people/Biographies_of_Important_Ancient_Peope_Famous_People.htm

"Eras — Major Events in the 3 Eras of Roman History"
    http://ancienthistory.about.com/od/romehistory/Ancient_Rome_Roman_History_Periods.htm

"Historians of Rome — Roman Historians"
    http://ancienthistory.about.com/od/romehistorians/Historians_of_Rome_Roman_Historians.htm

"Historians — Resources on Historians of Ancient Greece"
    http://ancienthistory.about.com/od/greekhistorians/Historians_Resources_on_historians_of_ancient_Greece.htm

"Historians and Philosophers: Classical Period (Until 500 A.D.)"
    http://www.scholiast.org/history/hp-clas.html
"Internet Ancient History Sourcebook"
    http://www.fordham.edu/halsall/ancient/asbook.html
"An Overview of Classical Greek History from Mycenae to Alexander"
    http://www.perseus.tufts.edu/cgi-bin/ptext?doc=Perseus%3Atext%3A1999.
    04.0009&query=toc
"Roman Empire — The Empire of Rome"
    http://ancienthistory.about.com/od/romeempire
"Roman Empire — Ancient Rome and Its Empire"
    http://ancienthistory.about.com/od/romanempire/Roman_Empire_Ancient_
    Rome_and_Its_Empire.htm
"The Roman Empire — Children's Section"
    http://www.roman-empire.net/children/index.html

EXERCISES

1.   Give the base of each of the following words and the meaning of the base, then explain the meanings accordingly:

Example: **annals**
Base: *ann-* [or *annal-*]
Meaning of base: *year* [or *yearly*]
Meaning of English word: *historical record structured chronologically by years*

    a. **investigation**   c. **memorial**
    b. **objective**   d. **record**

2.   (a) Give the meanings of the following Greek and Latin words.

        Example: **graphein**
        Greek or Latin word: *graphein*
        Meaning: write

        1. *logos*   5. *aevum*
        2. *dare, datum*   6. *vestigium*
        3. *archē*   7. *primus*
        4. *annus*   8. *curare, curatum*

(b) Using bases either by themselves or in combination from the words listed in 2(a), form three English words relevant to the study of history. Give the meanings of the words you form.

Example:
English word: **historiography**
Meaning: *The writing of history*

	English Words	Meaning
Base 1		
Base 2		
Base 3		

3. Complete the following sentences with appropriate English words formed by combining bases, prefixes, and/or words selected from the following list.

1. *graphein*
2. *scribere*
3. *ana-*
4. *autos*
5. *histor*

6. *chronos*
7. *bios*
8. *finis*
9. *datum*
10. *pre-*

a. No written records exist from _____ times.

b. It would be _____ to claim that the policies of a past government were influenced by the policies of the present administration.

c. An _____ cannot be regarded as an entirely reliable historical source because it is bound to be selective and influenced by personal interests.

4. There are two Greek words for time: *chronos* and *kairos*. What is the difference in meaning between them?

5. What types of *primary sources* are available to historians in the following categories?

Written Sources	Archaeological Sources	Other Sources

6. Give the meaning of the Greek word *histor* and explain the significance of this meaning in terms of Herodotus' understanding of his purpose as an historian.

7. Based on what the ancient historians say in the extracts from their prefaces in this chapter, which of these writers is more concerned with accuracy and objectivity? Do you think any of these writers is likely to be as accurate and objective as a modern historian?

APPENDIX 1

GREEK AND LATIN ALPHABETS

W. J. Dominik, J. L. Hilton, and A. P. Bevis

Greek Letter	Roman Letter	Greek Letter in English	Greek Name	Approximate Pronunciation of Greek and Latin
A α	A a	A a	Alpha	Greek and Latin: c**u**p; f**a**ther
B β	B b	B b	Beta	Greek and Latin: **b**
Γ γ	G g	G g, ng	Gamma	Greek and Latin: **g**et (Greek: before another γ and before κ, χ, ξ, and probably μ pronounced like the "n" in "finger" or the "ng" in "sing")
Δ δ	D d	D d	Delta	Greek and Latin: **d**
E ε	E e	E e	Epsilon	Greek and Latin: p**e**t (Latin: also w**ai**t)
Z ζ	Z z	Zd zd (later Z z)	Zeta	Greek: wis**d**om, later pronounced as **z**; Latin: **z** (taken over from Greek)
H η		E e	Eta	Greek: t**ê**te (French)
Θ θ		Th th	Theta	Greek: **t**, later **th** (with an "h" sound, later as **th**)
	H h			Latin: **h**
I ι	I i	I i	Iota	Greek and Latin: d**i**p, d**ee**p (Latin: also **y**acht)
K κ	C c, K k	K k, C c	Kappa	Greek and Latin: **k**
Λ λ	L l	L l	Lambda	Greek and Latin: **l**
M μ	M m	M m	Mu	Greek and Latin: **m**
N ν	N n	N n	Nu	Greek and Latin: **n** (Latin: before "c," "g", and "qu" pronounced like "n" in "finger" or "ng" in "sing")
Ξ ξ		X x	Xi	Greek: **ks/x**
	X x			Latin: **x**
O o	O o	O o	Omicron	Greek and Latin: g**o**t (Latin: also g**oa**t)
Π π	P p	P p	Pi	Greek and Latin: **p**
	Q q			Latin: **qu**ick
P ρ	R r	Rh rh, R r	Rho	Greek and Latin: **r**
Σ σ, ς	S s	S s	Sigma	Greek and Latin: **s** (Greek: before β, γ, δ, and μ pronounced like English "z")

Greek Letter	Roman Letter	Greek Letter in English	Greek Name	Approximate Pronunciation of Greek and Latin
T τ	T t	T t	Tau	Greek and Latin: **t**
Υ υ	Y y	U u, Y y	Upsilon	Greek and Latin: **u** (like German ü, as in "für"; this was a Greek, not native Roman, sound)
	V v			Latin: p**u**t, f**oo**l, wa**x**
Φ φ	F f	Ph ph	Phi	Greek: **p**, later **f** (with an "h" sound, later changed to **f**); Latin: pronounced as **f**
X χ		Kh kh, Ch ch	Chi	Greek: **k**, later "lo**ch**" (with an "h" sound, later changed to **ch**)
Ψ ψ		Ps ps	Psi	Greek: **ps**
Ω ω		O o	Omega	Greek: s**aw**

DIPHTHONGS

Greek Letters	Roman Letters	Greek Letter in English	Approximate Pronunciation	English Examples from Greek with Variant Spellings
αι	ae	ai, ae, e	r**i**de	**Aithiopia, Aethiopia, Ethiopia**
αυ	au	au	h**ow**	**auto** (self)
ει	ei	ei, i, e	w**ai**t	**chiropractor, cheiropractor**
ευ	eu	eu	**ēh – oo**	**Euripides**
οι	oe	oi, oe, e, i	b**oy**	**amoibe, amoeba, ameba, Oidipous, Oedipus**
ου		ou, u	p**oo**l	**Muse, Mousa**

APPENDIX 2

WRITING OF GREEK WORDS IN ENGLISH

W. J. Dominik, J. L. Hilton, and A. P. Bevis

There are two main conventions for writing Greek words in English. The first convention, which tends to be used in recent works, keeps as closely as possible to the original Greek spelling. Greek has two letters for "e," *epsilon* (short "e") and *ēta* (long "e") and two letters for "o," *omicron* (short "o") and *omega* (long "o"). In English the long vowel is sometimes indicated by using a macron (for example, *hēdonē, erōs*). A *gamma* before another *gamma* ("g"), *kappa* ("k"), *chi* ("kh," "ch"), or *xi* ("x") is written as an "n" (for example, *angelos,* "angel"; *ankulos,* "ankle"; *phalanx,* "phalanx"; and *ankhō,* "throttle"). The Greek diphthongs are written in English as "ai," "au," "ei," "eu," "oi," and "ou/u." At the beginning of a word a vowel may or may not have an "h" in front of it.

The *final* syllable *-ē* in Greek is represented in English as *-a* or *-e* or is omitted (for example, Greek *amoibē* changes to English **amoeba;** Greek *phialē* changes to Latin *phiala,* which appears in French as *phial* and in English as **phial**), but final *-n* is sometimes dropped (for example, Greek *Platōn* is written as **Plato** but the Greek spelling of *Kimōn* is retained in English.

The second convention for spelling Greek words in English Latinizes them. In general, older books use the Latinized forms. Even in more recent works, however, some very common words and names will be found in their Latinized forms.

Greek Spelling		Latinized Spelling	
ai	**ai**gis, **Ai**thiopia	**ae**	**ae**gis, **Ae**thiopia
		e	**E**thiopia (late)
ei	S**ei**ren, Med**ei**a	**i**	S**i**ren
		e	Med**e**a
k	Sō**k**ratēs, A**k**ropolis	**c**	So**c**rates, A**c**ropolis
kh	or**kh**ēstra	**ch**	or**ch**estra
ou	**Ou**ranos	**u**	**U**ranus
u	ph**u**sis; ps**u**chē	**y**	ph**y**sis, ps**y**chē

Note also the following word endings which are sometimes found in their Greek form and sometimes in the equivalent Latin form:

Greek		Latin	
-os	Dionys**os**	*-us*	Dionys**us** (The final Greek syllable *-os* sometimes does not change when Latinized (for example, **cosmos**).
-on	Mousei**on**, stadi**on**	*-um*	Muse**um**; stadi**um**
-on	Plat**ōn**; Di**ōn**	*-o*	Plat**o**; Di**o**
-oi	Delph**oi**	*-i*	Delph**i**

You will also find that *-e* and *-a* alternate in the spelling of some words, especially feminine names; for example, the name of the Greek goddess *Athenē*, whose Latinised spelling is *Athena*. Some other examples of Greek names and their Latinized forms follow.

Greek Spelling (Variant)	Latinized Spelling (Traditional)
Aischylos	Aeschylus
Aristophanēs	Aristophanes
Aristotelēs	Aristotle
Euripidēs	Euripides
Helenē	Helen
Homēros	Homer
Platōn	Plato
Sōkratēs	Socrates
Sophoklēs	Sophocles

ROUGH AND SMOOTH BREATHINGS

Greek uses the sound spelled "h" in English, but does not use a separate letter to represent it. It is shown by the rough-breathing sign ʽ written over the vowel of the syllable, as in the word ἥλιος (written as *helios*, "sun"). This sign appears mainly at the beginning of a word. A word with a vowel without the "h" sound at the beginning is written with the smooth-breathing sign ʼ over it, for example, ἰχθύς (written as *ichthys*, "fish," as in **ichthyology**). At the beginning of a word *rho* is pronounced with an "h" sound, as in the word ῥυθμός (written as *rhythmos*, "measure," as in **rhythmicality**).

NUMBERS AND COLORS

W. J. Dominik, J. L. Hilton, and A. P. Bevis

GREEK NUMBERS

Cardinal Number	Meaning	English Base	English Derivative
hen	one	hen-	henotheism
duo	two	dy-	dyad
treis	three	tri-	tripod
tettares	four	tetra-	tetrameter
pente	five	pent-	pentathlon
hex	six	hex-	hexagon
hepta	seven	hept-	heptagon
oktō / octō	eight	oct-	octopus
ennea	nine	ennea-	ennead
deka / deca	ten	dec-	decathlon
hekaton / hecaton	hundred	hect-	hectare
chilioi / khilioi	thousand	kil-	kilometer

Word for Word

LATIN NUMBERS

Cardinal Number (and Meaning)	Roman Numeral	English Derivative	Ordinal Number (and Meaning)	English Derivative
unus, una, unum ("one")	I	**unicycle**	*primus* ("first")	**primary**
duo, duae, duo ("two")	II	**duplicate**	*secundus* ("second")	**secondary**
tres, tria ("three")	III	**triad**	*tertius* ("third")	**tertiary**
quattuor ("four")	IV	**quaternary**	*quartus* ("fourth")	**quarter**
quinque ("five")	V	**quinquennial**	*quintus* ("fifth")	**quintessence**
sex ("six")	VI	**sexagenarian**	*sextus* ("sixth")	**sextillion**
septem ("seven")	VII	**September**	*septimus* ("seventh")	**septimal**
octo ("eight")	VIII	**October**	*octavus* ("eighth")	**octave**
novem ("nine")	IX	**November**	*nonus* ("ninth")	**nonagenarian**
decem ("ten")	X	**December**	*decimus* ("tenth")	**decimation**
centum	C ("one hundred")	**centennial**	*centesimus* ("one hundredth")	**centesimal**
mille ("one thousand")	M	**millennium**	*millesimus* ("one thousandth")	**millesimal**

GREEK COLORS

Greek Word	Meaning	English Base	English Derivatives
chloros	(light) green	**chlor-**	**chlorophyll**
chrysos	gold	**chrys-**	**chrysanthemum**
erythros	red	**erythr-**	**erythrocyte**
leucos / leukos	white	**leuc-** **leuk-**	**leucocyte** **leukemia**
melas, melanos	black	**melan-**	**melancholy,** **melanoma**

ABOUT THE CONTRIBUTORS

A. P. Bevis is a former Lecturer in Classics at the University of Natal, Durban.

W. J. Dominik is Professor of Classics at the University of Otago.

A. Gosling was Senior Lecturer in Classics at the University of Kwazulu-Natal, Durban.

J. L. Hilton is Professor of Classics at the University of Kwazulu-Natal, Durban.

S. M. Masters is Junior Lecturer in Classics at the University of Stellenbosch.

INDEX OF NAMES
AND CULTURAL TOPICS

This index contains select names and cultural topics mentioned in the text, mainly in chapters 4–9. It does not include the names and topics mentioned in the exercises in each chapter.

A

abortion 121, 161
Achilles 91–92
acropolis 21, 145, 148; see *Acropolis*
Acropolis 145; see *acropolis*
Adam 236
Adams, John 157
Aegean Sea 175, 179
Aegisthus 91, 212
Aeneas 92
Aesculapius 105, 124; see *Asklepios*
Africa 158–159, 163, 173–174, 179, 181, 236, 237
Africa, East 181
Agamemnon 91, 148, 212
Aglaion 209
agriculture, Greek 172
agriculture, Roman 79, 84, 171–173, 185
Ajax 91
Alexander the Great 148, 203
Alexandria 114, 116, 118, 173, 175, 231
Amazons 87
Amistad 183
anatomy 105, 111, 114, 116, 135
Anaxagoras 197
Anaximander 196
Anaximenes 196
Anchises 92
Antigone 98–99
Antoninus Pius 114
Antony, Mark 176, 237
Aphrodite 79–80, 90, 211; see *Venus*
Apollo 79–82, 89, 95–96, 105–106
Arabia 181–182
Archagathus of Sparta 112
Ares 79; see *Mars*
Aretaeus 121
aretē 200, 205–206
Argos 98, 146
Ariadne 88–89

Ariminum 180
Aristogeiton 149
Aristophanes 172
Aristotle 7, 114, 146, 170–172, 183, 195, 203, 205, 210–211
Artemis 79, 86; see *Diana*
Asclepiades of Bithynia 112, 125
Asia 174, 180
Asia Minor 90, 105, 114, 118, 234
Asklepion 123
Asklepios 105–106, 123–124; see *Aesculapius*
assemblies, Roman 151–154, 173, 178
Athena (-e) 79, 81, 85–86, 90; see *Minerva*
Athenaeus 113
Athens 84, 88–89, 145–146, 149–150, 169, 175, 179, 183–184, 198–200, 203, 235
Atlas 87–88
Atomists 197, 202
Attica 169, 172
Augeas 86
Augustine, Saint 147
Augustus 154, 156, 171, 176, 178, 231, 237–238, 241; see *Octavian*
Aurelius, Marcus 114
Avebury 231
Azania 181

B

Bacchanalian cult 178
Bacchus 79–80; see *Dionysus*
Baltimore 157
Barbary apes 114
Black Sea 172, 179
Bodrum 234
Bononia 180
Britain 1–2, 154, 181, 238; see *England*
Britain, Roman 2
Brundisium 180
Brutus 237
business, Roman 177–178, 184

C

Caecilius 120
Caesar, Julius 173, 231, 237
calendars 231
calendar, Gregorian 231
calendar, Julian 231
Caligula 180
Capua 180
Carthage 154, 179, 181, 184, 236
Cassandra 92, 212
Cassius 237
Cato 172, 233
Celsus 125
Cerberus 87; see *Kerberos*
Ceres 79–80; see *Demeter*
Chaos 75, 197
Charon 82
Charybdis 94–95
childbirth 112, 115, 117–119
Chiron 105
Church, Christian 2, 147
Cicero 7, 153, 178
Circe 93, 95
Cithaeron, Mount 96, 212
class structure, Roman 153
Claudia 230
Claudius Pulcher, Gaius 178
Claudius 238, 241
Cleanthes 116
Cleisthenes 149
Cleopatra 171, 176
clubs, Roman 178–179
Clytemnestra 91, 212
commerce 169–186; 170–171, 179
commodities 180–181
company organization 177–178
contracts 152, 162, 178, 229
contraception 120, 121
Cooper, Thomas 157
Corinth 96, 98, 114, 212, 236
Coriolanus 242–244
Cos 105
Crassus, Publius Licinius 173
creation of the world 75, 231
Creon 98–99
Cretan bull 86, 89
Crete 76, 86, 88–89
Ctesibius 185
Cupid 79–80, 211; see *Eros*
Cyclops 93, 95

Cynics 204
Cyrene 174
Cyrus 235

D

Darius 234
Delphi 81–82, 95–97, 212
Delphic oracle 81–82, 199, 212
Demeter 79, 84; see *Ceres*
democracy 19, 149–151, 179
Democritus 197, 204
Descartes, René 202–203
Diana 79; see *Artemis*
Diaulus 113
Diocletian 171
Diogenes 204
Diomedes 87
Dion 201
Dionysius I 201
Dionysius II 201
Dionysius of Halicarnassus 153
Dionysus (-os) 36, 79, 89; see *Bacchus*
doctors 106–107, 109–118, 121–123, 125–128
doctors, female 115, 117
doctors, military 116
doctors, training of 113–114
Domitian 238
drachma 126, 174–175
Draco 151
drugs 105, 107–108, 110, 113, 115, 119
Dutch 158

E

economic theories, Greek 169–171
economic theory, Roman 171
economics, Greek 172, 174–176, 179, 184–185
economics, Roman 172–185
Egypt 171, 173, 175–176, 179–181, 231, 235
Electra 212–213
Eleusis 84
Empedocles 197
Empire, Roman 154, 171, 176, 180, 184–185, 238
England 2–3, 157; see *Britain*
Ephesus 115, 118, 196
Epicureans 204
Epicurus 204
Epidaurus 105
Eros 79, 80, 211; see *Cupid*

Erymanthos, Mount 86
Eteocles 98
ethics and etiquette, medical 105, 109–110
Europe 114, 154, 157, 172, 231
Europe, Western 157
Eurydice 99
Eurystheus 85–87, 89
Eurytion 87
exposure 120–121

F

Fabius 243
fasces 152, 155
finance, Greek 175
fisc, Roman imperial 176
food welfare 173
Freud, Sigmund 98, 213
Freudian psychology 213

G

Gaia 75; see *Ge*
Galen 114, 121
Galilee 236
Gaul 154, 181, 237
Ge 75; see *Gaia*
Germany 154, 238
Geryon 87
Glaucon 208–210
gods 1, 9, 75–87, 92–93, 95, 105–106, 123–124,
     169, 199, 204, 207, 227, 242
Gracchus, Tiberius Sempronius 178
Greece 78, 81, 86–87, 89–90, 95, 105, 113, 146,
     148, 169, 172, 175, 179, 181, 183, 191, 212,
     234–236
Grotius, Hugo 157
gynecology 105, 111–112, 115, 118–122

H

Hades (god) 79, 83–84, 87; see *Pluto*
Hades (underworld) 82–84, 206–207
Hadrian 118
Haemon 98–99
Halicarnassus 153, 234, 239
Hannibal 237
Harmodios 149
Hateria Superba 119
Haterius Ephebus, Quintus 119
healing, divine 124–125
Hector 92, 206

Hegel 199
Heineccius, Gottlieb 157
Helen 90
Hellespont 179
Hephaestus (Hephaistos) 79, 81, 91; see *Vulcan*
Hera 78–79, 90; see *Juno*
Heracleitus 196, 202
Heracles 85–89; see *Hercules*
Heracles, labours of 85–88
Herculaneum 116
Hercules 85, 88; see *Heracles*
Hermes 79, 85, 90, 211; see *Mercury*
Herodotus (-os) 172, 225, 233–235, 238–239
Heron of Alexandria 185
Hesiod 169–170
Hesperides, Garden of the 87–88
Hieron II of Syracuse 185
Hippocrates 105–107, 109–110, 125, 172
Hipparchus 149
Hippias 149
Hippolyta 87
historians 169, 184, 191, 227–229, 233–244
history 6, 120, 123, 147, 150, 153, 178, 180,
     199, 203, 227–249
Hoffman, David 157
Homer 93, 95, 145, 148, 205, 206–207, 233
humor, medical 125–127
humors, theory of 108–109, 135
Hydra 86, 88
hysteria 121–122, 134, 213

I

India 180–182
instruments, medical and surgical 116, 118,
     120, 128, 132, 135–137
Iolaus 85–86
Ionia 195
Ionian philosophers 195
Iraq 154
Iris 79–80
Ismene 98
Italy 19, 147, 154–155, 172–173, 175, 180–181,
     185, 196, 235

J

Jefferson, Thomas 157
Jewish War 236
Jocasta 97–98, 212
Josephus, Flavius 236
Jove 77; see *Jupiter, Zeus*

Judea 2, 181, 236
Jugurtha 237
Juno 79, 176–177; see *Hera*
Jupiter 77, 79; see *Jove, Zeus*
Justinian 9, 157–158

K

Kent, James 157
Kerberos 87; see *Cerberus*
Keryneia 86
Kronos 75–78 ; see *Saturn*
Kyme 126–127

L

Laius 96–98, 212
Laughter-lover, The 125
law, American 157–158
law, commercial 157, 162
law, private 161
law, Roman 113, 154, 155–159, 171, 177, 185
law, South African 158–159
legal actions, Roman 159
legal concepts, Roman 158–159
legal principles, Roman 157–158
Leontios 209
Lethe 82
Livy (Titus Livius) 153, 178, 233, 237–238, 241–243
Lucian 180
Lucius Verus 114
Lucretius 204
Lugdunum 176
Lyceum 203
Lyon 176
Lysias 183

M

Macedonia 184, 236
Marathon 86, 89, 234
Marcius 242
Mars 11, 79, 80, 231; see *Ares*
Martial 113
maxims, Roman 157–158
Mecca 231
medicine, Greek 105–112
medicine, "rational" 105–106
medicine, Roman 112–125
Medina 231

Mediterranean, the 2, 154, 175, 181, 195, 236, 238
Megara 178
Menander 169
Menelaus 90–91
Meno 200
Mentor 95
Mercury 79–80, 171; see *Hermes*
Merope 96, 212
Mesopotamia 23, 175, 234
Middle East 176
Miletus 195
Milesian school 195
Minerva 79; see *Athena*
Minos 88
Minotaur 88
Mohammed 231
monarchy 148–149, 237
money, Roman 171, 176–178
money and coinage, Greek 174–175
Monists 197
Mucianus 123
Muses 79, 82
Muslim 206
Mussolini 155
Muza 181
mythology 75–99, 105, 191, 195, 211–213

N

Narcissus 212–213
Nemea 85
Nemean lion 85
Neptune 79; see *Poseidon*
Nero 238, 241
Nestor 91–92
New Orleans 157
Nikon 114
Normans 3

O

Octavian 176, 237; see *Augustus*
Odysseus 91–95, 148, 207
Odysseus, wanderings of 93–95
Oedipus 95–99, 172, 212, 213
Olympus, Mount 78, 90
ophthalmology 118, 122–123
Orthros 87
Ostia 173
Ozene 182

P

Palestine 235
Pandora 169
Paris 90, 92
Parmenides 197
Patroclus 206
Peiraieus 209
Peisistratus 149
Peleus 91
Peloponnesian War 150, 235, 239–240
Penelope 93–95
Pergamum 114
Pericles 150
Persephone 84; see *Proserpina*
Persia 146
Persian empire 148
Petronius 180
Phaedrus 200
Philadelphia 157
Philip V 236
philosophy 4, 114, 158, 191–213
physiology 105, 111, 114
Piraeus 179
Plato 170, 172, 198–203, 205, 208–211
Plato's forms 201–202, 211
Pliny 120, 123, 180
Pluralists 197–200, 202, 204
Plutarch 116
Pluto 79, 80; see *Hades*
Polybius 178, 236, 238, 240
Polybus 96, 212
Polynices 98
Polyphemus 93
Pompeii 116
Pompey 237–238
Poseidon 79; see *Neptune*
Pre-Socratics 195
Priam 90–92
Procrustes 89
proletarian 153, 156
property 121, 151, 153, 156, 161–162, 170–171,
    177, 179, 184, 229
Proserpina 84; see *Persephone*
Psychē 1, 211
psychē 10, 82, 206–211
psychology 81, 98, 130, 137, 191, 213–219
Ptolemaic Egypt 175
Pufendorf, Samuel von 157
Puteoli 177
Pylos 91

Pythagoras 196–197
Pythagoreans 196–197
Pythia 81–82, 95–96

R

Red Sea 181–182
Remus 147
Republic, Roman 120, 151–154, 156, 178–181,
    185, 237
Rhapta 181
Rhea 75–76
Rhine-Danube River 154
Rome 92, 112, 114, 118, 123, 125, 147–157 *pas-
    sim*, 171–184 *passim*, 228–244 *passim*
Romulus 147, 155
Rutilius, Publius 178

S

Salamis 234
Sallust 173, 237
Sarapis 177
Saturn 77, 176; see *Kronos*
Satyros 114
Scipio Aemilianus 236
Scylla 94–95
Scythia 234
sea power, Athenian 179
Senate, Roman 151–156, 173, 176, 178, 237–238
Servilius Nonianus, Marcus 123
Sibyl 95–96
Sicily 81, 175, 181, 201
Silphium 120, 174
Sinis 89
Sinon 90
Sirens 93–95
Sisyphus 83
slavery 125, 183–185, 242
Smyrna 114
Socrates 195, 198–200, 202, 205, 208–210,
    235
Sophists 200, 205
Sophocles 172
Soranus of Ephesus 115, 118–122
Spanish 1, 4, 151, 232
Sparta 112, 146, 235
Spartacus 184
Sphinx 96–97, 212
Stentor 91
Stoa 204

Stoics 204
Stonehenge 231
Stymphalis, Lake 86
surgery 105–108, 110, 113, 115–116, 118, 122, 136
Syracuse 185, 201
Syria 181, 235

T

Tacitus, Cornelius 180, 238, 241
Tantalus 83–84
technology 184–186
Teiresias 207
Telemachus 94–95
Telesphoros 105
terminology, medical 127–139
tetradrachm 176
Thales 196
Thanatos 83
Thebes 95–99, 146, 212
Theseus 86, 88–89
Thrace 87, 235
Thucydides (Thoukudides) 150, 169, 235, 238–240
Tiber Island 123
Tiber River 173
Tiberius 125, 154, 180, 241
Titans 75, 78
trade, Greek 179
trade, Roman 180–182
Trajan 118
transport, Roman 180
treatments, folk 123–124
treatments, medical 105–111, 113–114, 123–125
treasury, Roman 176, 178, 180

Trimalchio 180
Trojan War 90–93, 95, 212
Troy 90–93, 148, 207, 212
Turkey 114, 195

U

underworld 79, 82–84, 87, 206–207
United States 146, 157–158, 163
Uranus 75, 77

V

Venus 79–81; see Aphrodite
Verona 157
Vespasian 236
Veturia 242–243
Volsci 242
Volumnia 242
Vulcan 79, 81; see Hephaestus

W

Western Cape 158
wills 161, 229

X

Xenophon 170, 172, 175, 179, 184, 235
Xerxes 234

Z

Zanzibar 181
Zeno 204
Zeus 76–81, 83–84, 90; see Jupiter, Jove
Zeus Ammon 174
Zosime, Julia 119

INDEX OF
WORD-BUILDING TOPICS

This selective index mainly contains the more common word-building topics mentioned in the text, mainly in Chapters 1–3 and 5.

Greek

adjective-forming suffixes 7, 36, 60–61: -ac 36; -ic 36; -oid 36

adjectives 21–25: acr- 21; all- 21; arist- 22; aut- 22; cac- 22; heter- 22; hier- 22; hol- 22; hom- 22; home- 23; idi- 23; macr- 23; mega-, megal- 23; mes- 23; micr- 23; mon- 24; neo- 24; olig- 24; orth- 24; pale- 24; pan-, pant- 24; poly- 24; pseud- 25; scler- 25; therm- 25

adverb 25: eu- 25

alphabet 19

bases 19, 25, 29, 132–138: arthr- 132; cardi- 132; cephal- 133; chlor- 133; cirrh- 133; dendr- 133; enter- 133; hydr- 134; hyster- 134; leuc-, leuk- 134; mast- 134; melan- 135; my- mus-, myos- 135; myc-, mycet- 135; nephr- 135; neur- 136; ophthalm- 136; oste- 136; ot- 137; phleb- 137; psych- 137; sthen- 137; tachy-, tach- 137; tox- 138; xanth- 138

changes in meaning 8–10

combining forms 19–21, 129–132: -archy, -arch 19; -cracy, -crat 19; -ectomy 129; -graphy, -graph 20; -logist 130; -logy 20, 130; -mania 20; -meter 130; -metry 20; -nomy 20; -path 131; -pathy 20, 131; -philia, -phile 21; -phobe 21; -rrhea 131; -skopy, -skope 21; -therapy 132; -tomy 132

influence upon English 1–3

noun-forming suffixes 34–35, 129–132: -ac 34; -emia 129; -ic 6, 34; -ics 6, 34; -in, -ine 130; -is 35; -ism 35; -ist 6, 35; -ite 34; -itis 130; -oid 34; -oma 131; -osis 131; -ot 34; -y 35

prefixes 30–33: a-, an- 30; amphi- 30; ana- 30; anti-, ant- 30; apo- 30; cata-, cat- 31; dia-, di- 31; dys- 31; ec-, ex- 31; en-, em- 32; epi-, ep- 32; exo-, ecto- 32; hyper- 32; hypo-, hyp- 32; meta-, met- 32; para-, par- 33; peri- 33; pro- 33; syn-, sym-, syl-, sy- 33

singular and plural forms 13–14: -is, -es 13; -ma, -mata 14; -on, -a 13

verb-forming suffixes 36: -ize 6, 36

verbs 25–29: agog- 25; acou- 25; ball-, bol- 26; cri- 26; do- 26; gen- 26; gno- 26; graph-, gram- 26; id- 26; log-, lect- 26; ora- 27; opt- 27; path- 27; phen-, phan-, pha- 27; pher-, phor- 28; prag-, prac- 28; rheu-, rh- 28; skept- 28; skop- 28; sta- 28; tom- 29; the- 29; trop- 29; treph- 29

Latin

abbreviations 63

adjective-forming suffixes 60–62: -able, -ble, -ible 60; -ain, -an, -ane, -ine 60; -ant, -ent 61; -ar, -al, -ary 61; -arian, -ian 61; -ate, -ite 61; -ic 61; -id 62; -ific 62; -il, -ile 62; -ilent, -olent, -ulent 62; -ious, -ose, -ous 62; -ive 62; -ory 62

alphabet 10, 45

bases 45, 48, 50

changes in meaning 8–10

derivatives in legal vocabulary 158–164

expressions 63–65

influence upon English 1–5

legal phrases 163–164

noun-forming suffixes 55–60: -acy, -acity, -y 56; -ain, -an 58; -al 56; -ance, -ancy, -ence, -ency 56; -and, -end 58; -ane, -ine 55; -ant, -ent 58; -ar 58; -arian, -ian 58; -arium, -orium 59; -ary, -ory 59; -ate 58; -ation, -ion, -tion 56; -cle, -cule, -icle 59; -el, -le 59; -ety, -ity, -ty 57; -ice 57; -il 60; -ile 57; -ite 55; -itude 57; -ive 57; -ment 55; -mony 57; -or 57, 59; -ose 56; -ule, -ole 60; -ure 56

nouns 45–46: aqu- 45; gener- 46; grad- 46; jur- 46; patr- 46; sen- 46; serv- 46; tempor- 46; verb- 46; vir- 46 phrases 64

prefixes 49–55: *ab-, a-, abs-,* 49; *ad-, a-, ac-, af-, ag-, al-, an-, ap-, ar-, as-, at-* 49; *ambi-* 50; *ante-* 50; *circum-* 50; *com-, co-, col-, con-, cor-* 50; *contra-* 50; *de-* 50; *dis-, di-, dif-* 51; *equi-, equa-* 51; *ex-, e-, ef-* 51; *extra-* 51; *in-, il-, im-, ir-* 51; *infra-* 52; *inter-* 52; *intra-* 52; *multi-* 52; *non-* 52; *ob-, oc-, of-, op-* 53; *per-* 53; *post-* 53; *pre-* 53; *pro-* 53; *re-, red-* 53; *retro-* 54; *se-, sed-* 54; *semi-* 54; *sub-, suc-, suf-, sug-, sup-, sus-* 54; *super-* 54; *trans-, tra-, tran-* 55; *ultra-* 55

quotations 65

singular and plural forms 13–15: *-a, -ae,* 15; *-ex, -ix, -ices* 15; *-um, -a* 14; *-us, -i* 14; *-us, -ies, -era/-ora, -ies* 15; *-yx, -x, -yces, -ces* 15

verb-forming suffixes 63: *-ate* 63; *-efy, -ify* 63; *-esce* 63

verbs 47–48: *ag-, act-, ig-* 47; *capt-, cept-, -ceive* 47; *-ced, -ceed, cess-* 47; *-cid, cis-* 47; *dat-, dit-* 47; *fac-, fact-, fect-* 47; *leg-, lect-* 48; *-mit, mitt-, miss-* 48; *pon-, pos-, posit-* 48; *ven-, vent-* 48

Other

adjectives 6–7, 11–12

Anglo-Saxon 8, 10

bases 1, 3–4, 6, 12–13; definition of 5

combining form 5, 19, 129–132; definition of 5

combining vowel 5

English 1–15

English, Old 2–3

English derivatives 10, 12–13, 19–36, 45–63

French 1, 3–4, 10–11

French, Old 3

hybrid 1

Italian 1, 4

Latin borrowings 2, 4

Latinate register of English 8

Latinate vocabulary 8

loan words 3–4

medical terminology 129–139; medical term, definition of 7

nouns 6–7, 11–13; abstract noun, definition of 7; agent noun, definition of 7; diminutive noun, definition of 7; general noun, definition of 7; locative noun, definition of 7

Portuguese 1, 4

prefix, definition of 5

pronouns 11–12

Renaissance 3–4

scientific language 1, 8, 129

Spanish 1, 4

spelling, changes in 10

suffix, definition of 5

verbs 6–7, 12–13

vowel changes 13

word changes 8–10

word forms, changes in 11–13

word structure 6–7

INDEX OF ENGLISH WORDS AND PHRASES

This index lists English (and some foreign) words and phrases in bold and italics that are mentioned, analyzed, or discussed for their etymological or cultural features, meanings, or origins. In addition, it not only contains nouns and phrases derived from mythological and historical figures but also Latin abbreviations and phrases commonly used in English.

A

a fortiori 64
a priori 64
ab initio 163
A.D. 63
a.m. 63
abduct 6, 69, 160
abject 49
abortion 121, 161
abridgement 55
abrogate 69
abscond 160
abstract 49, 70
academic 200
academy 200
accept 49
accuracy 245
Achilles, heel of 91
acoustic 25
acrobat 148
acromegaly 148
acronym 21, 148
acrophobia 148
acropolis 21, 145, 148
actio in rem 163
action 47, 67
ad hoc 64
ad hominem 64
ad litem 163
ad nauseam 64
addendum (-a) 14, 58
adduce 69
adhesive 57
adjacent 70
adjective 70
adjudicate 162
adjudication 162
administer 161
admit 49

adopt 161
advent 68
advocate 176
aediles 152
aegis 81, 102
Aeneas 92
affix 49
agendum (-a) 58, 228, 244
agent 47, 67
aggregate 49
agnostic 26, 192
agonize 36
agrarian 61, 171
agriculture 56, 171, 188
agronomy 171
aichmophobia 216
ailurophile 217
alga (-ae) 15
alias 160
alibi 160
allegation 160
allergy 21, 129
allocate 49
altar 3
alumna (-ae) 15, 64
alumnus (-i) 17, 64
amatory 62
Amazon 102
ambidextrous 50
amnesia 30, 226
amnesty 41
amoeba 253
amphibious 30
amputate 118
anabolic 186
anachronism 30, 232, 244
anagram 44
analysis (-es) 13
analyze 43
anarchy 166

anatomy 111, 141
anesthesia 5
anesthetic 193
Anglican 60
animadvert 211
animal 211
animate 211
animism 211
animosity 211, 226
animus 163, 211
animus testandi 163
annalist 244
annals 244, 247
announce 49
annual 244
annuity 162
annul 161
anorexia nervosa 216
anosmia 30
antagonism 30
antecedent 50
antenatal 138
antenna (-ae) 15
anterior 138
anthology 9
anthropophobia 216
anthropoid 34
anthropology 1
anthropomorphism 41
antibiotic 41
antidote 41
antimelanin 130
antinomy 20
antipathy 30, 41
antiquarian 244
antithesis 43
antitoxin 130
apathy 27
aphrodisiac 18, 80
apodeictic 193
Apollo 80
apologize 192
apology 30, 41
appellant 162
appendectomy 129
appendicitis 130
appendix 17
apportion 68
apprehend 49, 182
aquarium 45, 188
aqueduct 6, 45
arbor 61

arboreal 61
archaeology 244
archive (-s) 244
Ariadne's thread 89
aristocracy 19, 22
aristocrat 19
army 3
arrogant 49, 69
arthrectomy 132, 142
arthritis 130, 132, 143
ascend 11
ask 11
aspire 49, 68
assault 160
assent 49
associate 183
asteroid 36
asthenopia 137
astronaut 76
asymmetry 6
atheist 192
athlete (-s) 35
athletics 34
atlas (-es) 88
atom 29, 198
atrium (-a) 14, 138
atrophy 29
attract 49
atypical 43
audi alteram partem 163
auditorium 59
Augean 88, 102
Augean stables 88
aureole 60
autobiography 244
autocracy 149
autocrat 149
autograph 4
automobile 22
autonomy 22
avert 49, 68
aviophobe 216

B

Bacchanalia 80
bacillus (-i) 14
bacterium (-a) 17, 117
ballistic 26, 186
barbarism 35
basis (-es) 13
beauty 3

beef 8
bellicose 62
beneficiary 161
benefit 4
bibliography 20
bibliomania 20
bibliophile 21, 41
bigamist 18
bigamy 18
binocular 123
biography 76, 244
biology 1
biped 139
bipedal 139
bishop 2
bona fide 163
booklet 60
bovine 60
bulimia 216
butter 2

C

c. 63
c.v. 63
cacti 17
cacophony 22
calculus (-i) 14
calligraphy 20
calyx (-yces) 15
canine 55
capital 160
capsule 60
captain 58
captive 47
carcinoma (-mata) 14, 107
cardiac 36
cardiograph 132
cardiologist 130
cardiology 132
cardiopathy 142
carditis 143
Cassandra 92
catalogue 41
catastrophe 31, 42
catharsis 213
catholic 31
caveat emptor 163
caveat scriptor 163
celestial 77
censor 152

censorship 152
centennial 256
centesimal 256
centuriation 173
cephalitis 133, 142
cephalopod 133
cereal 80, 101
cerebellar 61
cerebral 139
certain 60
cf. 63
chaos 75, 102
chaotic 75
chaste 10
chastity 10
cheese 2
chemotherapy 132
chlorine 133, 143
chloroma 133, 142
chlorophyll 133, 256
choleric 108
chromosome 5
chronic 232
chronicles 244
chronology 244
chrysanthemum 256
Circe 95
circus 9
circumnavigate 50
cirrhosis 133, 143
citadel 147
citizen 147
city 147
civic 61, 147
civics 147
civil 62, 147
civilian 147
civility 147
civilization 147
civilize 147
client 184
clientele 184
codex (-ices) 15
codicil 161
co-ed 50
collate 5
college 178
colloquium 50, 67
colonies 154
colonoscopy 21
colossus (-i) 14

commemorate 245
commerce 171, 188
commodity 177
communism 171
commute 6
compare 50
competition 171
complete 155
complex 129
compos mentis 163
compose 5
comprehend 182
computer 8
conception 121
conclusion 67
concoction 57
conducive 69–70
confer 5
confirmation 70
confound 13
confuse 13
consanguinity 161
conscience 193
conscious 50
consciousness 193
conscription 67
consortia 17
conspiracy 160
constitute 148
constitution 148
constitutional 148
consulate 67, 152
consuls 152
consumable 70
consumptive 70
contraception 121
contract 162
contradict 50
Contras 66
controversy 8
convalesce 63
convene 13, 49
convenient 13
convention 13, 48, 70, 182
conventional 182
convert 6
conveyance 162
convince 67
co-operate 50
co-opt 50
co-ordinate 50

corporal 7, 12, 67, 70
corporate 7
corporeal 7, 70
corpse 8
corpus (-ora) 8–9, 15, 17
corrigendum 58
corrupt 50
cosmetic 76
cosmic 76
cosmogony 76
cosmography 76
cosmology 76
cosmonaut 76
cosmopolitan 76, 101
cosmos 75–76, 222
co-star 50
counterclaim 50
countercurrent 50
counterpoint 50
countershaft 50
countersign 50
course 9
covenant 162
co-worker 50
creator 59
creature 56
credit 177
creditor 162
creed 3
crime 3, 160
criminal 160
crisis (-es) 17, 26, 35
criterion (-a) 4, 13
critic 26, 34
crux (-ces) 15
culpa lata 163
culpable 160
cum laude 64
Cupid's arrow 102
cupidity 80
curate 244
curator 163, 228
curator bonis 163
curriculum (-a) 14
custody 56, 161
cyclic 232
cyclist 35
Cyclopean 95
cyclophobia 216
Cynic 204
Cypriot 18

D

datum (-a) 17, 47, 228, 245
de facto 163
de iure 163
de minimis non curat lex 163
deacon 2
debt 177
de-bus 50
decathlon 255
December 256
deception 47
decimation 256
declaration 56
de-clutch 50
deduct 69
defame 162
defection 47
defendant 162
defoliate 70
dehydrate 134
deify 78
dejected 50
Delphic 82, 101
demagogue 25, 151
demand 171
democracy 19, 149
democrat 19, 149
democratic 149
demography 151
demonize 18
dendroid 133
dendrologist 133, 142
dendrite 34
dependence 56
dependency 226
depose 69
derogatory 69
despot 151, 170
despotic 170
despotism 170
detain 160
detention 160
deterrent 160
deus ex machina 64
diabolic 41
diachronic 31, 232
diagnosis (-es) 17, 26, 107, 141
diagram 26
dialect 26
dialectic 222

dialectics 203
dialogue 43, 203
diaphanous 41
diarrhea 28, 131
dictate 155
dictation 155
dictator 152, 155
dictatorial 152, 155
diction 155
dictionary 155
different 51
digest 51
digital 8
dinar 176
Dionysiac 36, 41
diorama 31
disbelief 52
discern 51
disciple 3
discus 2
dish 2
divorce 161
doctor (-s) 117
doctorate 117
dogmatist 35
doli capax 163
doli incapax 163
dolus 163
domicile 161
Dominate 157
dormitory 59
dorsal 139
dose 26
draconian 151
dramatic 6
dramatics 6
dramatist 6
dramatize 6
drive 13
driven 13
drove 13
duckling 60
duct 6
ductile 6
duplicate 256
durable 60
dyad 255
dyarchy 154
dynamite 34
dysentery 133
dyslexia 31

dyslexic 226
dystrophy 41

E

e.g. 63
ecclesiastic 151, 166
ecology 171
economy 35, 171
ecosphere 171
ecosystem 171
ecstasy 31
ecstatic 31
ectoplasm 32
ecumenical 171
edifice 152
effluent 51
egocentric 214
egoist 214
egotist 226
eject 51
Electra complex 213
electrocardiogram 132
electroencephalograph 128, 133
elocution 67
emancipate 4, 182
emblem 186, 188
empathy 32
emperor 155
emphasis (-es) 13
empirical 222
encyclopedia 4
endemic 32
engine 186, 188
ennead 255
enterectomy 133, 142
enteritis 142
entrepreneur 182
ephemeral 32
epicurean 222
epidemic 41
epigraph 44
epilogue 26
epinephrine 130
epistemology 192
epitaph 32, 41
equanimity 51
equinophile 217
equivalent 51
eros 12
erotic 12, 80, 101

erratum (-a) 14
eruption 56
erythrocyte 256
essences 7
esteem 176
etc. 63
ethereal 7
ethics 18, 111
etiology 222
eugenic 25
eulogy 20, 25, 41
euphemism 25
euphony 25, 43
evident 67
evolution 67
ex facie 163
ex gratia 64
ex officio 64
ex parte 163
ex tempore 64
exact 4
exclude 67
excursion 4
exegesis (-es) 13
exigent 47
exodus 31
exogamy 32
exoneration 160
expose 51, 121
extenuation 160
extortion 160
extramural 51

F

facile 47
faction 245
factory 47
factual 245
fallacy 56
fascist 155
fast 11
favorite 61
fear 11
federation 154
femoral 139
femur 139
finance 177, 188
finesse 188
finish 245
firm 11

fiscal 177
fluency 56
forceps 118
formula 9, 17
forum 9
fracture 56
fragment 55
frigid 62
fungus (-i) 14

G

galeophobia 216
gastric 185
gastrotomy 132
gene 186
generality 46
generosity 46
genesis 26
genius 186, 188
genus (-era) 12, 15, 46, 193
geography 20, 41, 76, 101
geology 41, 76
geometry 20, 77
George 77
geothermal 77, 101
gestation 57
gladiolus (-i) 14
globular 61
glossotomy 132
glucose 56
government 3
gradation 46
gradualism 46
graduand 58
graphite 34
graphology 1, 26
gymnasium (-a) 14
gynarchy 19
gynecology 112

H

habeas corpus 163
Hades 82
harmony 35
hectare 255
hector 92
hedonist 35
heir 161
Helen of Troy 90

heliotherapy 132
hematology 11
hematoma 131
hemorrhage 11
henotheism 255
heptagon 255
Heracles, labors of 88
herculean 88
hereditary 161
hesitancy 56
Hesperides, apples of the 88
heterosexual 22
hexagon 255
hieroglyphics 22
hippopotamus 17
historian 228, 245
historic 228
historical 228
historiographer 228
historiography 41, 245, 248
history 227–228, 245
hobophobia 216
holocaust 22
holy 11
homogenize 41
homeopath 23
homicide 47, 160
homonym 41
homophobia 41
homosexual 22
horrific 62
horror 11
humility 57
hydra-headed 88
hydraulics 186
hydrocephalus 134
hydrochloride 186
hydrogen 186
hydropathy 131, 142
hydrotherapy 142
hyperthermia 32
hyphen 32
hypnosis 131, 213
hypodermic 32, 129
hypothesis (-es) 13, 43
hypothesize 41
hysterectomy 134, 142
hysteria 122, 141, 213
hysterical 122
hysterogenic 134
hysterotomy 134

I

i.e. 63
ibid. 63
ichthyology 254
idea 26, 195
idiom 23
idiosyncrasy 23
idiot (-s) 34, 219
illegal 51
illuminate 51
immediate 51
immigrate 51
imperative 155
imperial 155
imperialism 155
imperialist 155
imperious 155
impose 69
imposition 5, 70
impulse 67
impulsive 62
in camera 64
in loco parentis 163
in re 163
in toto 64
inactive 51
incarcerate 160
inch 10
incision 47
indices 17
induce 69
industrial 182
industrious 182
industry 179, 182
infanticide 121
infection 117
infelicitous 51
infer 67
inflation 172
infrastructure 52
ingenious 186
inject 51, 70, 139
injection 139
injunction 162
inquire 67
insistent 61
insulate 182
insulin 182
intellectual 226
inter alia 64, 163

intercede 47
interject 52
intermission 57
intermittent 48
internet 52
interrogate 11
intervene 48
intestate 161
intoxicate 138
intranet 52
investigation 247
iota 37
ipso facto 163
ipso iure 163
iridescence 80
iridescent 101
irresistible 51
irrigate 51
island 182
isle 182
isobar 151
isochronous 151
isometric 151
isomorphic 151
isonomia 151
isosceles 151
isotherm 151
isotonic 151
isotope 151
isotropic 151
issue 10
iusta causa 163

J

Jove 77
jovial 77
jugular 139
Jupiter 77, 79, 80
jurisdiction 162
jurisprudent 46
jurist 46

K

kaleidoscope 41
kilometer 255
kingly 11
kleptomania 20
know 192

L

labyrinth 89, 102
labyrinthine 89
lachrymal 139
lacuna (-ae) 15
larva (-ae) 15
latent 162, 219
lateral 139
lawful 11
lecture 48
legacy 161
legal 11, 12
legatee 161
legible 48, 60
lethargic 82, 101
lethargy 82
Lethe, waters of 82
leukemia 129, 134, 142, 256
leucocyte 134, 256
leucoderma 134
leucoma 134
liable 162
liberty 184
library 59
lieutenant 11
liquefy 63
liter 175
literate 61
litigant 58
lobotomy 132
locate 5
locus (-i) 11, 14, 163
locus standi 163
logic 18
logorrhea 131
loquacious 62
lotus-eaters 95, 102
loyal 11
lunar 61

M

machine 186
macrocosm 23
macroeconomics 23, 41
magistrate 58, 155
majority 161
mala fide 163
malice 57
manage 171

Manchester 2
mandate 171
maneuver 184
maniac 34
manic depression 218
manikin 60
manual 67, 184
manufacture 184
manumit/-ted 184
manure 184
manuscript 184
March 80
Mars 80
martial 12, 80, 101
Martian 61
martyr 151, 166
masochism 219
mastectomy 134, 142
master 3
mastitis 134, 143
mastodon 134
mastoid 134
matrimony 57
matrix (-ices) 15
maxillary 139
May 80
mechanical 186
mechanize 186
media 17
medical 113
medicate 113
medication 113
medicinal 113
medicine 3, 113
megabyte 23
megalomania 20, 23
megaphone 23
melancholic 108
melancholy 135, 256
melanin 135, 143
melanoderma 135
melanoma 131, 143, 256
melanosis 135, 142
melodrama 6
memorandum (-a) 14, 58
memorial 247
memory 245
mens rea 163
mentor 95, 101
mercantile 171
merchandise 81, 171

merchant 171
mercurial 80, 102
Mercury 80
mercury 81, 171, 188
mercy 171, 189
meretricious 171
merriment 55
Mesopotamia 23
metabolism 26
metal 186
metallic 186, 188
metalloid 186
metallurgy 186
metamorphosis (-es) 17, 32, 41
metaphor 43
metaphysics 195
metathesis 43
metempsychosis 41
methane 55
method 32
metropolitan 76
miasma (-mata) 14
microcephalic 133
microgram 23
microscope 23
microscopy 35
mile 17
military 61, 72
millennium (-a) 14, 256
millesimal 256
minority 161
mint 2, 177
misogyny 41
missile 48, 57, 67
missionary 67
modus operandi 163
molecule 59
monarch 19, 148
monarchist 41
monarchy 41, 148, 165
money 177
monopoly 172
monotonous 24
monument 245
moratoria 17
morsel 59
mount 11
multiplication 52
mundane 60
municipality 154
muscle 59, 135, 139

muse 82
museum 82
music 34, 82
musical 82
musician 82
mutatis mutandis 64
mutual 177
myalgia 135
mycetoma 135, 142
mycology 135, 142
mycosis 135, 143
myograph 135
myology 135, 142
myositis 135, 143
myosthenia 137
myotomy 142
mysticism 18
mythography 101
mythology 75, 101

N

n.b. 63
narcissism 213
narcissistic 222
narrate 245
narrative 245
nasal 139
nature 56
nausea 64, 182, 188
nauseated 182
nauseous 182
nautical 182
navigate 10, 63, 182
navigation 10
navy 182
nebula (-ae) 15
necrophilia 217
negotiate 183, 188
neolithic 24
neologism 18
nephritis 135, 142
nephrolith 136
nephrology 142
Nestor 92
neuralgia 111, 136
neurasthenia 137
neurodermatitis 136
neurologist 136, 142
neurology 111
neuroma 111

neuropathy 131, 142
neuropsychiatry 136
neurosis 136, 143
neurasthenia 142
neurosurgery 136
nitrite 55
noble (-s) 148, 165
non compos mentis 163
non sequitur 64, 205
nonagenarian 256
non-American 52
nonbeliever 52
noncandidate 52
nonevent 52
nonplussed 52
nonprofit 52
nonsense 52
nonsensical 52
nonslip 52
nonverbal 52
nonviolent 52
nonwhite 52
novelty 57
November 256
numismatics 174

O

obelisk 174
obiter dictum 164
object 53
objective 245, 247
obstetrics 117
occur 53
octave 256
October 256
octobrach 255
octopus 255
ocular 139
oculist 123
Odysseus 92
odyssey 102
Oedipus complex 98, 213, 222, 226
offer 53
oligarchy 24, 148
ontology 226
ophthalmia 122, 136
ophthalmologist 122, 136, 142
ophthalmology 142
ophthalmoscope 136
opponent 48

oppose 67, 70
opposite 53
optic 27
optician 122, 142
optometrist 41, 122, 141
opulent 62
opus (-era) 15
oration 151
oratory 151
orthodontist 24
osteoarthritis 130
osteologist 142
osteology 1
osteoma 131, 136, 143
osteopath 131, 136
osteopathy 5, 131, 142
osteotomy 136, 142
ostracism 35
ostracize 36, 150
otiose 183, 188
otomycosis 137, 142
otorrhea 137, 142
otoscope 137

P

p.m. 63
p.s. 63
pacify 63, 183
pact 183
paleography 24
panorama 27
pantheist 21, 24
pantomime 21, 24
paradox 33
paragraph 43–44
parallel 33
paralysis 41
parapsychology 41
parataxis 41
parenthetic 41
Paris, judgment of 90
parliament 3
parochial 171
particle 59
patent 162
patrician (-s) 46, 152, 155
patrilineal 46
patriot 34
patrons 179
pectoral 139

pedagogue 25
pediatrician 112, 141
pediatrics 112
pedophile 12
pedophilia 21
penal 160
pencil 60
Penelope 95
penicillin 5
penitentiary 160
pentathlon 255
people 3
per annum 164
per capita 164
per se 164
pericardium 132
perimeter 41
periphery 33
periscope 28, 43
permit 53
persona non grata 164
perversion 70
pestilent 62
phantom 27
pharmacist 108
pharmacology 108
pharmacy 108
phase 27
phenomenon (-a) 13, 27
pheromone 28, 41
phial 253
philodendron 133
philology 41
philosophy 191
phlebectomy 137, 142
phlebitis 137, 142
phlebosclerosis 137
phlebostenosis 137
phlegmatic 108
phobia 129, 216
phonetician 58
phosphorescent 28
photogenic 186
photograph 20
physics 34
physiology 111
picture 56
piety 9
pious 11
placenta 112
plagiarize 18

plastic 18
Plato 253
platonic 203
plebeian (-s) 152, 155
Pluto 80
plutocracy 149, 179
plutocrat 149, 179
pneumonia 4
poetic 36
pogonophobe 216
police 145
policy 145
politic 42, 145, 166
political 145, 165
politician 145
politicize 42, 145
politico 145
politics 34, 42, 145
polity 42, 145
polychrome 24
polygraph 20
polytheism 39
populace 183, 188
popular 184
pork 8
position 5, 48
posthumous 160
postpone 53, 67
posture 48
poultry 8
power 9
practical 28
praetor (-s) 152, 155
pragmatic 28, 42
pragmatics 42
pragmatism 42
pragmatist 42
prefects 176
prehistory 245
preposition 53
preposterous 53, 66
prerequisite 67
Pretoria 152
prima facie 164
primary 256
primeval 244–245
primitive 245
Principate 156
prison 49
pro forma 164
pro rata 164

problem 186
procedure 67
proceed 47
procession 70
Procrustean 102
Procrustes, bed of 89
procurators 176
profit 188
prognosis (-es) 13, 33, 107
program 26, 41, 44
project 53
prolegomenon 17
proletarian 156
proletariat 156, 166
prologue 41, 43
propeller 67
proposition 67
prosecutor 162
prosthesis 43
protohistoric 245
protohistory 245
provision 67
pseudonym 25
psyche 10, 206
psychedelic 191
psychic 191
psychogenetic 191
psychokinesis 191
psychology 1, 130, 137, 191
psychopath 131, 142
psychopathology 137
psychopathy 142
psychosis 41, 131, 143, 191
psychotherapy 132, 142
public 155
publican 155, 183
publish 155, 183
pulmonary 139
puncture 56
python 82

Q

quaestors 152, 179
quantum 5
quarter 256
quaternary 256
question 11, 152
qui facit per alium facit per se 164
quicksilver 81
quid pro quo 164
quinquennial 256

quinsy 130
quintessence 7, 256
quorum 64

R

radiant 61
radio 8
radiotelegraphy 8
radius (-i) 9, 14
receive 47
recession 47, 67
record (-s) 244, 247
redemption 53
reduce 69
reduction 70
referendum 58
regal 11
regent 148
regimen 125
regulate 166
reject 53, 67
remember 245
remit 48
removal 56
renal 139
repentance 56
repose 69
residuary 161
respondent 58
retrospect 54
reverend 58
revolve 67
rheostat 41
rhetoric 166
rheumatism 28
rhythmic 18
rhythmicality 254
rise 11
Rochester 2
rodent operatives 8
rostrum (-a) 14
row 8
royal 11
rupture 56

S

sacred 9, 11
sacrosanct 183
sanctify 183
sanctimonius 183

sanction 183
sanctuary 183
sanguine 108
Saturday 77
Saturn 77
scalpel 118
schizoid 218
scholar 58
schools 178
science 193
scientist 193
sclerosis 25
scribble 67
scribe 13, 176
script 13
scruple (-s) 59–60
Scylla and Charybdis 95, 102
secede 67
secondary 256
sedition 54
seduce 69
seducible 70
seduction 54, 70
seductive 70
seismograph 20
seizure 56
semiannual 54
semiotics 245
Senate 151, 166
senescent 46
senile 151
senility 46
senior 151
señor 151
señora 151
señorita 151
September 256
septicemia 129
septimal 256
servant 184
serviceable 46
service 185
servile 184, 188
servitude 46
sexagenarian 256
sextillion 256
sine die 64
sine qua non 164
siren 95, 102
Sisyphean task 83
skeleton 111
skeptical 28

social 183
socialism 35
society 183
sociology 1, 183
Socratic method 203
Socratic irony 203
soldier (-s) 176
solitude 57
sophistry 203
sovereign 148
specialize 177
species 15
specimen 188
specious 188
spectacle 188
spectrum (-a) 14
stable 11
static 28
stellar 61
Stentor 91
stentorian 91, 102
sthenia 137
stimulus 17
stoically 222
Stoicism 41
story 228
stratum 17
street 2
streptomycin 135
Stygian 83, 102
sub judice 164
subcutaneous 139
subject 54
subliminal 219
succinct 54
suffer 54
suggest 54
suggestion 57
superglue 54
superheat 54
superimpose 6
supervise 54
support 54
suppose 69
suprasensible 195
surgery 108
surrogate 69, 70
suspect 54
syllogism 33
symbol 26, 29
symbolic 36
sympathy 33, 41

synagogue 25
synchronic 33, 41, 232
synchronize 36
synoptic 27
synthesis (-es) 13, 43
synthetic 29
system 33

T

tachometer 137, 142
tachycardia 137, 142
tachylogia 137
talent 178
tantalize 84
technique 186
technobabble 186
technocracy 186
technocrat 149
technology 186
telegram 13, 26
telegraph 13
telepathy 20, 41
telephone 5, 41
telescope 21
television 8
temperature 4
temple 3
temporal 245
temporary 46
temporization 46
tenacity 56
terminus (-i) 14
terminus ante quem 64
terminus post quem 64
terrain 77
terrarium 59
terrestrial 77
terrible 77
terrier 77
terrific 77
terrify 77
territory 77
terror 11
terrorist 77
terrorize 77
tertiary 256
testament 161
testate 161
testify 161
tetrameter 255

thanatology 101
theogony 76, 78, 101
theology 1, 20, 78, 101
thermometer 4, 130
thermostat 25
thesis (-es) 17, 29
titanic 78
Titanic 78
titanium 78, 101
tonsillectomy 128, 129
tonsillitis 130
toxicology 138, 142
toxin 138, 143
tracheotomy 132
trachoma 131
tradition 47, 245
traduce 55, 69
tranquil 55
transmit 55, 67
transpose 69
trapeze 175
trapezium 175
trauma (-mata) 14, 213
triad 256
tribe 147
tribunal 152
tribune (-s) 152, 166
tribute 176
trigonometry 41
tripod 255
triskaidekaphobia 216
Trojan horse 90
Trojan, work like a 92
trope 29
tropics 29
tuberculosis 131
tyrannical 6, 149
tyrannize 149
tyranny 149, 165
tyrant 149

U

ultraviolet 55
unbeliever 52
under the aegis 81, 102
unhappy 51
unicycle 256
union 56
Uranus 77
urban 147

urbane 147
urbanity 10, 147
urbanization 147
urbanize 147
usufruct 161
usury 177
uterine 139
uterus 139
utility 188
utopia 4

V

v. 63
vacuum 4
valor 57
variety 57
vegetarian 58
venereal 12, 81
Venus 80
verbal 46
verbiage 46
vernacular 186
vertebrae 17
vertex (-ices) 15
veteran 58
vexation 57
vice versa 64
victory 67

violent 62
virile 46
virilization 46
virus 117
vitamin 5
vitreous 62
volatile 62
voluble 60
vortex (-ices) 15
vulcanology 81, 101

W

wine 2

X

xanthemia 138, 142
xanthin 138, 142
xanthoderma 138
xenophile 217
xenophobe 21
xenophobia 226

Z

zoology 1
zootoxin 138

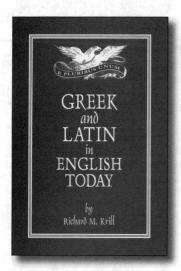

Greek and Latin in English Today

Richard Krill

vi + 250 pp. (1990)
Paperback, ISBN 978-0-86516-241-9
Cassettes, ISBN 978-0-86516-248-8

Greek and Latin in English Today is a vocabulary-builder par excellence, with the added advantage that it builds understanding of the critical roles Greek and Latin played in the development of English. The book's incremental approach and reinforcing exercises bring vocabulary building into everyone's reach.

The book also includes lucid explanations of the metric system, Roman numerals, and other classification systems; and exercises aimed at reinforcing each chapter's lesson. A section deals with Greek and Latin in the development of specialized nomenclature in science, medicine, law, and the arts. Two audio cassettes provide the proper pronunciation of the main Greek and Latin words and phrases. The book can be used with or without the cassettes.

Features

- 32 brief chapters on the Latin and Greek derivatives of both common and technical/professional contemporary vocabulary
- Charts including geologic time, Indo-European family of languages, sub-atomic particles, and early alphabets
- Over a dozen anatomical diagrams, map showing the spread of language in Europe, map of the moon, plus other images from antiquity
- Lists of animal names, educational degrees, cognates, vocabulary, and more
- Hundreds of exercises

BOLCHAZY-CARDUCCI PUBLISHERS, INC.
WWW.BOLCHAZY.COM

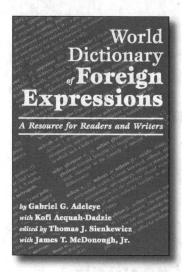

World Dictionary of Foreign Expressions

A Resource for Readers and Writers

Kofi Acquah-Dadzi and Gabriel G. Adeleye; Eds. James McDonough, Jr. and Thomas J. Sienkewicz

xxviii + 411 pp. (1999)
Paperback, ISBN 978-0-86516-423-9
Hardbound, ISBN 978-0-86516-422-2

The *World Dictionary of Foreign Expressions* is an excellent resource for those who encounter the foreign words and phrases that permeate spoken and written English and seek a fuller understanding of them. It contains abbreviations, single words, and phrases from a wealth of languages including: Afrikaans, Arabic, Aramaic, Chinese, Dutch, French, Greek, German, Italian, Hawaiian, Hebrew, Hindi, Inuit, Japanese, Latin, Persian, Portuguese, Provençal, Russian, Sanskrit, Spanish, Turkish, and Yiddish.

Features

- Identification of the language of origin and a polished translation for each expression
- Literal word-by-word explication of each entry
- Models for proper usage through quotations from recent scholarship or journalism
- Easy-to-follow format that is gentle on the eyes

"...a good one-stop guide to non-English expressions that occur in English contexts..."
– W. Miller, Florida Atlantic University, Choice

"Nothing else like this around ... The research and presentation are of the highest quality, informative, and enthusiastic."
– Margaret Richek, Northeastern Illinois University

"Rarely have I seen anything that is such a must-have for writers."
– Alex Krislov, Compuserve Online Services

BOLCHAZY-CARDUCCI PUBLISHERS, INC.
WWW.BOLCHAZY.COM

A Glossary of Terms in Grammar, Rhetoric, and Prosody for Readers of Greek and Latin

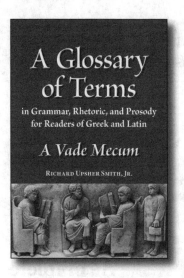

A *Vade Mecum*

Richard Upsher Smith, Jr.

xii + 140 pp. (2011)
Paperback, ISBN 978-0-86516-759-9

From *ablaut* to *zeugma* this glossary explains terms in grammar, rhetoric, and prosody that readers of Greek and Latin commonly encounter in their first three years of study. While English grammar is the focus, the links with Greek and Latin grammar are also explained and some Greek and Latin constructions that do not occur in English are defined. Common rhetorical and prosodical terms encountered in the annotations on Greek and Latin texts are explained and illustrated with Greek and Latin quotations.

Features

- All AP* Vergil rhetorical and prosodical terms
- Quotations from Greek, Latin, and English masterpieces
- Tables of verbal aspect, types of nouns, English personal pronouns, English relative pronouns, the English verb *to be*, and more

Richard Upsher Smith, Jr. is a professor of Classics at the Franciscan University of Steubenville. He holds a BA in Ancient History and Biblical Studies, a MDiv from Harvard Divinity School, and a PhD in Classics from Dalhouise University. Smith served in the Angelican ministry for 20 years. He has published in the fields of Classics, Medieval Studies, and on the Reformation. Smith teaches Greek, Latin, and in the Great Books (Honors) Program.

*AP is a registered trademark of the college Entrance Examination Board,
which was not involved in the production of, and does not endorse, this product.

BOLCHAZY-CARDUCCI PUBLISHERS, INC.
WWW.BOLCHAZY.COM